European Regional Policy and Development

The shortcomings of traditional regional policies led to a major policy. Thus, regions have become more active in the design and implementation of policies, following a bottom-up approach and involving the participation of the local community in strategic planning, as opposed to the traditional top-down method. This book addresses regional development theories and policies, with a special focus on forgotten places, and raises emerging questions about recent theoretical advances, as well as trends and challenges in the field.

It examines two main and related issues: the crucial role of regional actors for development and the role of Forgotten Spaces. It emphasizes the spatial/territorial approaches from different theoretical perspectives, underlining place-based approaches, and compares the experiences of both successful and failed cases, attempting to identify lessons and policy recommendations, as well as adding empirical evidence to this field. The different cases presented, which focus on Forgotten Spaces, allow the reader to assess the role of different actors for regional development as well as some sectoral approaches. While there is a clear focus on European countries with different geographical, institutional, and sociocultural characteristics, the book also examines good and bad examples of regional development and policies related to forgotten places from different regions worldwide, including developed and developing countries.

The book benefits from contributions from over 20 authors from different nationalities, and a rich diversity of case studies, approaches, and methods of discussion. The authors discuss practical examples and more complex theoretical approaches, involving techniques of spatial analysis, spatial econometrics, social networks, content analysis as well as regional planning techniques. The book will appeal to an interdisciplinary audience and will provide academicians, politicians, and policy designers with original and detailed analyses.

María del Carmen Sánchez-Carreira is Associate Professor of Applied Economics at the University of Santiago de Compostela, Galicia, Spain.

Paulo Jorge Reis Mourão is Associate Professor in the Department of Economics at the University of Minho, Braga, Portugal.

Bruno Blanco-Varela is Lecturer of Applied Economics at the University of Santiago de Compostela, Galicia, Spain.

Routledge Advances in Regional Economics, Science and Policy

European Regional Policy and Development

Forgotten Regions and Spaces

Edited by
**María del Carmen
Sánchez-Carreira,
Paulo Jorge Reis Mourão
and Bruno Blanco-Varela**

Routledge
Taylor & Francis Group

LONDON AND NEW YORK

First published 2024
by Routledge
4 Park Square, Milton Park, Abingdon, Oxon OX14 4RN

and by Routledge
605 Third Avenue, New York, NY 10158

Routledge is an imprint of the Taylor & Francis Group, an informa business

British Library Cataloguing-in-Publication Data
A catalogue record for this book is available from the British Library

Library of Congress Cataloging-in-Publication Data
Names: Sánchez Carreira, María del Carmen, editor. | Mourão, Paulo Jorge Reis, editor. | Blanco-Varela, Bruno, editor.
Title: European regional policy and development : forgotten regions and spaces / edited by María del Carmen Sánchez-Carreira, Paulo Jorge Reis Mourão and Bruno Blanco-Varela.
Description: Abingdon, Oxon ; New York, NY : Routledge, 2023. | Series: Routledge advances in regional economics, science and policy | Includes bibliographical references and index.
Identifiers: LCCN 2023001343 (print) | LCCN 2023001344 (ebook) | ISBN 9781032187969 (hardback) | ISBN 9781032188003 (paperback) | ISBN 9781003256281 (ebook)
Subjects: LCSH: European Union countries—Economic conditions—Regional disparities. | Regional planning—European Union countries. | Regional economics—European Union countries.
Classification: LCC HC240 .E877 2023 (print) | LCC HC240 (ebook) | DDC 330.947—dc23/eng/20230505
LC record available at https://lccn.loc.gov/2023001343
LC ebook record available at https://lccn.loc.gov/2023001344

ISBN: 978-1-032-18796-9 (hbk)
ISBN: 978-1-032-18800-3 (pbk)
ISBN: 978-1-003-25628-1 (ebk)

DOI: 10.4324/9781003256281

Typeset in Bembo
by Apex CoVantage, LLC

Contents

Figures

Tables

Authors

Ariane Sept is Professor of Participative Spatial Development and Community Organizing at Munich University of Applied Sciences in Germany since October 2022. Prior to that, she worked as Research Associate at the Leibniz Institute for Research on Society and Space in Erkner (Germany). She studied urban and regional planning and holds a Ph.D. degree in sociology. Her main fields of study regard current spatial transformations, especially the interplay of rural and urban areas, social innovations as well as European urban and regional policies.

Bianka Plüschke-Altof is Lecturer in Qualitative Methods at the University of Tartu and a senior researcher in environmental sociology at Tallinn University (Estonia). Her research focuses on questions of socio-spatial and environmental justice in Central-Eastern Europe. In her Ph.D. thesis, she analyzed spatial inequalities, territorial stigmatization, and coping strategies in the case of Estonian rural areas and small towns. Her postdoctoral research lies in the field of human-nature interactions, focusing particularly on environmental justice concerns.

Bruno Blanco-Varela holds a Ph.D in Economics and Business from the Universidade de Santiago de Compostela (Spain). He is Lecturer in the Department of Applied Economics since 2021 at the same institution. His main research files are regional and local development; public policies and welfare state; socioeconomic mobility and education; and labor market insertion and quality of employment. He also works in other research fields, such as gender studies; social and territorial disparities; and management of public funds. He has publications in relevant journals in these issues, as well as participation in congress and conferences.

Carlos Costa is Assistant Professor in the Department of Economics, Sociology and Management (DESG), School of Human and Social Sciences (ECHS), University of Trás-os-Montes and Alto Douro (UTAD) (Portugal). He is a researcher at the Centre for Transdisciplinary Development Studies (CETRAD), UTAD. He holds a B.Sc in Agronomy and Ph.D. degree in rural economics. His main research fields are rural development, with emphasis on the competitiveness of quality agrifood products, and the use of local natural resources for rural and local development. He is a researcher and local coordinator of several European and national funded research and extension projects, related to the aforementioned research fields. He is author or coauthor of more than 20 scientific works, publications and technical production items, most of which are in these fields.

Francesco Silvestri is Assistant Professor of Applied Economics at the University of Modena and Reggio Emilia (Italy). His research focuses on local sustainable development and environmental economics. His interest in the Inner Areas Strategy originates from a personal involvement as an expert supporting the National Committee for Inner Areas during the period 2016–2020.

Giuseppe Lucio Gaeta is Associate Professor of Public Economics at the University of Naples "L'Orientale" and Associated Research Fellow at the CiMET05 Inter-University Centre for Applied Economics (Italy). His research focuses on public administration, political economy, education, and cultural economics.

Ina Drejer is Professor with special responsibilities in impact studies and innovation. She is head of the IMPAKT Centre for Impact Analyses of Investments in Knowledge and Technology at Aalborg University Business School (Denmark). Her work has been published in journals such as *Regional Studies*, *Technovation*, and *Research Policy*. Her research is based on both quantitative and qualitative methods, with research interests, including innovation and industrial dynamics, university-industry interaction, interfirm relations, regional economics, and place-based development. In addition to her research expertise, she has several years' experience as a policymaker, working on national and regional innovation policy.

Jacek Gancarczyk is Adjunct Professor of Management Science at the Institute of Entrepreneurship, Jagiellonian University in Kraków (Poland). His research and publication activities are focused on innovative ventures, small- and medium-sized enterprises (SMEs), regional development, and industrial clusters. He is also a member of the European Council for Small Business and Entrepreneurship (ECSB).

Joanna Stawska, Ph.D., is a researcher employed as Assistant Professor in the Department of Central Banking and Financial Intermediation at the Faculty of Economics and Sociology of the University of Lodz (Poland). Her research interests mainly include monetary policy, fiscal policy, policy mix, public finance, game theory, economic policy, corporate investments, and financial system stability. She is the head of a research project on the coordination of monetary and fiscal policy in the studies of monetary–fiscal interactions based on the game theory in the European Union countries, financed by the National Science Center Poland. She is the author of many publications published by renowned national and international publishing houses. She actively participates in many international conferences at home and abroad. She is also a reviewer for numerous international scientific journals. She has also been a lecturer at foreign universities under the Erasmus+ program. She cooperates with many scientists from foreign universities on a permanent basis.

Jon Mikel Zabala-Iturriagagoitia is Associate Professor at the University of Deusto in San Sebastian (Spain) and affiliated to University College of Southeast Norway in Kongsberg (Norway). He was previously Assistant Professor at CIRCLE, Lund University (Sweden). He has also been visiting scholar at the VTT Technical Research Centre of Finland (Finland) and HEC Montreal

(Canada). His research interests include innovation policy and innovation management strategies.

Jose Blanco-Álvarez is a Ph.D. candidate in economic and business at the University of Santiago de Compostela (Spain). He currently works at the innovation, structural change and development (ICEDE) research group, where his research interest is focused on contemporary migration, with a special focus on high skilled migration and brain drain. His dissertation develops methodologies to measure this high-skilled migration at the subnational level and applies it to the Galicia region.

Lea Holst Laursen is Associate Professor of Urban Design and Head of the Architecture and Urban Design Section, Department of Architecture, Design and Media Technology, Aalborg University (Denmark). Her research concerns urban and rural transformation with a place-based, human-centered objective – querying and discussing urban and rural pasts, presents, and futures. The central themes include place-making, local cocreated responses, site-specific development potentials, regional development, and shrinking territories. Her work has been published in journals such as *Ambiances, Nordic Journal of Architectural Research*, and *Policy Design and Practice*, including a recent major publication titled *Mobilising Place Management* by Routledge.

Manuel González-López is Associate Professor in the Department of Applied Economics and member of the innovation, structural change and development (ICEDE) research group at the University of Santiago de Compostela (Spain). His research focuses on regional innovation, innovation geography, and regional innovation policies. He is the author and coauthor of several papers and books on the referred issues.

Marek Reichel is Associate Professor of Economics and Vice-Rector of the Academy of Applied Sciences in Nowy Sącz, Malopolska (Poland). His research and publication activities focus on regional development, intraregional polarization, evaluation of public intervention, and local government competitiveness.

María del Carmen Sánchez-Carreira is Associate Professor in the Department of Applied Economics, University of Santiago de Compostela and a member of the Innovation, Structural Change and Development (ICEDE) research group. Her main research topics are regional and local development, regional policies, innovation policies, regional innovation policies, public procurement, targeted policies to develop new sectors (biomedicine, wind energy or eco-innovation), state-owned enterprises, privatization, and the Welfare State and Economics of Education. Apart from academic publications, she has participated in several international and national projects.

Marta Gancarczyk is Full Professor of Economics and Finance at the Institute of Economics, Finance and Management, Jagiellonian University in Kraków (Poland). Her research and publication activities focus on economic governance, entrepreneurial and financial ecosystems, entrepreneurship economics, firm growth, technology commercialization, industrial clusters, and public policy for small- and medium-sized enterprises.

Paulo Jorge Reis Mourão is Associate Professor with habilitation in the Department of Economics of the University of Minho (Portugal) and a member of the Centre for Research in Economics and Management (NIPE). He is the author of several scientific articles indexed by ISI Thompson and of some books. His research interests include economics, public finance, social economics, and sports economics. He frequently appears in national and international media for commenting on social and economic issues. Paulo Jorge Reis Mourão has been awarded several times for his scientific works.

Riccardo De Vita is Professor of Innovation Management at the University of Greenwich (United Kingdom), where he is also Head of School – Business, Operations and Strategy. He holds a PhD from Universita' Carlo Cattaneo – LIUC (Italy). In his research, he applies social network analysis, often in combination with other research methodologies, to explore innovation within organizational networks.

Stefano Ghinoi is Senior Lecturer in Economic Sociology at the School of Business, Operations and Strategy, University of Greenwich (United Kingdom) and Visiting Scholar at the University of Helsinki (Finland). His research focuses on innovation and sustainability, and the application of social network analysis for investigating business-related problems.

Stephanie Francis Grimbert is a Ph.D. candidate at the University of Deusto in San Sebastian (Spain) and an affiliated member of CIRCLE, at Lund University (Sweden). Her Ph.D. thesis approaches the theory and practice of innovation policy from a value creation perspective. In particular, she focuses on the inclusion of end users within the value creation constellation of actors. She holds an MBA from the Ecole Supérieure des Sciences Economiques et Commerciales (ESSEC).

Vítor Martinho holds a Ph.D. degree in economics from the University of Coimbra (Portugal). He was President of the Scientific Council, President of the Directive Council, and President of the Agricultural Polytechnic School of Viseu (Portugal) from 2006 to 2012. He was an Erasmus student at the Faculty of Economics from the University of Verona (Italy), participated in various technical and scientific events nationally and internationally, has published several technical and scientific papers, is a referee of some scientific and technical journals, and participates in the evaluation of national and international projects.

Acknowledgments

The editors are grateful to the authors of the chapters for their engaging and insightful contributions, their strict compliance with the deadlines, and their easy-going nature during all the process. They extend their thanks to the authors of the works that have not been accepted for publication for their interest in the project and understanding.

They would also like to thank the reviewers for their dedication, expertise, as well as the thoroughness of the review, their valuable comments and constructive suggestions. Each chapter was double-blind reviewed by a minimum of two experts, in addition to the review by the three editors. This review process contributes to achieve research contributions of high standard. Our deeper thanks to Alejandro López González, University of Leon (Spain); Ana Grdović Gnip, University of Primorska (Slovenia); Ana Paula Bastos, University of Brasilia (Brazil); Andrea Zatti, University of Pavia (Italy); Birgitte Gregersen, University of Aalborg (Denmark); Cadima Ribeiro, University of Minho (Portugal); Cristina Ares Castro-Conde, University of Santiago de Compostela (Spain); Cristina García Nicolás, University of Castilla-La Mancha (Spain); Elina De Simone, University of Tre Rome (Italy); Elisabeth Baier, Victoria International University of Applied Sciences (Germany); Federico Martín Bermúdez, University of A Coruña (Spain); Ivano Dileo, University of Naples Parthenope (Italy); Marie-France Gaunard-Anderson, University of Lorraine (France); Marta Nadja-Janoszka, Jagiellonian University (Poland); Martha Cecilia Jaramillo Cardona, Autonomous University of Baja California (Mexico); Radoslaw Witczak, University of Lodz (Poland); Richard Tuffs, Independent Expert, European Regions Research & Innovation Network (Belgium); Ruben Markosyan, Eurasia International University (Armenia); Salvatore Ercolano, University of Basilicata (Italy); Susana Franco, Orkestra – Basque Institute of Competitiveness (Spain); Vanda Marakova, Matej Bel University (Slovakia); and Ximena Alexandra Morales-Urrutia, Indomeric Technological University Ambato (Ecuador).

The editors express their gratitude to Routledge and specifically to the editorial team for their support, trust, and patience along all the process. Our appreciation for your hard work is boundless. Many thanks to Natalie Tomlinson, for the interest in our research and encouraging and guiding us in the initial step; to Kristina Abbotts, for all the warm support, effective work, willingness and responsiveness; and to Christiana Mandizha for the sound management for all the managing issues.

The authors are grateful to the Iacobus Program of the European Association for Cross-Border Cooperation Galicia-Norte de Portugal for supporting their stay at the University of Minho (Portugal) in 2020, which led to the idea of this book; and another stay in 2021, during which the project grew toward two interrelated books, given the interest shown and the high number of potential contributions. This project was supported by Xunta de Galicia (Consellería de Cultura, Educación e Ordenación Universitaria: predoctoral aid program, ED481A-2018/087, and consolidation and structuring of competitive research units. Mode A: competitive reference groups GRC and GI-1178, ED431C 2018/23); and the National Funds of the FCT – Portuguese Foundation for Science and Technology within the project "UIDB/03182/2020."

Introduction

Forgotten Spaces in the European regional policy and development

María del Carmen Sánchez-Carreira[1], Paulo Jorge Reis Mourão[2] and Bruno Blanco-Varela[3]

Regional Development is a well-established discipline within the economic and geographic sciences. If the regional development has conveniently cataloged the regions as developed or in development, then the existence of Forgotten Spaces has been neglected. Thus, the authors have identified a gap about these places, as well as the role of actors to foster these depressed areas, which is approached here.

This book attempts to increase the knowledge within the field of regional development and policies in the European area, with a focus on Forgotten Spaces. Regions have been increasing their role in the last few decades in the European context, where a regional development policy exists since the early beginning, increasing their relevance since the 1980s. This contribution allows identifying different paths of regional development and learning from several experiences around Europe. Overall, regions have followed different development paths and even facing different challenges. The regional disparities shown in different socioeconomic aspects involves assuming that it is not possible to apply the one-size-fits-all approach (Tödtling & Trippl, 2005). Even the European area shows a high level of heterogeneity both among and within countries and regions.

The cases analyzed in this book provide knowledge about diverse Forgotten Spaces in Europe, from both the theoretical and empirical perspectives. These experiences are not only successful but also failed to get best practices and lessons. The book analyses new and nontypical experiences with well-defined focuses, which makes it easier for policymakers to design the appropriate mechanisms and tools for future experiences on the regional intervention.

We identify European economies as developed. The experience of Europe from the regional perspective is truly enriching and relevant, because of the expressed political orientation of achieving territorial balance in the European Union (EU). The European regional policy, also known as cohesion policy, has been articulated since the beginning of the European integration process. In fact, regional policy, based on the structural and cohesion funds, is one of the important functions of the EU. Despite this policy, there are high disparities in socioeconomic terms and in the level of development of different areas, both between and within countries or regions (Iammarino et al., 2019). Therefore, Forgotten Spaces come into existence and survive. However, European policies often seem to devalue their own Forgotten Spaces with serious implications in the well-being of the living communities. This overlooking

DOI: 10.4324/9781003256281-1

of Forgotten Spaces also affects the abundant literature on European regional policy (Stahlecker & Koschatzky, 2010; McCann, 2015; Molle, 2016; Cuadrado-Roura, 2020, among others).

Hence, the cohesion policy with the purpose of achieving economic, social, and territorial cohesion should be considered a development policy (Barca, 2009; Bachtler et al., 2013), rather than a redistributive policy (McCann, 2015). Each enlargement process has increased regional disparities within the EU. The EU cohesion policy has changed over time, highlighting two key moments according to Ares (2020). Since the 1999 Berlin European Council, the goal has been to use the EU funding better and focus on making the EU more competitive. The second moment is 2013, when key adjustments for the programming period 2014–2020 were approved, establishing ex ante conditions to receive funds and an enhanced focus on delivering results were put at the forefront. Thus, smart specialization strategies have become key. Both policy innovations were introduced with the aim of improving EU funding. The main change in the rationale of the policy, at least rhetorically, consists of abandoning the compensation logic and the objective of helping the less favored regions to converge, in favor of investing more in those territories where more results can be achieved, with the purpose of enhancing the EU competitiveness (Medeiros, 2017; Ares, 2020).

This book will reflect on Forgotten Spaces. The main theoretical innovations in this book can be summarized in two major contributions. First, it approaches the concept of forgotten space within Europe. The neglect of such areas – often including the existence of abandoned and untreated industrial facilities – carries potential costs not only in environmental sustainability but also in other values such as landscape aesthetics. Thus, this book reflects on the dimensions of the identification of such Forgotten Spaces, on the design of policies focused on minimizing associated costs, and on the scope of programs to promote these areas, not only for upgrading them but also for promoting their environmental sustainability. The second theoretical contribution is evident in the significant diversity of expected contributions. With the presence of several authors from different nationalities and a diversity of case studies, this book allows any reader to enrich the literature with original and detailed analyses. With the richness derived from the diversity of approaches, methods of discussion, and experience in the sectors in question, it combines practical examples with more complex theoretical approaches, involving techniques of spatial analysis, spatial econometrics, social networks, content analysis, as well as regional planning techniques.

The contributions also provide a way of evaluating the path followed by the regional policy of the EU since its inception, as well as providing insights for the current programming period 2021–2027. In this sense, this interesting issue invokes the debate about the nature and definition of regional policies and, specifically, whether they are regional because they are made by regions or whether they are designed for regions. Other relevant questions that arise in the political sphere concern to know what regional policies exist for and the main problems facing European regions.

The content of the book combines two different parts. On the one hand, various chapters address some of the latest theoretical advances in regional development and policy, emphasizing the role of places, actors, and resources. Thus, the book mainly adopts a place-based approach. On the other hand, different experiences of Forgotten Spaces and regions in Europe are analyzed, including cases of success and failure. The book addresses interesting experiences in forgotten places in a developed area. It highlights the positive cases, which can be identified as well-succeeded experiences of regional change.

Regional development policies can adopt two main different approaches: the place-blind and place-based approaches (Varela-Vázquez et al., 2019; Hassink, 2020). On the one hand, the place-blind approach address development proposing the same measures regardless of the features of the region. Thus, these policies intend to improve the welfare of individuals, regardless of which region they live in (Barca et al., 2012). On the other hand, the place-based approach assumes that the territorial context, understood in terms of social, cultural, and institutional characteristics, matters for policy intervention. From a policy perspective, the particularities of regions make ineffective the 'one-size-fits-all' approach and, for this reason, the place-based approach suggests that development strategies should focus on mechanisms that build on local capabilities and promote innovative ideas (Barca, 2009; Varela-Vázquez et al., 2019). Moreover, it should be noted that place-blind policies are not neutral in their territorial effects. This leads to targeting for place-based policies, considering the singularities of each region.

Since the 1970s, place-based policies have increased their relevance within the framework of endogenous development theories and policies (Vázquez Barquero, 2002). The shortcomings of traditional regional policies lead to a major shift in regional development policies. Thus, regions become more active in the design and implementation of policies, following a bottom-up approach, which involves the participation of the local community in the strategies, as opposed to the traditional top-down approach. The place-based approach has been used by the EU cohesion policy since the programming period 2014–2020 and, particularly, in the smart specialization strategies. Therefore, the European regional policy evolves to mix cohesion and innovation goals.

There is a clear focus on European spaces with different geography, institutional and sociocultural characteristics, due to the long development in this topic driven by the EU policies and the fact that a new EU programming period is starting in 2021–2027. The comparative approach of the empirical part also allows providing knowledge and experience from EU regional policy and innovation approaches useful in other regions worldwide.

The concepts of region and Forgotten Spaces are ambiguous, undefined, and even changing with respect to time and a certain spatial context. Thus, the concept of regions has evolved over time from its identification with physical space to a more political conception. At the European level, the political definition of regions dominates, mainly for practical reasons, given the administrative boundaries and that it refers to an area where a specific set of policies or programs is applied. In addition, there is more availability of data for this definition of regions (Boudeville, 1961; Richardson, 1969). In this sense, the level of competences, resources, budgets, and capacities of each region are key aspects. The composition of regions is articulated as the grouping of resources, actors, and institutions interacting in one space uniformed by some common feature, such as geography, history, culture, social, political, or economic element (Boudeville, 1961; Richardson, 1969). The concept of region has also adapted to a new, more complex, and polycentric spatial organization (Velzt, 1996; Copus, 2011; Parr, 2004). The organization of the territory is being transformed and new forms are appearing. The trend is the replacement of hierarchies by networks. Thus, polycentric regions are configured as a network of cities and actors whose exchanges, productive, technological, and commercial relations make up an economic system. Hence, there is a diversity of spaces, with different activities, connected through a system of transport and communication.

This new context differs from the nodal regions identified by Boudeville (1961), which are characterized by the existence of a dominant node or hub. This hub tends to polarize, provoking internal flows and interdependencies. In this sense, Velzt (1996) uses the term archipelago network to refer to this new special organization, in which horizontal relations (between poles) predominate over vertical ones (between the poles and their surrounding areas or hinterland). Thus, we move from analyzing the territory from a zone perspective to a network perspective, where relationships take place between poles, which could be identified with the islands of the archipelago. Other spaces surrounding the poles are dipped and not integrated in the network. As the poles are far apart, it can also be said that long-radius relationships predominate over short-radius ones. Moreover, in the framework of the knowledge economy, the digital borders of the regions arise.

Given the building process, the region is not a rigid structural unit, but is open and in a constant process of self-determination. The manifestation of the regional sphere brings together, explicitly or implicitly, cultural, social, and economic factors, expressed as a product of the concretization of the community relationship with the natural and geographic environment.

The understanding of the concept of region can be approached at different levels. Thus, it can be distinguished into micro, macro, and meso aspects. At the macro level, the region refers to the determination of a supranational space in which production, trade, consumption, and distribution activities interact beyond the regional level. The concept of region can be studied at different levels that are organized hierarchically. The main territories range from the subnational to the supranational level. The most common definition is based on the delimitation of the political-administrative organization.

The economic space exceeds the geographical space, which makes it difficult to define regions. From an economic point of view, regions blur geographical boundaries by involving agents and resources that may be located in other territories. This situation becomes more relevant if one considers how the local level interrelates with participation in the globalized paradigm. Although it may seem paradoxical, in a globalized context, more local issues acquire higher relevance, which allows us to refer to glocalization.

Some of the utilities and applications of the regional perspective is the study of economic specialization, since it points out a unit of analysis that can be compared. It also analyzes the factors of spatial location, the level of economic concentration, and the consequences of these phenomena. A current trend is that in reality, disparities and concentration of population and economic activity are observed as a consequence of agglomeration economies. These trends are also associated with polarization effects in other areas, such as the geography of social discontent (Rodríguez-Pose, 2018; Rodrik, 2018; Iammarino et al., 2019; McCann, 2019; Dijkstra et al., 2020).

Analyzing smaller territorial units can be related to an increase in information on economic and social needs. It also exploits to a greater extent the potential of the agents, provides greater resilience or a higher commitment to the political project. Smaller territorial units may be less hierarchical than national organizations, and the lower technical or resource capacity may require larger cooperation between actors. Consequently, cooperation became a necessity.

Forgotten Spaces are those regions that are neglected by most of the citizens of a country, with serious difficulties in attracting investment, and with a significant threat of a reduction of well-being perceived by the residents. These spaces tend to exhibit low levels of population density, a low value of income per capita, and are located in peripheral areas (Mourao, 2020).

The socioeconomic concept of 'Forgotten Spaces' has also been used in several scientific works indexed by the Scopus database (accessed on October 31, 2022). To the fullest extent and considering the presence of these terms in the title, abstract, or keywords, we found 1,258 works with the term 'Forgotten Space(s)' in the Scopus database. If we restrict ourselves to the works filtered as 'Social Sciences' works, we have 557 identified. Finally, there are 17 works in the area of 'Economics, Econometrics and Finance'.

In terms of temporal evolution, these 17 works began in 1996, with the work by B. Page, 'Across the great divide: Agriculture and industrial geography', published in *Economic Geography*. Then, until 2021, the evolution was as follows: 2002, 1; 2006, 2; 2014, 2; 2015, 4; 2016, 1; 2019, 2; 2020, 2; 2021, 2.

These 17 works had the following configurations: 14 articles, 2 book chapters, and 1 review. Interestingly for our project, none of these 17 works is a book, which confirms our book as the first to be identified, in the future, by Scopus as centered on the term 'Forgotten Spaces'.

Looking now at the journals, the articles were distributed under the following titles: *Space Policy; Asian Social Science; Consumption Markets and Culture; Contemporary Economics; Critical Perspective on Accounting*; and *Economic Geography*.

Several terms appeared to be associated with keywords. However, we emphasize the keywords that identified places studied in the works: Lodz, Andalusia, Astana, China, Europe, and Siberia (all with one registration).

There are no repeat affiliations. Some affiliations are as follows: Instituto de Estadistica y Cartografia de Andalucia, Wojewódzki Inspektor Ochrony Środowiska (WIOS) Laboratory in Łódź, Birkbeck, University of London, University of Toronto, and Kazan Federal University. There are three Funding Sponsors: Economic and Social Research Council, Horizon 2020 Framework Program, and Norges Forskningsråd.

The authors of the 17 works under analysis come from the following countries: the United Kingdom (4), the United States of America (3), Australia (2), Canada

(2), Poland (2), Austria (1), Germany (1), Norway (1), Romania (1), Russian Federation (1), and Spain (1). The English (16 works) and Spanish (1 work) are the languages used in these works by 19 authors.

The contents of this book are organized into eight chapters, in addition to the introduction and general conclusions. The main contributions of each of the chapters are highlighted below.

The first chapter entitled 'Comparative assessment of rural realities in the European Union: the main drivers of the rural population' is written by Vítor Martinho, Carlos Costa, and Bruno Blanco-Varela. It underlines the importance of Forgotten Spaces for a balanced regional development. In fact, these regions, with adjusted policies, can contribute to promote a more sustainable development, through alternative and innovative socioeconomic activities, compatible with the preservation of the environment in rural contexts and to avoid congestion and overpopulation in urban places. In these frameworks, institutions play a decisive role. This study also shows the relevance of economic sectors, specifically through small businesses, for the dynamics of the forgotten regions.

The Chapter 2, entitled 'Agglomeration of knowledge-intensive activities and brain drain: global cities and forgotten regions across Europe' and written by Jose Blanco-Álvarez and Manuel González-López, stresses one of the main challenges facing by forgotten regions: the flight of high skilled personal. The main hypothesis is that the agglomeration of knowledge-intensive business services (KIBS) in some dynamic regions acts as a major determinant of this migration flows. After a literature review where they draw the basic lines between KIBS, the emergence of global cities and migration, the chapter presents an empirical case study with data on Spanish provinces. Using business demographic and labor contract mobility data, it is constructed a pseudo-gravity model where KIBS agglomeration, measured with a regional relative specialization index, appears as one of the main factors driving high skilled migration flows between these regions. The political implications of these findings are of major importance when applied to the EU because mobility among Member States is relatively free and, therefore, this dynamic can exacerbate the unequal socioeconomic development and aggravate the situation of forgotten regions.

Bianka Plüschke-Altof and Ariane Sept are the authors of Chapter 3, entitled 'How to make Forgotten Spaces visible? Image making as a coping strategy of two European small towns', which starts the analysis of different cases of Forgotten Spaces in Europe. It explores two cases of small towns in Estonia and Germany as Forgotten Spaces, which convey the importance of negative images and invisibility that comes along with the peripheralization in two ways. First, the discursive dimension affects regional development by influencing the decision to leave or stay, visit and invest in places; and, thereby, strengthens processes of oblivion. Second, the discursive dimension strongly figures in coping mechanisms of Forgotten Spaces, where local decision-makers address material and immaterial difficulties with the help of discursive strategies.

The Chapter 4, entitled 'Italian Inner areas' strategic plans: a textual network analysis of the *Appennino Emiliano* and *Madonie* case studies' and authored by Riccardo De Vita, Giuseppe Lucio Gaeta, Francesco Silvestri, and Stefano Ghinoi, addresses one of the most integrated strategies to tackle remote areas social and economic issues, which is the Italian National Strategy for Inner Areas (SNAI), based on exploiting national finance and the European Structural and Investment Funds. This study proposes a textual network analysis of the strategic plans that two Italian areas developed during their participation in the SNAI pilot project. The study reveals that these plans have common traits that derive from the SNAI setting and dissimilarities that depend on the areas economic specificities.

Ina Drejer and Lea Holst Laursen are the authors of the Chapter 5 entitled 'Engaging with forgotten places: applying a multifaceted understanding of place in an analysis of two Danish cases', which analyses two local development initiatives in North Denmark. The chapter explores avenues to increase the likelihood of developing and implementing successful smart specialization-inspired policies in remote places. It also illustrates how a broadened approach to place-specific development has the potential to facilitate local, bottom-up processes in challenged remote areas, as well as showing the issues that may occur. The research reveals how such a broadened place-specific approach should look beyond the elements usually emphasized in regional and local development processes and additionally address more intangible elements, including subjective meanings, conceptions, and emotional aspects. Furthermore, this chapter emphasizes that identifying actors is essential to a broadened place-specific development approach, where attention should also be given to elements that can reveal where civil society engagement could serve as a driver of local economic development. The chapter introduces two very different local development initiatives from North Denmark that illustrate how a broad approach to place-specific development can facilitate local, bottom-up processes in disadvantaged remote areas.

The Chapter 6 entitled 'Revitalizing Forgotten Spaces through local leadership and social entrepreneurial ecosystems: the case of Muszyna Commune' written by Marta Gancarczyk, Jacek Gancarczyk, and Marek Reichel, identifies the mechanisms of resurgence and industrial path renewal of a formerly underdeveloped territory. The authors identify and describe bottom-up and local leadership-based processes and practices that formed a social entrepreneurial ecosystem conducive for revitalization and successful development of this commune. The country-level and regional policies were not direct drivers of progressive change, but rather external opportunities, which were efficiently exploited through local processes. This research contributes to the literature on entrepreneurial ecosystems, in particular, to social entrepreneurial ecosystem. The unique value of the chapter rests on emphasizing local place-based leadership as cocreating social entrepreneurial communities from the process perspective. Moreover, the chapter contributes to the path literature and the coevolutionary strand in regional studies. It explains the interactions of local agents in project-based mechanisms of collective action to generate an industrial path renewal. This study also aims to inform the development policy in peripheral and Forgotten Spaces by proposing how institutional voids can be filled by social leadership generating local institutions.

The Chapter 7 entitled 'The specificity determinants of monetary and fiscal policy in the V4 countries: comparative economics perspective' by Joanna Stawska, addresses the comparison of monetary and fiscal policy in the Visegrad Group (V4) countries in the context of economic shocks in 2000–2020. The Visegrad Group is an association of four countries: Poland, the Czech Republic, Slovakia, and Hungary, whose main objective is to deepen economic cooperation and European integration. The analysis of the last 21 years of existence of the V4 Group showed how these countries coped with economic shocks, primarily the global financial crisis, then the debt crisis and the COVID-19 pandemic. All these countries have belonged to the structures of the EU since 2004, and Slovakia has been a member of the eurozone since 2009. The agreement within the V4 Group has been in place for more than 30 years, and it should be noted that during this period there were moments of greater or lesser cooperation.

Stephanie Francis Grimbert and Jon Mikel Zabala-Iturriagagoitia are the authors of the Chapter 8 entitled 'Public procurement as a transformative innovation policy instrument: urban rehabilitation in Malmö'. This chapter shows how innovation policies can be instrumental in revitalizing urban spaces through the definition of sustainability agendas. It focuses on the Western Harbor local investment program for ecological development in the city of Malmö (Sweden), which was targeted through public procurement. Thus, the chapter provides evidence about the potential of public procurement for innovation as a transformative policy instrument to revitalize a declined area. They characterize 'Transformative Public Procurement of Innovation' as encompassing not only first-degree effects (capacity to meet given objectives) but also second-degree effects related to the environment, the economy, or societal well-being. The chapter concludes by identifying the conditions deemed necessary for a successful implementation of the 'Transformative Public Procurement of Innovation' tool in urban contexts and by discussing how the lessons learned through this innovation policy instrument can be transferred to other forgotten places that also aim to counter-effect environmentally related grand challenges.

Finally, the book ends with a conclusion chapter, which summarizes its main findings and provides some lessons and policy implications from the addressed experiences. The future paths are also addressed, as well as the transferability of these European cases to other regions worldwide.

Furthermore, the development of Forgotten Spaces is complemented by the analysis of Forgotten Spaces at the global level in another connected, but independent volume, which comprises 12 chapters. The complementary book deals specifically with the Forgotten Spaces of Africa and Latin America, but also includes experiences that are more general. Despite the territorial focus on diverse places, this diversity should be understood as a key aspect. The greater number of experiences analyzed allows for a richer analysis and contributes to increase the readers' knowledge of Forgotten Spaces worldwide.

The book aims mainly at the academic and policy audience. Furthermore, policymakers at different levels of government should find the book useful. This interest is not only for regional governments, because many policies implemented by other levels have regional effects, which are diverse. Apart from the public and policy spheres, other secondary audiences can be journalists or regional actors, including some interest from companies.

Notes

1 Associate Professor, Department of Applied Economics, ICEDE Group, Faculty of Economics, CRETUS, Universidade de Santiago de Compostela, Spain, email: carmela. sanchez@usc.es (ORCID: 0000–0001–9265–2521).
2 Associate Professor with habilitation, Department of Economics & NIPE, Economics & Management School, University of Minho, Portugal, email: paulom@eeg.uminho.pt (ORCID: 0000–0001–6046–645X).
3 Lecturer, Department of Applied Economics, Faculty of Economics and Business Administration, University of Santiago de Compostela, email: b.blanco.varela@usc.es (ORCID: 0000–0001–5319–6578).

References

Ares, C. (2020). EU regional development policy. From regional convergence to development through innovation. In M. González-López, & B. T. Asheim (Eds.), *Regions and innovation policies in Europe. Learning from the margins* (pp. 92–112). Cheltenham: Edward Elgar.

Bachtler, J., Begg, I., Charles, D., & Polverari, L. (2013). Evaluation of the main achievements of cohesion policy programmes and projects over the long term in 15 selected regions, 1989–2012. *Final report to the European Commission.* London: University of Strathclyde and London School of Economics, European Policies Research Centre.

Barca, F. (2009). An agenda for a reformed cohesion policy: A place-based approach to meeting European Union challenges and expectations. *Independent Report prepared at the request of Danuta Hübner, Commissioner for Regional Policy.* Brussels: European Commission.

Barca, F., McCann, P., & Rodríguez-Pose, A. (2012). The case for regional development intervention: Place-based versus place-neutral approaches. *Journal of Regional Science, 52*(1), 134–152.

Boudeville, J. R. (1961). *Les espaces économiques.* Paris: Presses Universitaires de France.

Copus, A. K. (2011): From core-periphery to polycentric development: Concepts of spatial and aspatial peripherality. *European Planning Studies, 9,* 539–552.

Cuadrado-Roura, J. R. (2020). European regional policy: What can be learned. In M. Fischer, & P. Nijkamp (Eds.), *Handbook of regional science.* Berlin: Springer.

Dijkstra, L., Poelman, H., & Rodríguez-Pose, A. (2020). The geography of EU discontent. *Regional Studies, 54*(6), 737–753.

Hassink, R. (2020). Advancing place-based regional innovation policies. In M. González-López, & B. T. Asheim (Eds.), *Regions and innovation policies in Europe. Learning from the margins* (pp. 30–45). Cheltenham: Edward Elgar.

Iammarino, S., Rodríguez-Pose, A., & Storper, M. (2019). Regional inequality in Europe: Evidence, theory and policy implications. *Journal of Economic Geography, 19*(2), 273–298.

McCann, P. (2015). *The regional and urban policy of the European union: Cohesion, results-orientation and smart specialisation.* Cheltenham: Edward Elgar.

McCann, P. (2019). Perceptions of regional inequality and the geography of discontent: Insights from the UK. *Regional Studies, 54*(2), 256–267.

Medeiros, E. (2017). For smart growth to European spatial planning: A new paradigm for EU cohesion policy post-2020. *European Planning Studies, 25*(10), 1856–1875.

Molle, W. (2016). *The economics of European integration: Theory, practice and policy.* London: Routledge.

Mourao, P. (2020). *Economia do Esquecimento.* Braga: UMinho Editora.

Parr, J. B. (2004). The polycentric urban region: A closer inspection. *Regional Studies, 38*(3), 231–240.

Richardson, H. W. (1969). *Elements of regional economics.* London: Penguin Books.

Rodríguez-Pose, A. (2018). The revenge of the places that don't matter (and what to do about it). *Cambridge Journal of Regions, Economy and Society, 11*(1), 189–209.

Rodrik, D. (2018). Populism and the economics of globalization. *Journal of International Business Policy, 1*(1), 12–33.

Stahlecker, T., & Koschatzky, K. (2010). Cohesion policy in the light of place-based innovation support: New approaches in multi-actors, decentralised regional settings with bottom-up strategies? *Working Papers Firms and Region No. R1/2010,* Fraunhofer ISI.

Tödtling, F., & Trippl, M. (2005). One size fits all?: Towards a differentiated regional innovation policy approach. *Research Policy, 34*(8), 1203–1219.

Varela-Vázquez, P., González-López, M., & Sánchez-Carreira, M. C. (2019). The uneven regional distribution of projects funded by the EU framework programmes. *Journal of Entrepreneurship, Management and Innovation, 15(3),* 45–72.

Vázquez Barquero, J. A. (2002). *Endogeneous development.* London: Routledge.

Velzt, P. (1996). *Mondialisation, villes et territoires: Une économie d'archipel.* Paris: Presses Universitaires de France.

Part I

Regional development and policies in Europe

Main theoretical advances and last trends and challenges

1 Comparative assessment of rural realities in the European Union

The main drivers of the rural population

*Vítor Martinho[1], Carlos Costa[2]
and Bruno Blanco-Varela[3]*

Introduction

The regional asymmetries, with overpopulated zones and underdeveloped rural areas, are always a concern for the several stakeholders, namely for the public institutions, at national level (Jermolajeva et al., 2017), and for the diverse international organizations, including for the European Union (EU) policymakers (Clarysse & Muldur, 2001).

The unbalanced regional development is, in fact, dramatic in some countries, where Portugal is not an exception. Portugal received significant funds in the last decades, after the adherence to the current EU, to converge with the European socioeconomic levels, specifically for the agricultural sector (Martinho, 2015). The farming sector assumes a special importance in the rural areas, considering their social, economic, and environmental dimensions (Martinho, 2020). Nonetheless, despite the amounts of financial funds received by the Portuguese institutions the regional asymmetries remain, especially in agriculture (Martinho, 2017).

The Portuguese framework is greatly impacted by the Spanish context, considering the proximity and the consequent socioeconomic relationships. The reality in Spain is not so different from that verified in Portugal, however with specific patterns, where the credit cooperatives, considering their specific characteristics, have had a relevant role to support the less favored regions (Alcaraz et al., 2021). The desertification of rural areas is a serious problem, where it is difficult to find solutions (Medina & Medina, 2020) and where the use and satisfaction with the information and communication technologies seem not enough to avoid problems related to the rural exodus (Pontones-Rosa et al., 2021).

Considering the context described, the main objectives of this research are to assess the rural frameworks in the EU Member States and to find the main determinants of the rural population (factors that affect the number of people in rural areas). A great part of the study is focused on the specific case of Portugal, considering their economic difficulties and the strongly asymmetric regional development between the coast and the inner (in the border with Spain) and between the north and the south (namely after Lisbon). As main insights, it is worth mentioning the importance of small businesses in attracting rural population.

DOI: 10.4324/9781003256281-3

To achieve these aims, statistical information from various databases was considered, specifically from the Eurostat (2021), Pordata (2021), and INE (2021). These data were explored through several approaches and methodologies, including those associated with classification and regression trees techniques, following the IBM SPSS (2019) procedures.

After this section for introduction, the remaining chapter is divided into four sections. They are "Literature review", "Rural realities in the European Union: the specific case of Portugal", "The main determinants of the rural population in the Portuguese municipalities" and, finally, "Discussion and conclusions".

Literature review

In this section, we will address the main highlights from the scientific literature about the following topics: rural development in the EU; rural policies in the EU; and Forgotten Spaces.

Rural Development in the European Union

The rural development is, indeed, a concern for several European stakeholders, including policymakers, because of its importance for the sustainability and due to the different complexities involved. The creation of employment and economic dynamics in rural areas has been the focus of diverse studies, including for rural health enterprises (Apostolopoulos et al., 2020).

The diversification of incomes in the rural regions, in complement of the agricultural activities, is often an alternative to improve well-being and food security (Bojnec & Knific, 2021). The agricultural multifunctionality and the interrelationship between the farming activities and other dynamics that may be developed in the rural zones are crucial to increase the farms survival and resilience.

The rural development of these regions has several endogenous characteristics that open possibilities to increase their sustainability. The small towns may have here a determinant contribution (Stoica et al., 2020). However, there are still constraints that needed to be addressed by the operators involved.

The organic farming sector is an example with great opportunities, but also with diverse constraints (Bryla, 2013), as well as the renewable energies (Chodkowska-Miszczuk et al., 2020), environmentally friendly farming practices (Despotovic et al., 2019), agroecology (Gargano et al., 2021), tourism (Petrovic et al., 2018), beekeeping (Pocol et al., 2012), forest diversification (Pra et al., 2019), and geographical indications (Torok et al., 2020).

The biomass, including farming and industrial waste, is considered as an important source of energy (McKay, 2006). In turn, the tourism is seen as a determinant activity for the rural revival in many rural territories (Sikorski et al., 2020). The younger farmers may bring significant contributions to the agriculture and the rural development (Spicka, 2020).

Another question is about the effects of the different European Union policies on the development of the territories. Considering the great heterogeneity of rural realities and diverse policies targeted for these territories, the impacts are not always the expected (Calegari et al., 2021). More coordination of these policies is needed (Krzyzanowski, 2018), especially for the times after 2020.

The Common Agricultural Policy (CAP), for example, as one of the main drivers of the European agricultural evolution (Rudnicki et al., 2019), suffered several reforms over the times (Michalcewicz-Kaniowska & Zajdel, 2019), including in the rural development strategies (Moyano Pesquera et al., 2017), but some adjustments are still needed.

In any case, the European funds have had positive impacts on the development of the territories, specifically on improving infrastructure (Surowka et al., 2021), nonetheless sometimes not in a balanced way between the richest and poorest spaces (Gospodarowicz, 2015). The adhesion to the EU, jointly with other international phenomena, has increased, in some countries, the asymmetries between the big cities and the rural areas (Laszlo, 2009).

Rural policies in the European Union

The rural development is faced with new challenges (van Eupen et al., 2012), but also new potentialities created by the new technologies, where the concept of "smart" came to stay (Adamowicz, 2018). The European rural policies are called to address properly these new realities.

The climate change is another concern for the institutions, as well as, the preservation of the natural heritage. These concerns led the European institutions to include rural landscape dimensions in the CAP post-2020 (Agnoletti et al., 2019). Nonetheless, these concerns are not new (Marriott et al., 2004) and have been in the mind of the European policymakers (Vlahos & Louloudis, 2011), namely since the CAP reform of 1992.

The rural policies are interrelated with several dimensions (Saraceno, 2013), but for a successful agricultural policy design the involvement of the several stakeholders is crucial. The same happens in the processes of policy implementation (Lacquement, 2012). Training courses and supporting services are, also, important (Cisilino & Monteleone, 2020), as well as, the ex ante assessments (Schleyer & Theesfeld, 2011) as a crucial part of the whole process (Theesfeld et al., 2010). The rural research initiatives are other opportunities to bring insights about the rural development (Eva, 2015) and support the creation of adjusted strategies (Donat et al., 2015).

In any case, the CAP instruments have been a fundamental support for the rural development, namely to interlink the agricultural productions with other dynamics, including agrotourism (Giaccio et al., 2018), with benefits for the sustainability (Mastronardi et al., 2015).

Forgotten Spaces

The process of desertification over several rural areas of the EU has caused the dramatic appearance of abandoned villages, which are Forgotten Spaces with negative consequences for a desirable sustainable development. In these cases, the preservation of the respective heritage is urgent and necessary (Caffio, 2018).

Of highlighting, however, that the concept of Forgotten Spaces is broader and has been considered by the researchers to address other contexts beyond the rural desertification and abandonment (Loggia & Govender, 2020). The expression "Forgotten Spaces" was considered by the scientific community to analyze, also, the following topics: human dignity with pandemic impacts (Fernanda Rivera-Hernandez et al., 2020); cultural landscape (Lopez Sanchez et al., 2021); new challenges for the Atlantic (Potofsky, 2008); and electrification impacts (Tomei et al., 2020).

Rural realities in the European Union: the specific case of Portugal

Considering data from the Eurostat (2021), on average for the period 2011–2018, Figure 1.1 shows that Ireland and Romania are the two EU countries with more than 50% of population in predominantly rural regions. The rural contexts have, in general, specific characteristics (low population densities and a great number of activities related to the agricultural sector) that bring concerns about the socioeconomic dynamics, but may be sources of environmental opportunities. The countries with less rural population (around 10% or less) are the following: Belgium, Spain, Italy, Lithuania, Netherlands, and Sweden.

Portugal, specifically, has a rural population around 30% that decreased from 2011 to 2018 (Figure 1.2). The decrease of population in the rural regions is, in fact,

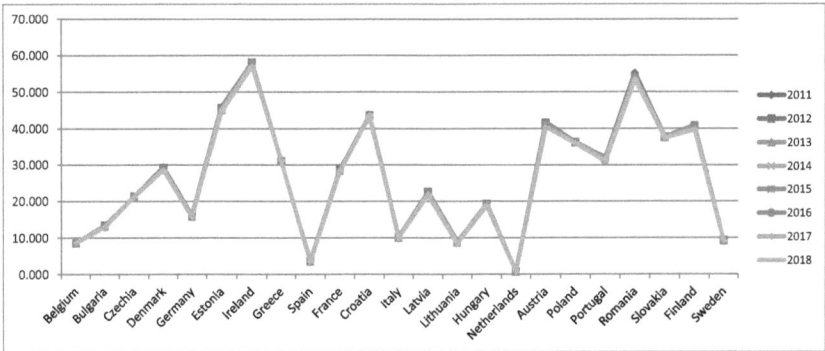

Figure 1.1 Percentage (%) of population in predominantly rural regions over the period 2011–2018 and across European Union countries

Source: Own elaboration considering Eurostat (2021) data

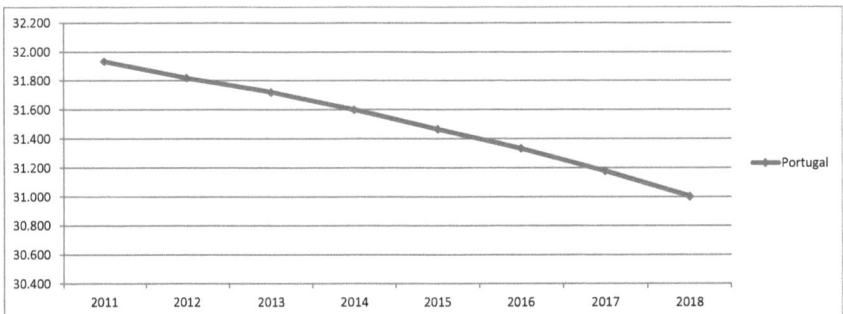

Figure 1.2 Percentage (%) of population in predominantly rural regions over the period 2011–2018 for Portugal

Source: Own elaboration considering Eurostat (2021) data

a problem that deserves special attention by, namely, the public institutions. The abandonment of rural areas creates several problems, including social (desertification) and environmental (unmanaged rural landscape).

Figure 1.3 was obtained through the software QGIS (2021) with shapefiles from dados.gov (2021) and data from Pordata (2021). This figure reveals that the municipalities around Lisboa and Porto are those with less rural population in 2011. The rural exodus creates a double problem with the rural regions abandonment and the congestion of urban areas.

The main determinants of the rural population in the Portuguese municipalities

One of the determinants of the rural population is the natural population balance (difference between the number of live births and the number of deaths) in rural regions. Because of the limited availability of time-series data for the rural population, disaggregated at municipality level, it was considered the natural rural population balance (obtained from INE (2021)) as explained variable in this section. Figure 1.4 presents that the natural population balances, between 2011 and 2018, were always worse in the rural regions and with a decreasing trend.

As independent variables the following were used: average number of nonfinancial companies per Km^2; spending on culture and sport as a percentage of total expenses; municipalities per capita expenditure on the environment (euro-ratio); gross value added of nonfinancial companies (thousand euros). These variables cover socioeconomic and environmental dimensions.

In a total of 2016 observations, over the period 2011–2018 and across the Portuguese municipalities, the averages for the several variables considered (Natural balance (Predominantly rural areas); Average number of non-financial companies per Km^2; Spending on culture and sport as a % of total expenses; Municipalities per capita expenditure on the environment (euro-ratio); Gross value added of non-financial companies (thousand euros)) were respectively the following (Table 1.1): −52 persons, 10 companies/Km^2, 10%, 61 euros per capita and 102187 thousand of euros. These results were obtained through the Stata software (2017a, 2017b; 2021).

To identify the main determinants of the natural rural population balance it was considered the classification and regression trees (Breiman et al., 1984) as main preliminary methodology, following IBM SPSS (2019) procedures. The main determinants of the rural natural balance are the economic variables related to the companies density and the gross value added (Table 1.2).

Figure 1.5 shows that a random Portuguese municipality has a higher probability of belonging to the node 1 (82.1%) for lower gross value added (less or equal to 168718 thousand euros). This random municipality has a higher probability (66.6%) of having a company's density inferior or equal to 11.05 and the same percentage (around 33%) of having a gross value added greater, lower, or equal to 22939.5 thousand euros. The worse natural rural balance was found for the terminal node 5 (−108.5 persons), with a probability of 11.4%. This context occurs in municipalities with a higher gross value added and a lower average number of companies per Km^2 (lower or equal to 22.7).

Figure 1.3 Percentage (%) of population in predominantly rural regions (0–1999 persons) in 2011 and across Portuguese municipalities

Source: Own elaboration considering Pordata (2021) data

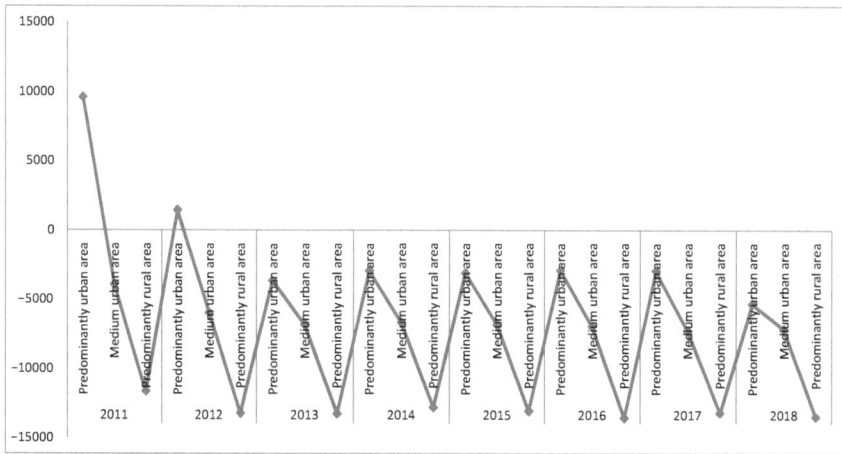

Figure 1.4 Evolution of the natural population balance for Portugal over the period 2011–2018
Source: Own elaboration considering INE (2021) data

Table 1.1 Summary statistics for several variables over the period 2011–2018 and across Portuguese municipalities

Variable	Observations	Mean	Standard deviation	Min	Max
Natural balance (Predominantly rural area)	2016	−51.705	50.445	−370.000	27.000
Average number of non-financial companies per Km^2	2016	9.625	11.977	0.500	116.900
Spending on culture and sport as a % of total expenses	2016	10.239	5.724	0.200	45.000
Municipalities per capita expenditure on the environment	2016	61.360	39.743	1.000	540.800
Gross value added of non-financial companies	2016	102,187.000	158,825.000	2078.000	1373,375.000

Considering these findings, a regression was carried out, following Stata procedures, and the results are presented in Table 1.3. To deal with problems of cross-sectional dependence and heteroscedasticity, it was considered to use panel-corrected standard error methodologies, following, for example, the suggestions of Torres-Reyna (2007).

Table 1.2 Importance of the independent variables for classification and regression tree methodology with natural balance (Predominantly rural area) as dependent variable over the period 2011–2018 and across Portuguese municipalities

Independent Variable	Importance	Normalized Importance
Average number of non-financial companies per Km²	547.565	100.000%
Gross value added of non-financial companies	386.648	70.612%
Municipalities per capita expenditure on the environment	63.350	11.569%
Spending on culture and sport as a % of total expenses	38.828	7.091%

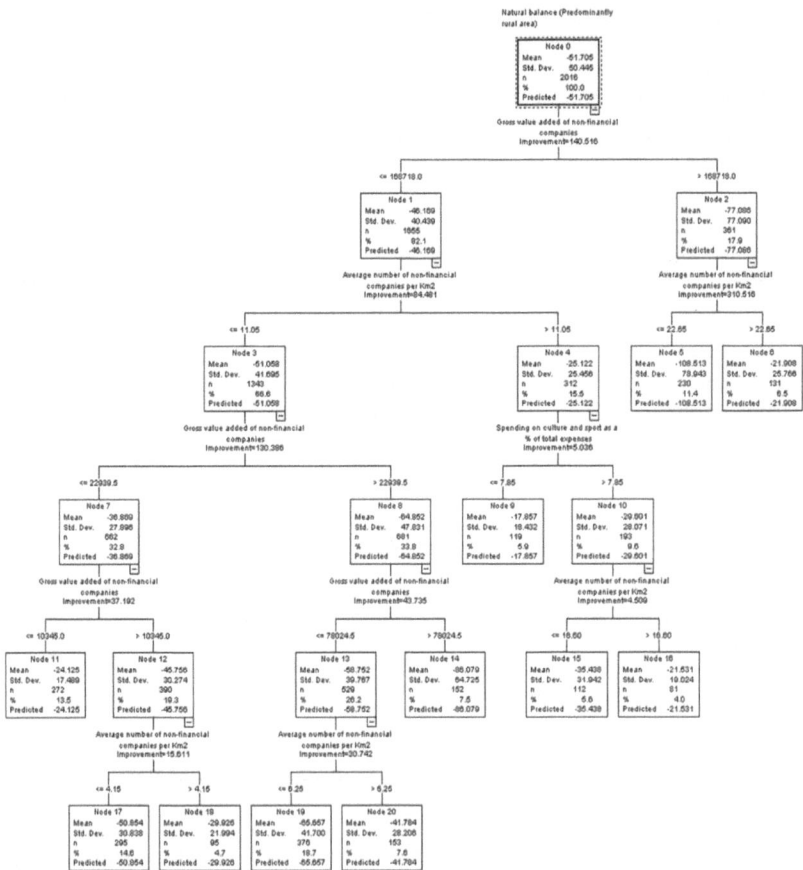

Figure 1.5 Results for classification and regression tree methodology with natural balance (Predominantly rural area) as dependent variable over the period 2011–2018 and across Portuguese municipalities

Source: Own elaboration considering INE (2021) and Pordata (2021) data

Table 1.3 Panel data results with natural balance (Predominantly rural area) as dependent variable over the period 2011–2018 and across Portuguese municipalities

Variables	Method (panel-corrected standard error (PCSE))
Constant	−61.868*
	(−33.430)
	[0.000]
Average number of non-financial companies per Km²	1.831*
	(45.090)
	[0.000]
Spending on culture and sport as a % of total expenses	0.163
	(0.920)
	[0.355]
Municipalities per capita expenditure on the environment	0.069*
	(3.740)
	[0.000]
Gross value added of non-financial companies	−0.000*
	(−26.710)
	[0.000]
Pesaran's test of cross-sectional independence	11.128*
	[0.000]
Modified Wald test for groupwise heteroskedasticity	35,290.390*
	[0.000]
Wooldridge test for autocorrelation	2.598
	[0.108]
Hausman test	23.440*
	[0.000]
VIF	1.330

*Statistically significant at 5%.

The natural rural population balance is explained by the average number of companies per Km² (marginal effect of 1.831), municipalities per capita expenditure on the environment (marginal effect of 0.069), and gross value added (almost null, but negative, marginal effect). This means that the rural natural balance is higher in municipalities with higher average number of companies per Km² and higher per capita expenditure on the environment. The municipalities with greater socioeconomic and environmental dynamics are able to spread positive effects for the rural regions and promote better natural balances in these areas.

Discussion and conclusions

This research aimed to analyze the rural realities in the EU and to identify the main drivers of the rural population, namely in Portugal (considering the problems of asymmetric development between the coast and the inland). To reach these objectives, the literature review focused mainly on the European context and the empirical part was dedicated to the case of Portugal, principally to identify the main variables that influence the rural population through classification and regression trees approach.

The main concern of the several stakeholders for the rural areas is to create social and economic dynamics, namely to promote the employment and avoid the desertification in these regions. The agricultural and rural policies, as well as, the diversification of activities and the multifunctionality of the farming sector are crucial to increase the resilience of the rural frameworks. The organic farming, agroecology, tourism, small manufacturing industry, alternative and renewable sources of energy, among others, are examples of dynamics that may support to increase the sustainability of the less favored zones. The concept of "smart" may open new perspectives for these contexts, as well as a deeper involvement of populations in the design and implementation of the various strategies. The survival of the rural areas in some countries will be a real challenge for the diverse institutions that will need changes in the associated paradigms. It is important to see and accept these contexts as real problems for the sustainability. In this perspective, it could be relevant to characterize these frameworks with the adjusted terms, expressions, and concepts. For example, the expressions "Forgotten Spaces" or "forgotten territories" are far from being vulgar terms among the diverse stakeholders. This seems to be symptomatic of a certain perspective of wanting to see solutions rather than problems and this may bias the design of strategies and programs implementation.

In the EU, some countries, such as Belgium, Spain, Italy, Lithuania, Netherlands, and Sweden, have lower percentages of population in predominantly rural areas. Inversely, Ireland and Romania had the greatest percentages of population in rural regions over the period 2011–2018. In these scenarios, Portugal had a rural population around 30% that decreased over the period considered. The decline of the rural population in Portugal brings problems of desertification in the inland and consequences of congestion in the coast municipalities, namely those around Lisboa and Porto.

To identify the main drivers of the rural population in Portugal, considering the availability of statistical information, the natural population balance (difference between the number of live births and the number of deaths) in rural areas was considered as dependent variables and the following as independent variables: average number of nonfinancial companies per Km^2; spending on culture and sport as a percentage of total expenses; municipalities per capita expenditure on the environment (euro-ratio); and gross value added of nonfinancial companies (thousand euros). These explanatory variables were considered to capture socioeconomic and environmental dimensions. The classification and regression trees approach reveals that the main determinants of the rural natural balance are the number of companies per Km^2 and the gross valued added (economic variables), highlighting that the companies are determinant to create employment and to capture population for the less favored zones. The regression results confirm these findings and highlight the importance of the small companies and the concerns of the municipalities with the environment to fix and attract population.

These insights highlight that one of the main focuses of the several stakeholders, namely the policymakers should be on the attraction of investment that promotes the creation of companies to increase the economic and social dynamics. The cooperation between public institutions, research organizations and companies is crucial for success in the rural regions (Dileo & Pini, 2021).

Acknowledgments

This work is funded by National Funds through the FCT – Foundation for Science and Technology, I.P., within the scope of the project Ref^a UIDB/00681/2020. Furthermore, we would like to thank the CERNAS Research Centre and the Polytechnic Institute of Viseu for their support.

Notes

1   Coordinator Professor with Habilitation, Department of Ecology and Sustainable Agriculture (DEAS), Agricultural School (ESAV) and CERNAS-IPV Research Centre, Polytechnic Institute of Viseu (IPV), Portugal, email: vdmartinho@esav.ipv.pt (ORCID ID: 0000–0001–9967–7940).
2   Assistant Professor, Department of Economy, Sociology and Management (DESG), School of Human and Social Sciences (ECHS) and CETRAD, University of Trás-os-Montes and Alto Douro (UTAD), Portugal, email: cfonseca@utad.pt (ORCID ID: 0000–0003–3324–6982).
3   Lecturer, Department of Applied Economics, Faculty of Economics and Business Administration, University of Santiago de Compostela, Spain, email: b.blanco.varela@usc.es (ORCID: 0000–0001–5319–6578).

References

Adamowicz, M. (2018). Normative aspects of rural development strategy and policy in the European Union. In A. Auzina (Ed.), *Rural development and entrepreneurship production and cooperation in agriculture* (Vol. 47, pp. 17–27). Latvia: Latvia University of Agriculture. https://doi.org/10.22616/ESRD.2018.001

Agnoletti, M., Emanueli, F., Corrieri, F., Venturi, M., & Santoro, A. (2019). Monitoring traditional rural landscapes. The case of Italy. *Sustainability*, *11*(21), 6107. https://doi.org/10.3390/su11216107

Alcaraz, M. C., Monteagudo, I. C., & Tormo, F. S. (2021). El papel de las cooperativas de crédito en el sostenimiento de la España vaciada a través del capital social. *REVESCO. Revista de Estudios Cooperativos*, *138*, e73866–e73866. https://doi.org/10.5209/reve.73866

Apostolopoulos, N., Ratten, V., Stavroyiannis, S., Makris, I., Apostolopoulos, S., & Liargovas, P. (2020). Rural health enterprises in the EU context: A systematic literature review and research agenda. *Journal of Enterprising Communities-People and Places in the Global Economy*, *14*(4), 563–582. https://doi.org/10.1108/JEC-04-2020-0070

Bojnec, S., & Knific, K. (2021). Farm household income diversification as a survival strategy. *Sustainability*, *13*(11), 6341. https://doi.org/10.3390/su13116341

Breiman, L., Friedman, J., Stone, C. J., & Olshen, R. A. (1984). *Classification and regression trees*. London: Taylor & Francis.

Bryla, P. (2013). Marketing of ecological food products – Results of a research study among polish processors. *Rocznik Ochrona Srodowiska*, *15*, 2899–2910.

Caffio, G. (2018). Drawing for the future: Micro-cities, villages and landscapes of Abruzzo. In G. Amoruso (Ed.), *Putting tradition into practice: Heritage, place and design* (Vol. 3, pp. 949–956). New York: Springer International Publishing Ag. https://doi.org/10.1007/978-3-319-57937-5_97

Calegari, E., Fabrizi, E., Guastella, G., & Timpano, F. (2021). EU regional convergence in the agricultural sector: Are there synergies between agricultural and regional policies? *Papers in Regional Science, 100*(1). https://doi.org/10.1111/pirs.12569

Chodkowska-Miszczuk, J., Martinat, S., Kulla, M., & Novotny, L. (2020). Renewables projects in peripheries: Determinants, challenges and perspectives of biogas plants – Insights from Central European countries. *Regional Studies Regional Science, 7*(1), 362–381. https://doi.org/10.1080/21681376.2020.1807399

Cisilino, F., & Monteleone, A. (2020). Designing rural policies for sustainable innovations through a participatory approach. *Sustainability, 12*(21), 9100. https://doi.org/10.3390/su12219100

Clarysse, B., & Muldur, U. (2001). Regional cohesion in Europe? An analysis of how EU public RTD support influences the techno-economic regional landscape. *Research Policy, 30*(2), 275–296. https://doi.org/10.1016/S0048-7333(99)00113-4

dados.gov. (2021). *Portuguese municipalities shapefiles.* https://dados.gov.pt/pt/datasets/concelhos-de-portugal/

Despotovic, J., Rodic, V., & Caracciolo, F. (2019). Factors affecting farmers' adoption of integrated pest management in Serbia: An application of the theory of planned behavior. *Journal of Cleaner Production, 228*, 1196–1205. https://doi.org/10.1016/j.jclepro.2019.04.149

Dileo, I., & Pini, M. (2021). The quadruple helix partnerships for enterprise eco-innovation in Italian macro-regions under the lens of smart specialization strategy. In M. Gancarczyk, A. Ujwary-Gil, & M. González-López (Eds.), *Partnerships for regional innovation and development: Implementing smart specialization in Europe.* London: Routledge.

Donat, K. A., Zsolt, F. J., & Eva, P. (2015). Definition, delimitation and classification of rural areas. *Ter Es Tarsadalom, 29*(1), 11–34. https://doi.org/10.17649/TET.29.1.2674

Eurostat. (2021). *Several statistics.* https://ec.europa.eu/eurostat

Eva, P. (2015). A complex rural research program conducted by the Hungarian academy of sciences and the Hungarian national rural network – An introduction. *Ter Es Tarsadalom, 29*(1), 3–10. https://doi.org/10.17649/TET.29.1.2698

Fernanda Rivera-Hernandez, C., Castillo-Forero, J., Yaneth Martinez-Sanchez, M., Magnolia Chingate-Hortua, N., & Milena Sanabria-Lopez, S. (2020). Forgotten spaces in human dignity during pandemic times. *Nodo, 15*(29), 99–113.

Gargano, G., Licciardo, F., Verrascina, M., & Zanetti, B. (2021). The agroecological approach as a model for multifunctional agriculture and farming towards the European green deal 2030-some evidence from the Italian experience. *Sustainability, 13*(4), 2215. https://doi.org/10.3390/su13042215

Giaccio, V., Mastronardi, L., Marino, D., Giannelli, A., & Scardera, A. (2018). Do rural policies impact on tourism development in Italy? A case study of Agritourism. *Sustainability, 10*(8), 2938. https://doi.org/10.3390/su10082938

Gospodarowicz, M. (2015). Social and technical infrastructure development of municipalities (gminas) in Poland. *Studies in Agricultural Economics, 117*(3), 147–154. https://doi.org/10.7896/j.1510

IBM Corp. (2019). *IBM SPSS statistics for windows, Version 26.0.* New York: IBM Corp.

INE. (2021). *Several statistics.* www.ine.pt/xportal/xmain?xpgid=ine_main&xpid=INE

Jermolajeva, E., Rivza, B., Aleksejeva, L., Sipilova, V., & Ostrovska, I. (2017). Smart growth as a tool for regional convergence: Evidence from latgale region of Latvia. *Economics & Sociology, 10*(4), 203–224. https://doi.org/10.14254/2071-789X.2017/10-4/16

Krzyzanowski, J. (2018). Tasks of the CAP after 2020. In M. Wigier, & A. Kowalski (Eds.), *Common agricultural policy of the European Union – The present and the future: Eu Member States point of view* (pp. 18–26). Institute of Agricultural & Food Economics, National Research Inst-Iafe-Nri. https://doi.org/10.30858/pw/9788376587431.1

Lacquement, G. (2012). Local governance practices in Eastern Germany: Institutional trans-fers, social learning and 'network logics' in the EU's Leader Program, 2007–2013. *Revue D Etudes Comparatives Est-Ouest*, *43*(3), 57.

Laszlo, J. (2009). Sectoral background of urban-rural economic development inequalities in Visegrad Countries. In M. Bucek, R. Capello, O. Hudec, & P. Nijkamp (Eds.), *Cers 2009–3rd central European conference in regional science, International conference proceedings – Young scientists articles* (pp. 1085–1094). Slovakia: Technical University of Kosice.

Loggia, C., & Govender, V. (2020). A hybrid methodology to map informal settlements in Durban, South Africa. *Proceedings of the Institution of Civil Engineers-Engineering Sustainabil-ity*, *173*(5), 257–268. https://doi.org/10.1680/jensu.19.00005

Lopez Sanchez, M., Linares Gomez Del Pulgar, M., & Tejedor Cabrera, A. (2021). Historic construction of diffuse cultural landscapes: Towards a GIS-based method for mapping the interlinkages of heritage. *Landscape Research*, *46*(7), 916–931. https://doi.org/10.1080/01 426397.2021.1921717

Marriott, C. A., Fothergill, M., Jeangros, B., Scotton, M., & Louault, F. (2004). Long-term impacts of extensification of grassland management on biodiversity and productivity in upland areas. A review. *Agronomie*, *24*(8), 447–462. https://doi.org/10.1051/agro:2004041

Martinho, V. J. P. D. (2015). Output impacts of the single payment scheme in Portugal: A regression with spatial effects. *Outlook on Agriculture*, *44*(2), 109–118. https://doi.org/10.5367/oa.2015.0203

Martinho, V. J. P. D. (2017). Insights from over 30 years of common agricultural policy in Por-tugal. *Outlook on Agriculture*, *46*(3), 223–229. https://doi.org/10.1177/0030727017729896

Martinho, V. J. P. D. (2020). Agricultural entrepreneurship in the European Union: Contribu-tions for a sustainable development. *Applied Sciences*, *10*(6), 2080. https://doi.org/10.3390/app10062080

Mastronardi, L., Giaccio, V., Giannelli, A., & Scardera, A. (2015). Is agritourism eco-friendly? A comparison between agritourisms and other farms in Italy using farm accountancy data network dataset. *Springerplus*, *4*, 590. https://doi.org/10.1186/s40064-015-1353-4

McKay, H. (2006). Environmental, economic, social and political drivers for increasing use of woodfuel as a renewable resource in Britain. *Biomass & Bioenergy*, *30*(4), 308–315. https://doi.org/10.1016/j.biombioe.2005.07.008

Medina, M. S., & Medina, J. S. (2020). Resiliencia territorial y sostenibilidad en la Es-paña vaciada. In G. X. Pons, A. Blanco-Romero, R. Navalón-García, L. Troitiño-Torralba, & M. Blázquez-Salom (Eds.), *Sostenibilidad turística: Overtourism vs undertourism*. (pp. 31–42). Societat d'Història Natural de les Balears. https://dialnet.unirioja.es/servlet/articulo?codigo=7593075

Michalcewicz-Kaniowska, M., & Zajdel, M. (2019). Rural development in European Union policy. In A. Auzina (Ed.), *Economic science for rural development 2019* (Issue 50, pp. 140–146). Latvia: Latvia Univ Life Sciences & Technologies. https://doi.org/10.22616/ESRD.2019.017

Moyano Pesquera, P. B., Miranda Escolar, B., & Gordo Gomez, P. (2017). The involvement of economic and social stakeholders in the revitalization of rural municipalities. *Investiga-ciones Regionales*, *38*, 91–115.

Petrovic, M. D., Vujko, A., Gajic, T., Vukovic, D. B., Radovanovic, M., Jovanovic, J. M., & Vukovic, N. (2018). Tourism as an approach to sustainable rural development in post-socialist countries: A comparative study of Serbia and Slovenia. *Sustainability, 10*(1), 54. https://doi.org/10.3390/su10010054

Pocol, C. B., Marghitas, L. A., & Popa, A. A. (2012). Evaluation of sustainability of the beekeeping sector in the North West Region of Romania. *Journal of Food Agriculture & Environment, 10*(3–4), 132–138.

Pontones-Rosa, C., Pérez-Morote, R., & Santos-Peñalver, J. F. (2021). ICT-based public policies and depopulation in hollowed-out Spain: A survey analysis on the digital divide and citizen satisfaction. *Technological Forecasting and Social Change, 169*, 120811. https://doi.org/10.1016/j.techfore.2021.120811

Pordata. (2021). *Several statistics*. www.pordata.pt/

Potofsky, A. (2008). New perspectives in the Atlantic. *History of European Ideas, 34*(4), 383–387. https://doi.org/10.1016/j.histeuroideas.2008.08.006

Pra, A., Brotto, L., Mori, P., Lattes, E. B., Masiero, M., Andrighetto, N., & Pettenella, D. (2019). Profitability of timber plantations on agricultural land in the Po valley (northern Italy): A comparison between walnut, hybrid poplar and polycyclic plantations in the light of the European Union Rural Development Policy orientation. *European Journal of Forest Research, 138*(3), 473–494. https://doi.org/10.1007/s10342-019-01184-4

QGIS.org. (2021). QGIS geographic information system. *QGIS Association*. www.qgis.org

Rudnicki, R., Jezierska-Thoele, A., & Biczkowski, M. (2019). The impact of common agricultural policy on socio-economic development in Poland. In T. Loster, & T. Pavelka (Eds.), *13th international days of statistics and economics* (pp. 1309–1318). Libuše Macáková, Melandrium. https://doi.org/10.18267/pr.2019.los.186.131

Saraceno, E. (2013). Disparity and diversity: Their use in EU rural policies. *Sociologia Ruralis, 53*(3), 331–348. https://doi.org/10.1111/soru.12017

Schleyer, C., & Theesfeld, I. (2011). Agricultural and environmental policies from an institutional economics perspective: A method for ex-ante policy assessment. *German Journal of Agricultural Economics, 60*(3), 186–199.

Sikorski, D., Latocha, A., Szmytkie, R., Kajdanek, K., Miodonska, P., & Tomczak, P. (2020). Functional changes in peripheral mountainous areas in east central Europe between 2004 and 2016 as an aspect of rural revival? Klodzko County case study. *Applied Geography, 122*, 102223. https://doi.org/10.1016/j.apgeog.2020.102223

Spicka, J. (2020). Socio-demographic drivers of the risk-taking propensity of micro farmers evidence from the Czech Republic. *Journal of Entrepreneurship in Emerging Economies, 12*(4), 569–590. https://doi.org/10.1108/JEEE-09-2019-0143

Stata. (2021). *Stata: Software for statistics and data science*. www.stata.com/

StataCorp. (2017a). *Stata 15 base reference manual*. College Station, TX: Stata Press.

StataCorp. (2017b). *Stata statistical software: Release 15*. College Station, TX: StataCorp LLC.

Stoica, I. V., Tulla, A. F., Zamfir, D., & Petrisor, A. I. (2020). Exploring the urban strength of small Towns in Romania. *Social Indicators Research, 152*(3), 843–875. https://doi.org/10.1007/s11205-020-02465-x

Surowka, M., Poplawski, L., & Fidlerova, H. (2021). Technical infrastructure as an element of sustainable development of rural regions in Malopolskie Voivodeship in Poland and Trnava Region in Slovakia. *Agriculture-Basel, 11*(2), 141. https://doi.org/10.3390/agriculture11020141

Theesfeld, I., Schleyer, C., & Aznar, O. (2010). The procedure for institutional compatibility assessment: Ex-ante policy assessment from an institutional perspective. *Journal of Institutional Economics, 6*(3), 377–399. https://doi.org/10.1017/S1744137410000056

Tomei, J., Cronin, J., Agudelo Arias, H. D., Cordoba Machado, S., Mena Palacios, M. F., Toro Ortiz, Y. M., Borja Cuesta, Y. E., Palomino Lemus, R., Murillo Lopez, W., &

Anandarajah, G. (2020). Forgotten spaces: How reliability, affordability and engagement shape the outcomes of last-mile electrification in Choco, Colombia. *Energy Research & Social Science, 59*, 101302. https://doi.org/10.1016/j.erss.2019.101302

Torok, A., Jantyik, L., Maro, Z. M., & Moir, H. V. J. (2020). Understanding the real-world impact of geographical indications: A critical review of the empirical economic literature. *Sustainability, 12*(22), 9434. https://doi.org/10.3390/su12229434

Torres-Reyna, O. (2007). *Panel data analysis fixed and random effects using Stata (v. 4.2).* https://dss.princeton.edu/training/Panel101.pdf

van Eupen, M., Metzger, M. J., Perez-Soba, M., Verburg, P. N., van Doorn, A., & Bunce, R. G. H. (2012). A rural typology for strategic European policies. *Land Use Policy, 29*(3), 473–482. https://doi.org/10.1016/j.landusepol.2011.07.007

Vlahos, G., & Louloudis, L. (2011). Landscape and agriculture under the reformed common agricultural policy in Greece: Constructing a typology of interventions. *Geografisk Tidsskrift-Danish Journal of Geography, 111*(2), 131–147. https://doi.org/10.1080/001672 23.2011.10669529

2 Agglomeration of knowledge-intensive activities and brain drain

Global cities and forgotten regions across Europe – a case study with Spanish data

Jose Blanco-Álvarez[1] and Manuel González-López[2]

Introduction

At the beginning of the 21st century, the optimism for the so-called New Economy led to the popularization of theories advocating that globalization and the expansion of modern technologies had created a *flat world* due to the *death of distance* (Cairncross, 2001; Friedman, 2005). Nowadays, it is widely recognized that even when innovative technologies and globalization change permanently the rules of competition, geographical conditions still apply to location choices. The emergence of a selected group of *global cities* (Sassen, 1991), that combine the political power and the headquarters of multinationals that govern over the global value chains gave us a new expression: today we live in a "spiky world" where the spikes are the global cities (Florida, 2005b). According to this vision, instead of decreasing the regional disparities, modern technologies can indeed increase the gap between rich and poor regions. One of the reasons is that knowledge-intensive activities show a trend to agglomerate in certain regions. This is especially true for the "knowledge-intensive business services" (KIBS hereinafter) which need a critical mass of potential clients and some other conditions to become viable. Such agglomeration trends would explain the attraction of productive factors toward larger cities, including skilled labor, as KIBS activities are particularly intensive in the use of highly qualified personnel. On the other hand, less developed or peripheral regions would have difficulties in retaining highly qualified personnel, showing a *brain drain* problem and therefore reducing their growth and development potential. This issue could be amplified if these territories qualified as "forgotten regions", that is, not only socioeconomically underdeveloped but also unattended by policymakers.

The aim of this chapter is to understand the dynamics explaining the relationship between the agglomeration of knowledge-intensive activities, and particularly KIBS, and migration flows at regional level. Our main research hypothesis states that this agglomeration is one of the main factors driving migration flows, particularly those of high skilled work.

The biggest obstacle to conduct this analysis is the absence of regional (subnational) data to study the migration in the European Union (EU). We get over this inconvenience using a case study of the Spanish situation. Spain is an interesting

DOI: 10.4324/9781003256281-4

example for several reasons: it is a developed country but shows GDP per capita below the EU average, with remarkable regional differences. In recent years, the country saw a growing social movement demanding political actions to address the increasing concentration of economic activity in some urban areas (especially Madrid and to the least extent Barcelona). This led to sustained emigration flux, which aggravate the demographic perspectives of the "forgotten regions", poaching its human capital and therefore harming their efforts to also update to a knowledge-based economy which would help to socioeconomic convergence. We should also note that some policies aimed to foster research and development in the EU might increase the existent regional imbalance, as the excellence and free competition are the main rules of funding distribution (Varela-Vázquez & González-López, 2020).

For our purposes, the availability of Spanish data at the subnational level is helpful. We have access to quality data on labor migration, population, and wages at the provincial level, which allows us to test our hypothesis with a balanced panel from 2001 to 2018.[3] To measure the agglomeration of KIBS we employ business data that allows us to compute a Regional Relative Specialization Index showing the position of each province. We then use a pseudo-gravity model of migration to test the hypothesis that the degree of KIBS concentration in Spanish regions is positively correlated with the capacity of these territories to attract high skilled immigrants. If the hypothesis confirmed, the same roots of the normal functioning of contemporary economies will induce agglomeration of human capital and the counterpart, brain drain, from the forgotten regions. This finding will justify the implementing of specific policies aiming to correct this gap in the spite of regional cohesion.

The structure of this chapter is as follows: first, we do a literature review of the knowledge-based economy and the factors explaining its agglomeration, with special emphasis on the KBIS. Second, we do a proper review of the brain drain literature, aiming to understand its implications for regional (subnational) economies. Third, we try to reconcile the two literature bodies and draw the basic lines between them. As a fourth point, we focus on relationships between KIBS and migration both from the perspective of global cities and forgotten regions. With this, we are ready to start the fifth section with our case study of Spain. We start this part describing the general context of Spanish regions related to KIBS' agglomeration and migration patterns. Following, we explain the functioning of pseudo-gravity models we rely on to study migration flows and introduce our empirical specification. Next, we describe the data we collected and employ in this analysis. Finally, we present and discuss our main results. Our conclusions derived from the literature revision and the empirical case study close the chapter.

Knowledge-based economy and agglomeration

The concept of knowledge-based economies describes a long-term tendency observed within the last decades, for which the creation and accumulation of knowledge become the crucial factor for business competitiveness (Abramowitz & David, 1996; David & Foray, 2003; Lundvall & Foray, 1996; Powell & Snellman, 2004).

As it is conceived to be a productive paradigm change, it has consequences for the regional location of economic activity.

Inquiry into the spatial conditions that interact with economic factors experienced a revival following the developments of the "New Economic Geography" which emphasized the importance of increasing returns on production, scale economies and externalities as factors that mitigate the trade costs arising from distance and thus help to explain patterns of regional agglomeration (Hanson, 2001; Krugman, 1991, 1995, 1998).

Applied to the knowledge-based economy, the importance of *spillover* effects as transmission channels of this knowledge configure the degree of agglomeration of industries relying on them. This agglomeration is sector specific and depends crucially on the amount of tacit knowledge involved. Aside from theoretical models, empirical studies suggest that industries relying on knowledge tend to cluster where these knowledge inputs are more available (Vence-Deza & González-López, 2008).

Altogether with this general idea, it appeared the concept of "knowledge-intensive business services" (KIBS), first theorized in the decade of 90s to "describe services consisting in the creation, accumulation or dissemination of knowledge" (Miles et al., 1995). The development of modern technologies and the process of economic integration allow the division of the value chains, which become global. The manufacturing activities were then increasingly outsourced to developing nations, while the developed countries started to become postindustrial societies where the services had the main importance. In this context, the KIBS acts by creating new knowledge and by diffusing this knowledge through its relationship with its clients.

Inside this diversity of service sector, the two basic differentiations of KIBS are (Zieba, 2021): (i) their orientation to business, both public and private, and (ii) their intensive use of knowledge, understood as a type of capital or productive resource. If old classifications distinguish between capital- and labor-intensive sectors, then the KIBS are human capital-intensive. Regarding the location choices, there are several factors that explain the KIBS tendency to agglomerate in core regions, usually within urban areas. We summarize them in four points (Vence-Deza & González-López, 2014):

- First, the market size matters. The KIBS sell highly specialized services, which required a critical mass of potential buyers to become viable. Therefore, low densely populated areas (in terms of both population and business demography) are not suitable to host these companies.
- Second, the headquarters of multinational companies show a tendency to agglomerate in global cities, close together with the political power. As both of these structures are responsible for decision-making and constituted the principal clients of KIBS, they act as explainers of this agglomeration.
- Third, the KIBS merged with (are part of) the regional system of innovation (RSI) and shared its resources with these superstructures. To our purposes, it is especially relevant that there is a pool of high skilled workers with a high degree of embodied tacit knowledge.

- Fourth, counterintuitively, the improvement of transportation and the decreasing cost of telecommunications could increase the agglomeration of KIBS. As peripheral regions become closer in time to core regions, but lack the critical mass of potential buyers, their demand can be supplied by exportations from the KIBS headquarters.

High skilled migration and brain drain at the regional level

High skilled migration

One of the main characteristics of the evolution of international migration over the last decades is the increase in the proportion of high skilled migrants, defined as those with tertiary education (d'Aiglepierre et al., 2020). This trend raises concerns about the potentially harmful consequences for sending countries with high skilled emigration rates, an issue popularly known as "brain drain". To summarize, if we accept that high skilled individuals are the basic enablers of the knowledge-based economy, or more generally, if we draw from the endogenous growth models that use human capital as their main explanatory variable, this emigration will lead to a decrease in the human capital level remaining in the source country and *ceteris paribus*, decrease their development potential.[4] Some recent studies suggest the relevance of this negative effect in source countries. For example, Oliinyk et al. (2021) find a positive correlation between the attraction of high skilled migrants and various synthetic indexes related to country's competitiveness. Reversely, these indicators show a negative correlation with measures of brain drain. Kasnauskiene and Palubinskait (2020) used data on immigration to the United Kingdom to study the effects of the Eastern Expansion of the EU. They found that the surge of emigration from these new members have reduced their economic growth. Sometimes the relevance of the brain drain issue is downplayed by stating that modern migration paths are more resemblant of a brain circulation where high skilled individuals migrate only temporarily and can contribute to the development of their home territories by returning with the enhanced experience and knowledge gained at their destination. Empirical evidence, however, suggests that both brain grain and brain circulation coexist in the EU and are dependent on factors such as the country of origin and the main determinants of migration (Teney, 2021).

At theoretical level, the causes (or determinants) of this high skilled migration have been described as nearly the same from the start. The basic model has its roots in the conception of "useful skills and knowledge" being a type of capital inherent to individuals, commonly known as human capital (Schultz, 1961). If in the past, the "labor force" has being characterized as a rather homogeneous productive force together with the triad of land (resources) and (physical) capital, from this moment on it will be recognized as complex and heterogeneous. Human capital emphasizes not only the quantity but also the quality of the human beings involved in productive tasks. This human capital is not an innate characteristic, but the results of investments made in education and formal training. As any other investment, their owners seek to maximize their utility (or benefits). Therefore, the migration appears simply as a move to maximize this utility. Individuals move to regions where the return to their skills is bigger after discounting the cost of migration (Sjaastad, 1962).

The sociologist view has greatly contributed to improve these models with the introduction of the concept of "migrant networks" derived from the social capital and the social networks. According to the migration studies, these migration networks are defined as the set of social relationships that interconnect individuals with migrant background at both destination and sending communities. By reducing the problem of imperfect information and providing support, these networks greatly lower the cost of migration, thus acting as a bridge or enabler to the establishment of further migrants (Massey & García España, 1987; Portes & Sensenbrenner, 1993).

Reconciling high skilled migration with the regional perspective

Even when the first studies of migration pay considerable attention to internal migration, the topic soon becomes relegated in favor of the international migration, with the availability of data as a main problem. At a general level, the absence of significant legal barriers to internal migration and the cultural and geographical proximity reduces the costs of migration and should make individuals more able to move in response to smaller income gaps between regions.

Regarding brain drain, only a few studies incorporated some considerations of application to the regional perspective, either directly or indirectly. First, Miyagiwa (1991) argued that in the presence of increasing returns in education led to a sustained brain drain from less to more populated countries, as the "productivity of professional work increases with an increase in the number of similar professionals concentrated in one location". This corollary can be contested, and we believe that it is not only the gross population differences but also the density of high skilled jobs (closely related to market size for KIBS) which causes this brain drain. The model was applied to international migration, with the example of the USA and Taiwan, but their application to internal case yields the same results, but amplified, as there are no significant barriers to internal migration. More recently, Malul (2015) has developed a theoretical model to explicitly consider the internal brain drain from peripheral regions. In this case, it is the initial level of economic scope which explains, even without increasing returns to education, the migration to core regions. This is because he considers that the returns to education depend positively on the initial level of physical capital. Moreover, if the companies take their investment decisions considering the level of human capital, this dynamic can deepen the gaps between core and peripheral regions.

Aside from these interesting additions to the migration theory, the brain drain has not been empirically studied at subnational level on a holistic perspective. Instead, from our revision of literature, we can name three different topics related or applied to some degree to regional brain drain:

- Studies about the migration of postsecondary students. At international level, some studies show how the international postsecondary students usually have a high desire to remain in their host countries. Therefore, this temporal migration can become a brain drain. Applied to the regional (subnational) case, this problem seems to amplify. Without significant barriers to migration, students from low developed regions flow to core developed regions to study, and, with high probability, they enter the labor market here. The main determinant factors that explain this migration flows are the higher quality of educational institutions and the labor opportunities. On the other hand, the some-what abstract "feeling of belonging" (attachment) to their home region is the key to explain the decision to remain or return (García-Arias et al., 2021; Liu et al., 2017; Maleszyk, 2021; Thissen et al., 2010).

- The migration of scientific and researcher personnel. Another specific branch of studies analyzed the scientific mobility. Even when the international migration is their main area of interest, some studies address the competence between universities inside a country, namely China (Zhou et al., 2018). In nearly all cases, the best research institutions and infrastructure tend to agglomerate in core regions, therefore explaining this migration patterns.
- The impact of internal migration and convergence. Taking a macroeconomic perspective, some studies analyze the impact of human capital accumulation in the regional convergence. Drawing from the endogenous growth models, the presence of high skilled migration flows (i.e., brain drain) help to explain the persistence of regional disparities (Basile et al., 2019; Fratesi & Percoco, 2014).

To sum up, all these studies suggest that brain drain is potentially a bigger issue in the internal setting, where migration barriers are absent. Migration flows are generally directed from rural or less developed areas to urban and dynamic regions where the demand for high skilled jobs agglomerates. This process can damage the potential for economic convergence. Now, we are going to focus specifically on the links between global cities, KIBS and migration.

KBIS and high skilled migration, from global cities to "forgotten regions"

As we already mentioned in the introduction, the discussion about the relationship between dynamic cities and high skilled immigrants continues today. It is argued that we live in a global world where cities compete to attract high skilled (talented) individuals by providing more and better amenities and, in a broad sense, building tolerative and attractive environments. These efforts are justified because the current economy uses knowledge as its main input and a substantial share of this knowledge is tacit, that is, inherent to the individual, and so, hard, or impossible to codify and transmit. Therefore, these individuals by themselves, inserted in the correct framework, will help the economic growth of the city (region) by starting or engaging in innovative business and activities (Florida, 2002, 2003, 2005a).

Without challenging the core logic of these theories, some authors downplay the importance of amenities and tolerant environment to attract these workers and the ability of individuals by themselves to generate economic growth. From their perspective, the location of economic activity within the cities (i.e., the prevailing productive structure), specially of knowledge-intensive activities, is the main explainer of these immigration flows (Storper, 2010; Storper & Scott, 2009).

It is worth noting that both explanations are not exclusive: while it is true that international mobility has been increasing, it remains as the less liberalized productive factor. Moreover, the immigration policies of majority of countries make mandatory the existence of a job offer to get a residence permit. Only a few countries, those with the called points-system allow for legal immigration without job offer. Therefore, it is naïve to consider that talented people emigrate only basing their decision on the amenities of destination (Chaloff & Lemaître, 2009).

Related to this debate, is the concept of "global city": an abstract simplification to name the cities that excel in their contribution to contemporaneous society and economy either by its political, cultural or socioeconomic prominence at global level (Sassen, 1991). To decide what objective criteria can be used to define a city as "global" is a tricky question and, today, several classifications of global cities coexist.[5] Besides definition problems, the idea that the majority of migrants tend to agglomerate in urban areas and, within this, in the most prominent cities is well extended, with some recent empirical evidence (Kerr et al., 2017; Labrianidis et al., 2021).

However, if we consider internal migration, this agglomeration has a side effect not always recognized: the loss of population in the sending regions. As the migrants are usually positively selected from the base population (i.e, they are younger and more educated), this migration sustained over time will lead to the loss of the remaining human capital, in a process of internal brain drain. The magnitude of this migration could be potentially larger as there are no legal barriers to prevent it and its consequences could be more severe as some of the potentially countervailing mechanisms might not act in the internal scenario. On the other hand, the advantage of these regions is their insertion in a national framework where redistributive mechanisms exist and can be used to address this problematic.

Until this moment, the attention has been centered on the bright side of the process. Nevertheless, it is unrealistic to expect these "forgotten regions" to become global cities by any means. Instead, it would be more useful to open a debate and start thinking about how to use their own resources and capabilities to improve their positions and become less subordinated to these global cities.

We are aware that, at the current state of the art, it is nearly impossible to resolve the debate via proving casualty relationship between KIBS and high skilled immigration, or vice-versa. However, we have a solid theoretical basis to sustain our hypothesis that both variables are strongly correlated, and so we are going to try to prove that at empirical level in our next section.

Spanish case study

Context

Spain is a developed country with a high degree of decentralization starting from the process of transition to democracy in 1978. Today the country is organized into 52 provinces, which are grouped into 17 Autonomous Communities (regional level, equivalent to NUTS-2) according to their sociocultural similarities and historical trajectories.

These Autonomous Communities host regional governments responsible for a big share of public spending, including education and health services. Despite this political decentralization and the use of convergence funds, the economic differences persist. For example, with provincial GDP data from 2018, the richest province shows a GDP per capita roughly two times bigger than the poorest.[6] Some of these differences arise from the dysfunctional labor market, with national unemployment rates clearly above EU average, with important regional disparities.

In Figure 2.1, we present evidence of the agglomeration of KIBS in Spain, using the next regional relative specialization (RRS) index: (see next section with regard to the data sources and for precisions about calculation).

$$RRS_{kjt} = \frac{Emp_{kjt}}{\sum_{j} Emp_{kjt}} \Bigg/ \frac{\sum_{k} Emp_{kjt}}{\sum_{j}\sum_{k} Emp_{kjt}}$$

Where Emp_{kjt} is the employment at sector k in region j at year t. Table 2.4 in the annex depicts the average RRS for the period 2001–2018.

As we can see from Figure 2.1, only five provinces are specialized in this sector (RRS > 1), with the clear leadership of Madrid above all. These results are consistent with previous findings in the literature (González-López, 2009). Our main hypothesis is that this agglomeration of business (and employment) in KIBS will

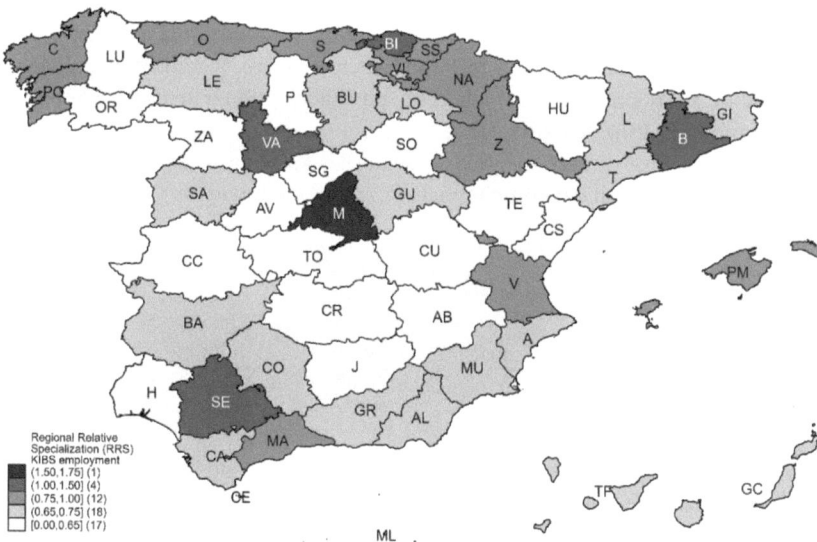

Figure 2.1   Regional relative specialization of KIBS employment in Spanish provinces, average for 1990–2020

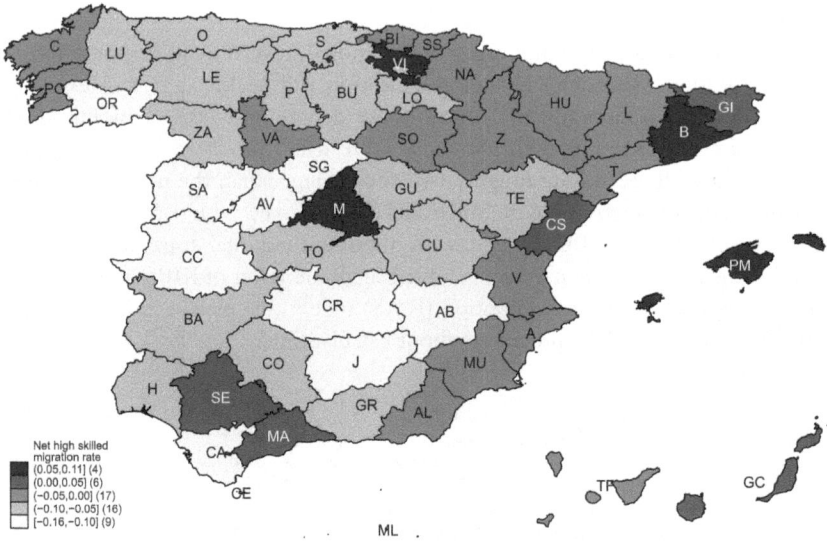

Figure 2.2   Net migration rate with labor contracts to high skilled workers by Spanish provinces, average for 2001–2018

mainly attract high skilled emigrants, as the job availability is the main determinant of internal migration. This might be particularly true for tertiary educated individuals who need to recover the costs incurred in their education investment. If the qualified jobs related to their field of specialization are scarce in their home provinces, they can opt for accepting jobs for which they are overqualified. However, this could be a suboptimal choice when the possibility to migrate there where these qualified jobs are available exists.

In Figure 2.2, we can see the same provincial map plotting a net migration rate (NMR) elaborated with data on contracts to high skilled workers with the formula.

$$NMR^h_{i=jt} \frac{I^h_{jt} - E^h_{it}}{T^h_{jt}}$$

$$I^h_{jt} = \sum_i^{i \neq j} n^h_{ijt} ; E^h_{it} = \sum_j^{j \neq i} n^h_{ijt} ; T^h_{jt} = \sum_i n^h_{ijt}$$

Where n^h_{ijt} is the number of labor contracts signed by high skilled workers (h) from origin province i in destination province j at year t. This NMR simply depicts the difference between high skilled immigration (I^h_{jt}) and high skilled emigration (E^h_{it}) in and out each province, divided by the total number of contracts signed *inside* the province (T^h_{jt}). Therefore Table 2.4 in the annex depicts the average NMR for the period 2001–2018.

Indeed, the agglomeration toward Madrid seems to be clear. During the considered period, the capital shows a net position of roughly 800,000 labor contracts, accounting for more than 10% of the total signed in the province (see Table 2.4 in annex). On the other hand, several provinces lose a considerable number of their high skilled workers in the annual migration to other regions, which is what we can define as "forgotten regions" in the Spanish context.

Empirical specification

To empirically test our hypothesis that the agglomeration of KBIS is positively correlated with the attraction of high skilled migrants, we rely on a pseudo-gravity equation built on a series of previous works (Czaika & Parsons, 2017; Grogger & Hanson, 2011).[7]

These types of models are micro-funded on the idea of individuals choosing the best possible location where their skills are more valuable, and so maximizing their utility after discounting the costs of migration (Sjaastad, 1962). Altogether with this theoretical explanation, the variables included in the gravity equation can be viewed as classic push and pull factors, which act in origin expelling and in destination attracting migrants, respectively (Lee, 1966).

With regard to specification, typically these models are divided into two different equations: scale and selection:

$$\ln n_{ijt}^{h} = \beta_1\left(\ln W_{jt}^{h}\right) + \beta_2\left(\ln A_{jt}\right) + \beta_3\left(\ln E_{jt}\right) + \beta_4\left(X_{ij}\right) +$$
$$\beta_5\left(\ln M_{ijt}\right) + \beta_6\left(K_{jt}\right) + \delta_{it} + \varepsilon_{ijt} \tag{1}$$

$$\ln\left(n_{ijt}^{h} \Big/ \sum_{S} n_{ijt}^{S}\right) = \beta_1\left(\ln W_{jt}^{h} - \ln W_{jt}^{S}\right) + \beta_2\left(\ln A_{jt}\right) + \beta_3\left(\ln E_{jt}\right) + \beta_4\left(X_{ij}\right) +$$
$$\beta_5\left(\ln M_{ijt}\right) + \beta_6\left(K_{jt}\right) + \delta_{it} + \varepsilon_{ijt} \tag{2}$$

The scale equation (1) regresses the number of migrants n with skill level h coming to destination province j from origin province i at time t. The log of this value should be positively correlated with the log of high skilled wage at destination W. The term A includes the amenities, that is, the pull factors, which act in the destination and attract the high skilled immigrants. The term E includes economic factors related to the cost of migration, which are destination specific. We take the unemployment level as the most practical measure of some of these costs. The term X includes time-invariant factors varying by pair source-destination, for example, the distance between region i and j, and some other dummies (share border, common language, common culture). The term M stands for the size of already established migration networks. Finally, the term K is our main variable of interest, a measure of agglomeration of KIBS in destination. The δ_{it} introduces fixed effects by province and time to remove concerns about any specific omitted variable. Finally, ε_{ijt} stands for the error term.

The selection equation (2) regresses instead the proportion of migrants with skill level h over the total number of migrants with all skill levels S. The only change in explanatory variables with respect to the scale equation is the inclusion of a high skilled wage premium, as the absolute difference between high skilled and average skilled wage.

Data

Our case study of Spain relies on a balanced panel data of provincial migration with 52 origins and 51 destinations, across 18 years from 2001 to 2018. To create this dataset, we merged the following data:

- Our basic data on migration come from the "Spanish Public Service of Employment" (hereinafter SEPE, its Spanish acronym). Under Spanish law, all (legal) labor contracts need to be registered before the starting date of the work. After a petition, we get access to a dataset containing all the labor contracts signed annually from 2001 to 2018, by nationality, level of studies, province of residence of the worker and province where the place of work is located. Therefore, we assume that if the two provinces differ, the contract implied a migration flow. We define the high skilled workers as those with an education level equal or superior to ISCED 5.[8]

- The wage data is released by the Spanish Tax Agency (hereinafter AEAT, its Spanish acronym) which published the annual income from work in the annual income tax. As the AEAT published the distribution by province and income groups (expressed as number of minimum wage), we can compute the high skilled wage as the corresponding wage to 80 percentiles. Then, we use a price index by province published by the Spanish Institute of Statistics (hereinafter INE, its Spanish acronym) to estimate the real wages.

- Unemployment by province is computed from Spanish Economically Active Population Survey (hereinafter EPA, its Spanish acronym) on a quarter basis and then transformed to an annual mean.

- The size of migration networks (i.e., the number of emigrants from province i living in j in year t), is computed from the Continuous (Population) Register, statistically exploited by the INE.

- Population by province comes from the official stats on population relying on the same Continuous (Population) Register.

- A dummy variable which takes the value 1 if the pair of source-destination provinces share a common border is computed with Stata, using a .shp file. The distance between provinces is measured with the same software, using the location of provincial capital in source and destination to compute the geodesic distance in kilometer. Another dummy takes the value 1 if the source and destination provinces share the same language or are part of the same Autonomous Community, which we take as a proxy of cultural proximity.

- Our main variable of interest is the Index of Regional Relative Specialization in KIBS, calculated as shown in the annex to be a proxy of the agglomeration of

KIBS in some provinces. This index is constructed with data from Statistical Use of the Central Business Register (hereinafter DIRCE, its Spanish acronym) for Spain, that records the number of business units and persons employed by NACE sector (at two digits), from 1999 to 2020 at provincial level.[9] A problem with this data is the break in the series, caused by the shift from NACE 1.1 to NACE 2.0 in 2010. We define the KIBS as the groups K72 (computer and related activities), K73 (research and development) and K74 (research and development) in NACE 1.1 (before 2010) and as the J62 (computer programming, consultancy and related activities), J63 (information service activities), M69 (legal and accounting activities), M70 (activities of head offices; management consultancy activities), M71 (architectural and engineering activities; technical testing and analysis), M72 (scientific research and development) and M73 (advertising and market research) in NACE 2.0 (from 2010).

The summary stats for our variables are shown in Table 2.1. One of the advantages of using exhaustive administrative data to define the migration is that we greatly reduce the number of zeros (i.e., migration corridors without any migrant at a particular time). Furthermore, these zeros are likely to be true zeros, compared with the use of migration data derived from surveys, which typically include zeros derived from sample errors. This allows us to use a standard ordinary least-squares (OLS) model instead of a Pseudo-Poison Maximum Likelihood model.[10]

Results

Our baseline results are presented in Table 1.2, showing the relevance of the pseudo-gravity model to explain the migration inside Spain. The model is well identified with an elevated level of precision, and all the relevant coefficients are significant and show the expected signs.

Table 2.1 Summary statistics data

	Mean	Std. Dev.	Min.	Max.
High skilled migrants (corridor)	128.09	479.88	0	14893
Low skilled migrants (corridor)	640.14	2207.87	0	63370
High skilled wage	19957.52	2851.98	13471.79	28291.38
Low skilled wage	9666.39	2020.72	3683.56	15265.8
High skilled wage premium	10291.13	1473.14	7190.23	15942.03
Population	864703.56	1092941	64754	6549519
Unemployment (%)	14.76	7.8	2.91	42.54
Migrant network size (corridor)	3285.35	9687.35	6	182607
Distance (corridor)	540.85	413.67	42.49	2284.7
Common border (dummy)	.08	.28	0	1
Common language (dummy)	.51	.5	0	1
Common culture (dummy)	.07	.26	0	1
Regional Specialization KIBS	.74	.22	.37	1.73

Panel data, N = 47736 = 52 provinces of origin × 51 provinces of destination × 18 years

Source: Own elaboration

From the scale equation displayed in column 1, we can say that the size of the high skilled migration flows by each corridor and year depend positively on the high skilled wage at destination, the size of population and the extent of migration networks (i.e., the current presence of past migrants from the same origin). On the contrary, it depends negatively on the distance and in the unemployment rate at destination. Sharing a border, a language, or a culture (the same Autonomous Community) have all a positive and significant impact on the size of this migration.

In column 2, we introduce our Regional Relative Specialization Index in KIBS as an additional explanatory variable. Our earlier conclusions remain valid and, more importantly, we confirm the relevance of this agglomeration as explanatory factor of the migration flows of high skilled workers. The interpretation is that a 1% increase in the specialization on this sector will be associated with an average 0.58% increase in the number of such immigrants. To account for the possible impact of the change in classification from NACE 1.1 to NACE 2.0 in the DIRCE stats, we separate this regression in two time periods. As we can see, the results remain robust.

When applying the selection equation in column 5, we are seeing the factors that contribute to increase (decrease) the proportion of high skilled workers among the immigrants. Not surprisingly, the wage premium has a positive effect on this proportion, while the unemployment and distance have a negative, although reduced effect. Sharing a border has a negative effect, meaning it acts by attracting more low skilled immigrants. Interestingly, population and migrant network size are not significative meaning it doesn't have a differentiated effect among low and high skilled. The culture proximity and the shared language have a positive and significant effect. We can conjecture that these variables that affect communication are more important for high skilled individuals and, significantly, for public servants as (usually) those working for regional administrations are required to speak all the official languages. Finally, our main variable is positive and highly significative: the agglomeration of KIBS not only increases the amount of high skilled immigrants but also the proportion of high skilled among all immigrants.

However, we should note that this specification only accounts for the pull factors, acting in the destination provinces. The push factors acting in the source provinces are captured by time fixed effects. We can run the same regressions with fixed effects for origin and time and disaggregate the explanatory variables for destination and origin as a robustness check. The results of this variation are shown in Table 2.3.

The most important result of this analysis is the relevance of unemployment rates to explain migration. It significantly depends positively on the unemployment at home province and negatively on the unemployment at destination. Observing the selection equation, we see that the proportion of high skilled among the immigrants is negatively related to the population in the origin province. We can theorize here that lowly populated provinces do not have the critical market volume to justify the presence of companies or public administrations hiring highly specialized talent. Therefore, all our results suggest that labor migration of highly skilled workers is related to the agglomeration of knowledge-intensive companies in a few regions with better labor market outcomes (wages and employment rates).

Table 2.2 Benchmark results with pull factors

	Scale				Selection
	(1)	(2)	(3)	(4)	(5)
	OLS	OLS	OLS Until 2010	OLS From 2010	OLS
High skilled wage (dest, log)	0.8497***	0.1774**	0.1904*	0.1490	
	(10.4540)	(2.0540)	(1.7962)	(1.5229)	
Wage premium (dest, log)					0.0562***
					(4.7324)
Population (dest, log)	0.5922***	0.4875***	0.4923***	0.4879***	−0.0002
	(27.0577)	(21.2881)	(20.7031)	(18.3694)	(−0.0599)
Unemployment (dest)	−0.0234***	−0.0252***	−0.0316***	−0.0226***	−0.0013***
	(−14.4203)	(−16.1087)	(−14.4167)	(−13.6631)	(−6.1445)
Migrant network (log)	0.4778***	0.4838***	0.4756***	0.4879***	−0.0014
	(30.3742)	(31.1499)	(28.5397)	(29.0273)	(−0.8623)
Distance (log)	−0.4403***	−0.4395***	−0.3837***	−0.4968**	−0.0063**
	(−18.3985)	(−18.3257)	(−14.8363)	(−19.7658)	(−2.3187)
Common border	0.6663***	0.6614***	0.6786***	0.6480***	−0.0138***
	(13.9220)	(14.1669)	(13.5988)	(13.2530)	(−2.8126)
Common language	0.2701***	0.2601***	0.2142***	0.3081***	0.0075***
	(11.3543)	(11.3408)	(8.1603)	(12.8510)	(2.6453)
Common culture	1.0461***	1.0338***	1.1178***	0.9556***	0.0509***
	(24.7127)	(24.9571)	(24.5630)	(22.5258)	(9.8309)
Spec. KIBS (dest, log)		0.5844***	0.6022***	0.5852***	0.0900***
		(15.1630)	(10.6705)	(12.5568)	(16.0216)
Observations	47736	47736	23868	23868	47736
R-squared	0.8695	0.8721	0.8619	0.8815	0.2174
Origin x Time FE	Yes	Yes	Yes	Yes	Yes

Source: t-values are in parentheses. Heterogeneous standard error clustered by pair origin-destination.

*** $p<.01$, ** $p<.05$, * $p<.1$

Scale equations regresses the size of high skill migration flows by corridor.

Selection equations regresses the proportion of high skilled in each corridor.

Table 2.3 Benchmark results with pull and pull factors

	Scale				Selection
	(1)	*(2)*	*(3)*	*(4)*	*(5)*
	OLS	OLS	OLS Until 2010	OLS From 2010	OLS
High skilled wage (dest, log)	0.8517*** (10.5841)	0.1798** (2.0889)	0.1892* (1.7992)	0.1497 (1.5418)	
High skilled wage (or, log)	0.0563 (0.3635)	0.0347 (0.2228)	0.4840* (1.6640)	−0.0063 (−0.0397)	
Wage premium (dest, log)					0.0558*** (4.7231)
Wage premium (or, log)					−0.0163 (−0.9557)
Population (dest, log)	0.5935*** (27.4353)	0.4889*** (21.5667)	0.4913*** (20.8860)	0.4882*** (18.5556)	−0.0004 (−0.1513)
Population (or, log)	0.6628** (6.0639)	0.6816*** (6.1729)	0.7665*** (4.8134)	0.0486 (0.1585)	−0.0667*** (−2.9742)
Unemployment (dest)	−0.0234*** (−14.5368)	−0.0252*** (−16.2331)	−0.0315*** (−14.5379)	−0.0226*** (−13.7666)	−0.0013*** (−6.1575)
Unemployment (or)	0.0098*** (6.3229)	0.0097*** (6.3361)	0.0007 (0.3565)	0.0025 (0.9719)	0.0003 (0.8180)
Migrant network size (log)	0.4766*** (30.6936)	0.4826*** (31.4602)	0.4764*** (28.9031)	0.4877*** (29.2716)	−0.0012 (−0.7391)
Distance (log)	−0.4410*** (−18.5987)	−0.4402*** (−18.5256)	−0.3831*** (−14.9596)	−0.4970*** (−19.9445)	−0.0062** (−2.2885)
Common border	0.6678*** (14.0830)	0.6630*** (14.3331)	0.6775*** (13.7003)	0.6483*** (13.3748)	−0.0141*** (−2.8987)
Common language	0.2699***	0.2599***	0.2143***	0.3080***	0.0076***

	(1)	(2)	(3)	(4)	(5)
Common culture	1.0466***	1.0343***	1.1174***	0.9557***	0.0508***
	(11.4488)	(11.4342)	(8.2353)	(12.9579)	(2.6849)
	(24.9511)	(25.1982)	(24.7701)	(22.7197)	(9.9078)
Spec. KIBS (dest, log)		0.5842***	0.6020***	0.5851***	0.0900***
		(15.1545)	(10.7393)	(12.6530)	(16.0382)
Spec. KIBS (or, log)		0.0554★	−0.0850*	0.0665	0.0067
		(1.7634)	(−1.8121)	(1.3718)	(1.0471)
Observations	47736	47736	23868	23868	47736
R-squared	0.8656	0.8683	0.8593	0.8792	0.1964
Origin + time fixed effects	Yes	Yes	Yes	Yes	Yes

Source: t-values are in parentheses. Heterogeneous standard error clustered by pair origin–destination.

*** $p<.01$, ** $p<.05$, * $p<.1$

Scale equations regresses the size of high skill migration flows by corridor.

Selection equations regresses the proportion of high skilled in each corridor.

Conclusion

In this chapter, we have approached the dynamics explaining the relationship between the agglomeration of knowledge-intensive activities, and particularly KIBS, and migration flows at regional level. Such dynamics are relevant for understanding the position of forgotten regions in the economic space and so for designing policy tool kits in order to upgrade their position.

Although existing theories do not establish a straightforward relationship between KIBS agglomeration and the attraction of high skilled immigrants, our analysis of the Spanish case suggests that the concentration of these sectors in a few dynamic metropolitan regions (namely Madrid and Barcelona) has the potential to increase the imbalance of the human capital distribution.

This conclusion is based on the results of a pseudo-gravity log model that regress interprovincial migration flows on a set of explanatory variables in which the KIBS agglomeration is approximated through an Index of Regional Relative Specialization calculated with business demography data. The existence of a clear correlation between the agglomeration of KIBS and the attraction of high skilled migrants, confirms our main research hypothesis that this factor is an important pull factor.

The broader implications of our study are significant. As the Schengen area has lifted great part of mobility barriers in Europe, our results may be extrapolated and so raise concerns about the future of forgotten regions in the European context. If the EU wants to lead the knowledge-based economy, policymakers should bear in mind these lessons and develop strategies to advance toward a more balanced distribution of KIBS across regions.

Acknowledgments

We would like to express our gratitude to those who made this chapter possible. Specially, we would like to thank the Spanish SEPE for generously providing us with the data used in our econometric model.

Notes

1 Ph.D. candidate, Associate Professor, Applied Economics Department, University of Santiago de Compostela, Spain, email: jose.blanco2@usc.es (ORCID: 0000–0002–2902–022X).
2 Associate Professor, Applied Economics Department, University of Santiago de Compostela, Avda. do Burgo, Santiago de Compostela 15782, Galicia, (Spain), email: manuel.gonzalez.lopez@usc.es (ORCID: 0000–0002–2645–011X).
3 Fifty-two provinces of Spain, equivalent to NUTS-3 level for EU statistical purposes.
4 Some countervailing mechanisms (remittances, return migration, incentive effects on education investment, etc.) can mitigate these problems or even convert the brain drain into a brain gain (Beine et al., 2008; Docquier & Rapoport, 2012).
5 To name some of the more relevant, the "Global Power City Index" published by the Institute for Urban Strategies at the Mori Memorial Foundation or the "Global City Index" estimated by the consultant AT Kearney are defined as synthetic indexes that weigh a set of indicators across several dimensions. The ranking by the "Globalization and World

Cities" (GaWC) Research Network employs instead a measure of world city network integration in the field of advanced producer services.

6 Alava with a GDP per capita of 36.480€ against Cádiz with a GDP per capita of 18.039€ according to our own calculations with data from INE.

7 To see a comprehensive review of these models applied to migration, see Beine et al. (2016) and Ramos (2016).

8 In our case, the level of studies defined in SEPE data as "Higher technical-professional post-secondary studies" (*Estudios postsecundarios técnicos-profesionales superiors*), "First cycle post-secondary studies" (*Estudios postsecundarios primer ciclo*), "Second and third cycle post-secondary studies" (*estudios postsecundarios de Segundo y tercer ciclo*).

9 Unfortunately, DIRCE includes this number indirectly, by classifying the companies by employment group (e.g., number of companies with 20 to 49 employees). We take the medium point of the interval (34.5 in our example) or the lower limit in the upper group (100 or more employees) to estimate the total employment by sector. We are aware that this is not the optimal procedure, but it is strong enough to do our analysis.

10 Even when the number of zeros is low (3336 out of 47736, or approximately 6.99%), we need to apply the usual correction of adding 1 unit to each corridor to take logs in our regressions.

References

Abramowitz, M., & David, P. A. (1996). Technological change and the rise of intangible investments: The US economy's growth path in the twentieth century. In B. A. Lundvall, & D. Foray (Eds.), *Employment and growth in the knowledge based economy* (1st ed., pp. 35–60). Washington, DC: OECD Publishing.

Basile, R., Mantuano, M., Girardi, A., & Russo, G. (2019). Interregional migration of human capital and unemployment dynamics: Evidence from Italian provinces. *German Economic Review*, 20(4), 385–414. http://doi.org/10.1111/geer.12172

Beine, M., Bertoli, S., & Fernández-Huertas Moraga, J. (2016). A practitioners' guide to gravity models of international migration. *The World Economy*, 39(4), 496–512. http://doi.org/10.1111/twec.12265

Beine, M., Docquier, F., & Rapoport, H. (2008). Brain drain and human capital formation in developing countries: Winners and losers. *The Economic Journal*, 118(528), 631–652. http://doi.org/10.1111/j.1468-0297.2008.02135.x

Cairncross, F. (2001). *The death of distance: How communications revolution is changing our lives* (2nd ed.). Boston: Harvard Business School Press.

Chaloff, J., & Lemaître, G. (2009). Managing highly-skilled labour migration: A comparative analysis of migration policies and challenges in OECD countries. *OECD Social, Employment and Migration Working Papers*, 79. https://doi.org/10.1787/225505346577

Czaika, M., & Parsons, C. R. (2017). The gravity of high-skilled migration policies. *Demography*, 54(2), 603–630. http://doi.org/10.1007/s13524-017-0559-1

d'Aiglepierre, R., David, A., Levionnois, C., Spielvogel, G., Tuccio, M., & Vickstrom, E. (2020). A global profile of emigrants to OECD countries: Younger and more skilled migrants from more diverse countries. *OECD Social, Employment and Migration Working Papers*, 239. https://doi.org/10.1787/0cb305d3-en

David, P. A., & Foray, D. (2003). Economic fundamentals of the knowledge society. *Policy Futures in Education*, 1(1), 20–49. http://doi.org/10.2304/pfie.2003.1.1.7

Docquier, F., & Rapoport, H. (2012). Globalization, brain drain, and development. *Journal of Economic Literature*, 50(3), 681–730. http://doi.org/10.1257/jel.50.3.681

Florida, R. (2002). The economic geography of talent. *Annals of the Association of American Geographers, 92*(4), 743–755. http://doi.org/10.1111/1467-8306.00314

Florida, R. (2003). Cities and the creative class. *City & Community, 2*(1), 3–19.

Florida, R. (2005a). *The flight of the creative class: The new global competition for talent* (1st ed.). New York City: HarperCollins. http://doi.org/10.1111/1540-6040.00034

Florida, R. (2005b, October). The world is spiky. *The Atlantic Monthly*, 48–51.

Fratesi, U., & Percoco, M. (2014). Selective migration, regional growth and convergence: Evidence from Italy. *Regional Studies, 48*(10), 1650–1668. http://doi.org/10.1080/00343 404.2013.843162

Friedman, L. T. (2005). *The world is flat: A brief history of the twenty-first century* (1st ed.). New York City: Farrar, Straus and Giroux.

García-Arias, M. A., Tolón-Becerra, A., Lastra-Bravo, X., & Torres-Parejo, Ú. (2021). The out-migration of young people from a region of the "empty Spain": Between a constant slump cycle and a pending innovation spiral. *Journal of Rural Studies, 87*, 314–326. http://doi.org/10.1016/j.jrurstud.2021.09.008

González-López, M. (2009). Euro commentary: Regional differences in the growth patterns of knowledge-intensive business services: An approach based on the Spanish case. *European Urban and Regional Studies, 16*(1), 101–106. https://doi.org/10.1177/0969776408098939

Grogger, J., & Hanson, G. H. (2011). Income maximization and the selection and sorting of international migrants. *Journal of Development Economics, 95*(1), 42–57. http://doi. org/10.1016/j.jdeveco.2010.06.003

Hanson, G. H. (2001). Scale economies and the geographic concentration of industry. *Journal of Economic Geography, 1*(3), 255–276. http://doi.org/10.1093/jeg/1.3.255

Kasnauskiene, G., & Palubinskaite, J. (2020). Impact of high-skilled migration to the UK on the source countries (EU8) Economies. *Organizations and Markets in Emerging Economies, 11*(1). https://doi.org/10.15388/omee.2020.11.23

Kerr, S. P., Kerr, W., Özden, Ç., & Parsons, C. (2017). High-skilled migration and agglomeration. *Annual Review of Economics, 9*(1), 201–234. http://doi.org/10.1146/ annurev-economics-063016-103705

Krugman, P. (1991). Increasing returns and economic geography. *Journal of Political Economy, 99*(3), 483–499. http://doi.org/10.1086/261763

Krugman, P. (1995). *Development, geography, and economic theory* (1st ed.). Cambridge: MIT Press.

Krugman, P. (1998). What's new about the new economic geography? *Oxford Review of Economic Policy, 14*(2), 7–17. http://doi.org/10.1093/oxrep/14.2.7

Labrianidis, L., Sykas, T., Sachini, E., & Karampekios, N. (2021). Highly educated skilled migrants are attracted to global cities: The case of Greek PhD holders. *Population, Space and Place*, e2517. http://doi.org/10.1002/psp.2517

Lee, E. S. (1966). A theory of migration. *Demography, 3*(1), 47–57. http://doi. org/10.2307/2060063

Liu, Y., Shen, J., Xu, W., & Wang, G. (2017). From school to university to work: Migration of highly educated youths in China. *The Annals of Regional Science, 59*(3), 651–676. http://doi.org/10.1007/s00168-016-0753-x

Lundvall, B. A., & Foray, D. (1996). The knowledge-based economy: From the economics of knowledge to the learning economy. In B. A. Lundvall, & D. Foray (Eds.), *Employment and growth in the knowledge-based economy* (1st ed.). Washington, DC: OECD Publishing.

Maleszyk, P. (2021). Outflow of talents or exodus? Evidence on youth emigration from EU's peripheral areas. *REGION, 8*(1). http://dx.doi.org/10.18335/region.v8i1.283

Malul, M. (2015). The process of brain drain in peripheral regions. *Applied Economics Letters, 22*(17), 1419–1423. http://doi.org/10.1080/13504851.2015.1037429

Massey, D. S., & García España, F. (1987). The social process of international migration. *Science*, *237*(4816), 733–738. http://doi.org/10.1126/science.237.4816.733

Miles, I., Kastrinos, N., Bilderbeek, R., Hertog, P. den, Flanagan, K., Huntink, W., & Bouman, M. (1995). *Knowledge-intensive business services: Users, carriers and sources of innovation*. Brussels: European Commission.

Miyagiwa, K. (1991). Scale economies in education and the brain drain problem. *International Economic Review*, *32*(3), 743–759. http://doi.org/10.2307/2527117

Oliinyk, O., Bilan, Y., Mishchuk, H., Akimov, O., & Vasa, L. (2021). The impact of migration of highly skilled workers on the country's competitiveness and economic growth. *Montenegrin Journal of Economics*, *17*(3), 7–19. https://doi.org/10.14254/1800-5845/2021.17-3.1

Portes, A., & Sensenbrenner, J. (1993). Embeddedness and immigration: Notes on the social determinants of economic action. *American Journal of Sociology*, *98*(6), 1320–1350. http://doi.org/10.1086/230191

Powell, W. W., & Snellman, K. (2004). The knowledge economy. *Annual Review of Sociology*, *30*, 199–220. http://doi.org/10.1146/annurev.soc.29.010202.100037

Ramos, R. (2016). Gravity models: A tool for migration analysis. *IZA World of Labor*, *2016*(239). http://doi.org/10.15185/izawol.239

Sassen, S. (1991). *The Global City: New York, London, Tokyo* (1st ed.). Princeton: Princeton University Press.

Schultz, T. W. (1961). Investment in human capital. *The American Economic Review*, *51*(1), 1–17. www.jstor.org/stable/1818907

Sjaastad, L. A. (1962). The costs and returns of human migration. *Journal of Political Economy*, *70*(5–2), 80–93. http://doi.org/10.1086/258726

Storper, M. (2010). Why does a city grow? Specialisation, human capital or institutions? *Urban Studies*, *47*(10), 2027–2050. http://doi.org/10.1177/0042098009359957

Storper, M., & Scott, A. J. (2009). Rethinking human capital, creativity and urban growth. *Journal of Economic Geography*, *9*(2), 147–167. http://doi.org/10.1093/jeg/lbn052

Teney, C. (2021). Immigration of highly skilled European professionals to Germany: Intra-EU brain gain or brain circulation? *Innovation: The European Journal of Social Science Research*, *34*(1), 69–92. https://doi.org/10.1080/13511610.2019.1578197

Thissen, F., Fortuijn, J. D., Strijker, D., & Haartsen, T. (2010). Migration intentions of rural youth in the Westhoek, Flanders, Belgium and the Veenkoloniën, The Netherlands. *Journal of Rural Studies*, *26*(4), 428–436. http://doi.org/10.1016/j.jrurstud.2010.05.001

Varela-Vázquez, P., & González-López, M. (2020). The effects of projects funded by the EU framework programmes on regional innovation and scientific performance. In M. González-López, & B. T. Asheim (Eds.), *Regions and innovation policies in Europe: Learning from the margins* (1st ed., pp. 162–187). Cheltenham: Edward Elgar Publishing.

Vence-Deza, X., & González-López, M. (2008). Regional concentration of the knowledge-based economy in the EU: Towards a renewed oligocentric model? *European Planning Studies*, *16*(4), 557–578. http://doi.org/10.1080/09654310801983472

Vence-Deza, X., & González-López, M. (2014). Regional concentration of knowledge-intensive business services in Europe. *Environment and Planning C: Government and Policy*, *32*(6), 1036–1058. http://doi.org/10.1068/c11171r

Zhou, Y., Guo, Y., & Liu, Y. (2018). High-level talent flow and its influence on regional unbalanced development in China. *Applied Geography*, *91*, 89–98. http://doi.org/10.1016/j.apgeog.2017.12.023

Zieba, M. (Ed.). (2021). *Understanding knowledge-intensive business services – Identification, systematization, and characterization of knowledge flows* (1st ed., Vol. 10). London: Springer International Publishing.

Annex

Table 2.4 Migration and KIBS by Spanish province, 2001–2018

ISO code	Province	Cum. net flux of hs contracts	Net mig. rate hs contracts (%)	RRS KIBS
M	Madrid	802561	10.76	1.62
B	Barcelona	332446	5.43	1.21
PM	Baleares	69838	9.82	0.75
MA	Malaga	56447	4.41	0.85
VI	Alava	35599	6.46	0.89
SE	Sevilla	15411	0.73	1.15
NA	Navarra	11173	1.03	0.82
GC	Las Palmas	4797	0.66	0.73
CS	Castellon	4749	1.39	0.59
GI	Girona	2610	0.58	0.65
CE	Ceuta	590	0.96	0.74
SO	Soria	−55	−0.05	0.57
HU	Huesca	−822	−0.45	0.54
ML	Melilla	−1871	−3.16	0.86
AL	Almeria	−2830	−0.61	0.71
L	Lleida	−5474	−1.88	0.66
TE	Teruel	−6330	−6.34	0.48
C	Coruña	−8624	−0.64	0.90
BI	Bizkaia	−9808	−0.47	1.18
CU	Cuenca	−10097	−9.03	0.51
TF	Tenerife	−11251	−1.54	0.74
MU	Murcia	−11978	−1.18	0.68
ZA	Zamora	−12239	−7.43	0.59
P	Palencia	−12311	−6.19	0.61
SG	Segovia	−15516	−11.30	0.52
VA	Valladolid	−15650	−2.36	1.03
GU	Guadalajara	−19347	−9.56	0.70
LU	Lugo	−20045	−5.81	0.64
AV	Avila	−20945	−15.92	0.59
A	Alicante	−22247	−2.53	0.65
OR	Ourense	−25808	−11.85	0.63
LO	La Rioja	−26458	−9.04	0.67
Z	Zaragoza	−27960	−2.65	0.90

V	Valencia	−30804	−1.43	0.90
H	Huelva	−32144	−6.30	0.61
BU	Burgos	−32371	−7.34	0.75
AB	Albacete	−33531	−13.02	0.62
T	Tarragona	−35112	−6.06	0.72
LE	Leon	−36778	−9.85	0.73
CC	Caceres	−40362	−12.81	0.56
CR	Ciudad Real	−46031	−13.71	0.60
TO	Toledo	−46240	−12.20	0.53
SS	Guipúzcoa	−46332	−3.93	0.78
BA	Badajoz	−46524	−7.76	0.67
PO	Pontevedra	−50987	−4.75	0.78
SA	Salamanca	−54139	−15.12	0.66
S	Cantabria	−63626	−9.86	0.78
J	Jaen	−66668	−11.27	0.63
CO	Cordoba	−77094	−9.72	0.67
GR	Granada	−83471	−9.39	0.71
O	Asturias	−101365	−8.05	0.87
CA	Cadiz	−124976	−10.77	0.65

Part II

Comparative analysis of regional experiences on Forgotten Spaces in Europe

3 How to make Forgotten Spaces visible?

Image making as a coping strategy of two European small towns

Bianka Plüschke-Altof[1] and Ariane Sept[2]

Introduction

Small towns are at risk of becoming Forgotten Spaces, both in academic and public discourses. In the former, small towns often fall into a structural attention gap, "because the small town systematically falls between metropolitan and rural studies" (Steinführer et al., 2021, p. 18). In the latter, in particular, small towns located in typical transit areas tend to be passed by and immediately forgotten. Next to invisibility, small towns facing problems of structural weakness or decline might also face stigmatizing discourses (Bürk et al., 2012). Reflecting this structural attention gap, current research on small towns is particularly concerned with their peripheralization (Bürk et al., 2012; Kühn & Weck, 2012; Porsche et al., 2021). In the case of two small towns located in Estonia and Germany, the chapter discusses the coping strategies of forgotten small towns to escape oblivion. In both cases, these focus on overlooked spaces in discussions on regional development: the negative image and invisibility that comes along with the peripheralization of Forgotten Spaces (Meyer & Miggelbrink, 2013). While the coping strategy in the Estonian small town addresses national and international audiences by showcasing its cultural heritage, the German town is based on a membership in the international network *Cittaslow*.[3] Despite focusing on different aspects, decision-makers in both cases have recognized the importance of the discursive dimension of peripheralization and are employing image making to overcome it.

Inspired by research on discursive peripheralization (Christmann, 2017; Görmar & Lang, 2019; Meyer & Miggelbrink, 2013; Plüschke-Altof & Grootens, 2019; Steinführer, 2015), the chapter seeks to widen the notion of Forgotten Spaces to the discursive level. Against the increasing focus of regional policies on competitiveness, which also encourages small towns to be entrepreneurial "place-sellers" (Bristow, 2010, p. 160), discursive peripheralization creates a situation where the resource that promises to boost regional development – a positive and visible image to attract residents, tourists and investors – is exactly what is missing. Our cases introduce two discursive strategies employed by small towns that aim to face this challenge. The first is image reversal (Bürk et al., 2012) to positively reinterpret negative associations with small towns. The second is scale jumping (Ernwein, 2014), which searches for collaborators and visibility across established spatial scales of action. The aim of this

DOI: 10.4324/9781003256281-6

chapter is to discuss the discursive dimension of Forgotten Spaces and the strategic ways small towns can address this, asking if and how Forgotten Spaces can reach visibility, and with what consequences.

In order to shed light on small town attempts for visibility and discuss image making as a coping strategy, the chapter first conceptualizes small towns as Forgotten Spaces that face material and discursive peripheralization ("Small towns as Forgotten Spaces facing material and discursive peripheralization"). This is followed by an elaboration of the methodology applied in conducting the individual case studies and comparatively analyzing them ("Methods and database: a multi-sited individualizing comparison of two small towns"). After these case study introductions, the empirical analysis ("The dynamics of image making in small and forgotten towns") focuses on the dynamics of image making in small and forgotten towns, which are critically discussed in the conclusion ("Conslusion").

Small towns as Forgotten Spaces facing material and discursive peripheralization

Addressing the structural attention gap in small town research and the performative role of discourses in regional development, we treat small towns as Forgotten Spaces facing material as well as discursive challenges. In urban development and planning, Forgotten Spaces indicate informal settlements or low-income migrant neighborhoods in globalizing cities (Elsheshtawy, 2008; Shatkin, 2004), as well as urban "leftover" or ignored spaces (Najjar & Ghadban, 2015). The notion is also used in educational studies in cases where rural areas are considered to be forgotten by educational policies (Oyarzún, 2020; Reynolds, 2017). From a historical perspective, the term denotes places of formerly great importance that are hardly noticeable today or whose significance is forgotten (Esfanjary & Alikhani, 2021; Rodgers et al., 2016). Finally, the philosophical idea of forgetfulness brings the "economics of oblivion" into play, connecting a forgotten space to a previously dynamic economy that has lost attention, value and agents interested in its development (Mourão, 2020).

A similar yet different idea is that of invisible places and spaces.[4] This can also be a matter of formerly significant places losing relevance. The notion refers to places that are not perceived as politically or spatially relevant today: they are invisible because they are not seen, discussed or heard. Invisible places, mainly in urban peripheries, are considered anonymous non-places (van Neste, 2020) or "in-between" spaces (Young & Keil, 2014). Although urban peripheries have come to embody the idea of invisible spaces, recent studies also apply the notion of invisibility to small towns and rural areas (Steinführer et al., 2021; Grootens, 2019). In this sense, we understand invisible places to include all types of spaces that are not represented in general, political or scientific discourses. The problem of invisibility is often particularly relevant for small towns, being comparatively little researched or subsumed under rural areas even though their inhabitants tend to value them for their "urban qualities" (Steinführer et al., 2021). The same is true for funding policies, as there are hardly any funding programs specifically tailored to small towns (Porsche, 2021).

Both notions of forgotten and invisible spaces meet in debates on small town peripheralization. Peripheralization describes a "multidimensional and multi-scalar process of descent that can encompass economic, infrastructural, political, and social-communicative processes" (Kühn & Lang, 2017, p. 6). It includes processes of demographic out migration, geographic disconnection, political dependency, economic downturn and negative discursive attributions (Kühn & Lang, 2017; Kühn & Weck, 2012; Weck & Beißwenger, 2014). Discourses form an inherent part of peripheralization (Meyer & Miggelbrink, 2013; Görmar & Lang, 2019), as they are mutually related with the other processes. As demonstrated in studies on residential decision-making (Kährik et al., 2012), place-marketing (Kauppinen, 2013), place attachment (Paasi, 2013) or territorial stigmatization (Bürk et al., 2012), the image and degree of visibility in public discourse can influence decisions to move and stay, visit or invest in certain places. We thus argue that the image of small towns as "slow" or "peripheral" and their invisibility in public discourse can be interpreted as a discursive act of peripheralization that reinforces the structural disadvantages that lead to economic and political oblivion as Forgotten Spaces.

While peripheralization dynamics result in multiple interrelated challenges, they also offer room for agency of local actors who try to cope or revise these processes (Kühn, 2015; Kühn & Lang, 2017; Weck & Beißwenger, 2014). In the same tune, the literature on discursive peripheralization highlights the agency of people and places to negotiate the images they are subjected to (Meyer & Miggelbrink, 2013, Willett, 2020). Albeit embedded in power relations, studies (e.g. Bürk et al., 2012; Kauppinen, 2013; Plüschke-Altof & Grootens, 2019) convey that peripheralized places can and do make use of discursive room for maneuver by actively engaging in image making. Image making as a coping strategy is also incentivized by the growing neoliberalization of European regional policies (Loewen & Schulz, 2019). The focus on regional competitiveness developed over recent decades (Bristow, 2010) urges places to utilize their endogenous resources in order to boost regional development. Also, spatial images are seen as such a resource because they have the potential to externally strengthen place marketing and regional product branding or to internally enhance social capital and place attachment (Bristow, 2010; Kašková & Chromý, 2014; Paasi, 2013; Semian & Chromý, 2014), although the fact that the grounding of strategic discourses in lay discourses needs extra attention and resources to be devoted by local decision-makers (Willett, 2020).

A positive and visible image is exactly the resource that forgotten small towns are lacking, and they are faced with the challenge of how to reverse negative ascriptions and put themselves (back) on the map. In consequence, image reversal is a popular response to discursive peripheralization (Bürk et al., 2012). By replacing negative with positive ascriptions, image reversal turns existing socio-spatial hierarchies on their head. Studies on peripheralized German small towns (Bürk et al., 2012) and stigmatized urban neighborhoods in the United States (Elwood, 2006) convey three common image reversal strategies. First, they refer to alternative spatial discourses or ascribe positive meaning to hitherto negative associations with place (Bürk et al., 2012). Second, they form asset narratives that illustrate existing spatial resources or potentials. Third, they use accomplishment narratives that foreground the achievements of communities and places in coping with difficulties (Elwood, 2006). Another discursive strategy to highlight is scale jumping. Building on a relational understanding of space, spatial scales are seen as constructions that exist only through the discourses and practices creating them (Ernwein, 2014). In the example of spatial activism, spatial narratives have been used to jump between different scales, thereby extending, narrowing or shifting the boundaries of spaces to one's own benefit (Ernwein, 2014). Scale jumping is thus used to negotiate scales, including scales of action, engagement, recognition and belonging. The (over)use of scale as an analytical category has been critically discussed in the literature (e.g. Marston et al. 2005). In this chapter – inspired by debates on scale jumping in social movements – we follow a constructivist approach to scale to describe how regions draw on images and relationships at different scales to press for advantage. While image reversal is the primary method used to overcome negative ascriptions, scale jumping rather addresses the problem of experienced invisibility, when the main aim is to "be in the big picture, to be on the big plan" (Grootens, 2019, p. 93).

Methods and database: a multi-sited individualizing comparison of two small towns

The following sections discuss "multi-sited individualizing comparison" (Tuvikene et al., 2017) as an analytical method and describe the qualitative empirical data in more detail. This is followed by an introduction to the case studies in Estonia and Germany.

Linking two research projects

The discursive dimension of small towns as Forgotten Spaces is analyzed with the help of a "multi-sited individualizing comparison" (Tuvikene et al., 2017). This means that we link two distinct research projects under the common interest of discursive coping strategies and thereby reanalyze the existing data. Similar to Tuvikene et al. (2017), we do not aim to compare individual case studies, but to take them as starting points to conceptualize small towns as Forgotten Spaces and reflect on their different image-making strategies. The comparison is made using two small town case studies, Tõrva in Estonia and Berching in Germany, conducted between 2015 and 2017. Inspired by focused ethnography (Knoblauch, 2005), both are based on participant observation and in-depth interviews with local decision-makers, and contextualized with relevant policy and media documents.

In the case of Tõrva, the fieldwork was conducted in Tõrva municipality. It also considered the broader context of Valga County. In Berching, the fieldwork included observations at national and international network meetings of Cittaslow where central actors from Berching participated. Our analysis builds on 28 interviews[5] with local and regional decision-makers representing the fields of politics, administration, entrepreneurship, culture, media, tourism, journalism and social work (see Annex). In the case of Berching, residents and officials from the Cittaslow network were also included.[6] The interviews were conducted as scheduled single and group interviews or *ad hoc* during participant observation at major cultural, political or tourist events.

The interviews were conducted in the local language and transcribed for content analysis, employing a discourse analytical approach.

The cases of two small towns

Our case study selection illustrates the notion that core-periphery relations are relative (Kühn & Lang, 2017). Even though Tõrva and Berching and their respective contexts differ considerably in size and population densities, they are both similarly facing processes of material and discursive peripheralization. Adhering to a relational understanding of peripheralization, Tõrva and Berching as forgotten and invisible spaces are contextualized by referring to the national (Estonia) and regional (Bavaria, Germany) scale, respectively.

The town of Tõrva marks the center of the surrounding municipality of the same name. Next to this, 38 villages are situated in the 649 km^2 municipality, giving home to approximately 6,000 people (Tõrva vald, 2022). Tõrva municipality is part of Valga County, located on the Estonian border with Latvia and comprises three main areas: Otepää area in the east, Valga area in the south and Tõrva area in the north. The County is among the areas of Estonia most heavily affected by the post-socialist restructuring of the rural economy after Estonia regained its independence in 1991, which caused a rapid drop in agricultural production and employment – from 20.8% in 1989 to 3.9% in 2014 (Annist, 2017). Although new jobs have been created in the service sector, especially in rural tourism (Raagmaa & Noorkõiv, 2013), the structural loss of employment in agriculture has far outweighed these new income opportunities. As a result, a polarization process manifested in Estonia, whereby human and economic capital is concentrated in the metropolitan areas while small towns and rural areas are subject to peripheralization. On the administrative level, these processes reinforce decreasing levels of public service provision (Plüschke-Altof et al., 2020).

Next to this material peripheralization, Estonian small towns and rural areas also suffer from a tangible discursive peripheralization. The countryside has historically been positively connoted, building on an idea of Estonians as "country people". The recent media analyses convey increasingly negative ascriptions to rural areas and small towns as economically lagging behind, geographically remote, politically dependent or institutionally weak and their residents as socially problematic, resistant to "modern" development and trapped in a "kolkhoz[7] mentality" of the Soviet past (Plüschke-Altof et al., 2020). In Valga County, discursive peripheralization figures as invisibility and territorial stigmatization – the latter also affecting the local population in the form of self-stigmatization (Plüschke-Altof, 2019). In an image study commissioned by the County government, up to 36% of respondents across Estonia did not associate anything with Valga County or knew much about it (Valga Maavalitsus, 2011). The interviews with decision-makers in Valga County and Tõrva also confirm the feeling of "not being on the map" (Egert) and of people from outside seeing nothing but a "periphery" (Reili and Raigo) or a place "somewhere at the Latvian border" (Gregor). Moreover, they feel that the region is stigmatized as "arse end of nowhere" (Kaarel) or "back of beyond" (Reili and Raigo) and are convinced that the unfavorable image of Valga County also clouds Tõrva's image.

Incentivized by an Estonian regional policy that is based on the premise of competitiveness (Loewen & Schulz, 2019), small towns and rural municipalities have developed coping strategies to peripheralization. The most common strategies include the fostering of community engagement and image making or a focus on heritage culture, place leadership and rural tourism, which are partly supported by project-based funding schemes on national and EU levels (Lang et al., 2021; Leetmaa et al., 2015). In 2018, 83% of Estonian municipalities including the municipality of Tõrva set image making as one of their development strategies (Plüschke-Altof et al., 2020). In line with incentivized regional development strategies, Tõrva focuses on its *Mulgi* cultural heritage. Mulgimaa (*land of the Mulgi*) represents a cultural-historical region in southern Estonia that today is divided between Viljandi and Valga counties, the latter including Tõrva. To revive and promote the cultural heritage of the region, a comprehensive institutional framework was established which includes the Mulgi County Development Chamber and the Mulgi Culture Institute (Plüschke-Altof, 2019). While the former concentrates on socioeconomic development, the latter is active in the field of culture, organizing and promoting popular events and workshops that (re-)introduce people to Mulgi language, culture and history.

The municipality of Berching includes 42 villages and neighborhoods spread over 131 km², making it one of the largest municipalities by area in the federal state of Bavaria. Within the Bavarian state development program of central places – the basis of regional development – Berching shares the functions of a middle-order center with Freystadt. Approximately 8,500 people live in Berching (GENESIS-Online Datenbank, 2016), of whom around 3,000 live in the central town (Schober Architekten, 2012, p. 16). In a way, Berching is a double periphery. On one hand, the town is far from larger urban centers, highways and train lines. The Berching railroad line was gradually shut down in 1987. On the other hand, the town center has suffered from a loss of inhabitants and functions in recent decades, while the villages have experienced an influx of people. Services such as supermarkets and stores increasingly left the center and settled in large areas outside or in neighboring towns. Over the years, the center has thus become the periphery and, in a sense, a forgotten place – a development that occurs in other small towns as well and is widely discussed in policy debates (Porsche, 2021). Since the mid-1970s, Berching's historic district has been redeveloped with the help of several public funding programs, but the redevelopment needs and vacancies were still high in the 2000s (Stadt Berching, 2015). In 2012, the integrated urban development concept attested that the center "is no longer a place to feel good" (Schober Architekten, 2012, p. 51).

From a discursive perspective, since the early 20th century in Germany, the image of small towns as "slow" has been established. According to Simmel, small towns had a "slower, more habitual, more evenly flowing rhythm" (Simmel, 1995 [1903], p. 117). What still sounded relatively neutral in Simmel's work has increasingly developed into negative attributions to small towns as "petty bourgeois, boring or provincial" (Schiemann & Steinführer, 2021, p. 210), even if this is again changing in more recent times. In this sense, the German terms for "slow" (*lang*sam) and "boring" (*lang*weilig) are very close to each other, hence for small towns: "often, associations with the term 'slowness' cause difficulties. There is a fear that it would be associated with an image of being 'sleepy'" (Medvei, 2011, p. 34). While there is hardly any public discourse about Berching's attractiveness – one could even say that the town is discursively forgotten – narratives by local people repeatedly show signs of self-stigmatization reducing the town's image to general boredom and an unattractive old town. Economically, the municipality is doing comparatively well, although it is not among the most prosperous regions in Bavaria. Some companies would like to expand locally but are unable to do so due to a shortage of skilled workers (Klaus). According to local politician Klaus, one of the reasons is that other places would be more attractive to live in. Thus, looking to the future, there is a risk of a further downward spiral to a "forgotten economy" (Mourão, 2020), fueled by an interplay of material and discursive peripheralization. It remains to be seen to what extent strengthening the town as a middle-order center can counteract this development.

To address the different dimensions of material and discursive peripheralization, Berching became the twelfth town in Germany to apply for membership in the international network Cittaslow. Founded in Italy in 1999, the network's mission is to strengthen the quality of life in cities with fewer than 50,000 inhabitants (Sept, 2021). Cittaslow's basic idea was to transfer the philosophy of Slow Food to daily life, administration and development, strengthening slowness and slowing down as a potential. With now more than 280 member towns worldwide (Cittaslow, n.d.a), the network understood globalization from the very beginning in a positively connoted sense of international cooperation between smaller towns to make them more visible. To apply for membership, a unanimous municipal council resolution respecting 72 "requirements for quality" (Cittaslow, n.d.b)[8] is needed. The criteria cover fields such as energy and environmental policies, quality-of-urban-life policies, policies for hospitality, awareness and training and social cohesion (Sept, 2021). Berching became a member of Cittaslow on March 10, 2013, after the councilors concluded: "we want to live according to these criteria" (Klaus).

The dynamics of image making in small and forgotten towns

Escaping negative ascriptions to Forgotten Spaces: image reversal

The case analyses convey two central and intertwined image-making strategies to counteract typically negative ascriptions to small towns and reach more visibility in Forgotten Spaces: image reversal and scale jumping. In terms of image reversal, the two towns actively utilize asset narratives and positive reinterpretations of negative ascriptions, while accomplishment narratives are comparatively less widespread. Responding to national discourses on small towns, reversal strategies mainly address negative images of spatial peripherality in Tõrva, whereas Berching's strategy concentrates on negative temporal images portraying small town life as too slow.

Similar to other Forgotten Spaces in Estonia, Tõrva's image reversal strategy uses peripherality as a trump card (Grootens, 2019). Despite visible self-stigmatization through local reproduction of negative images in Tõrva and its surrounding Valga County (Plüschke-Altof, 2019), in the image reversal, the same peripherality that is negatively connoted in the national public discourse gets a positive spin by painting a rural idyll (Halfacree, 2006) where the emptiness and remoteness of rural areas becomes the source for "beautiful nature," "clean forests" and "pleasant farms" (Reili, Raigo, and Egert) that cannot be found in densely populated metropolitan areas. This positive image of peripherality is distributed foremost in marketing, media and cultural institutions. It also appears in the tourist sector which makes use of nationwide campaigns such as *Tule maale* ("Come to the country") that highlight positive aspects of small town and rural life such as strong communities (as opposed to anonymity) and safety (as opposed to unsafe urban environments) (Plüschke-Altof et al., 2020). At the same time, negative aspects of metropolitan areas, such as intense traffic, unsafe surroundings and a hectic life, are foregrounded: "Every time I go to [Estonia's capital] Tallinn, I just quickly want to get out of there" (Imbi). These positive images of peripherality are combined with asset narratives that focus on local resources such as recreation as "everyone just loves our lake" (Peep), "favorable real estate prices" (Imbi and Andrus), "cheap labor" (as incentive for firm settlement, Kaarel), a safe environment for children (Leela), and foremost, Mulgi heritage as a commodity for marketing and branding, which can "give us an advantage" (Peep).

The main target groups for image reversal are, however, not only external with focus on tourists, investors or potential new residents but are also internal with the intention to enhance the pride and place attachment of local people and overcome tendencies of self-stigmatization. For politician Peep, internal and external images are interrelated: "When a person does not appreciate the place, then this is mirrored in their behavior and communication to the people from outside." Peep sees the role of local leaders in "keeping up the self-esteem and local patriotism of the people," to avoid having people "looking downwards with shame," thinking, "Oh my God, what a horrible place [we live in]." Aware of the discursive dimension of living in a forgotten space, he and his colleagues are convinced that it is "not so much a question of a [peripheral] location, but about where we are located in peoples' minds."

In Berching the image, reversal strategy focuses on temporal ascriptions to small town life. In the context of its Cittaslow membership, Berching provides an example of how negative attributions of slowness are transformed into positive ones. As in Tõrva, this image reversal is not only relevant to the outside but also for the local residents. Communication with the local population was not easy, since not everyone saw the Cittaslow membership in a positive light. Nevertheless, Berching's residents started to gradually accept it: "In the beginning it was, 'Ah yes, logical. Berching continues to sleep'" (Tom). Tourism officer Frank in a comparable Cittaslow town puts it this way: "[Y]ou have to be careful that it doesn't become a boomerang advertising slogan; that people say: 'Oh, we're lame, it's clear, we're Cittaslow'." The network, however, actively works on labeling slowness as "modern" and "sustainable", becoming the forerunner of a "new slowness" (Ravelli, 2005). This claim is expressed already in the Cittaslow logo (an orange snail) and the self-description as "International Network where Living is good" (Cittaslow, n.d.a).

Berching took advantage of Cittaslow's positive connotation and branded itself as "Space to live" (Stadt Berching, n.d.). With the discursive link between being slow and livable, an image develops that connects deceleration with the good life, and thereby redefines slowness in positive terms: Berching is particularly livable *because* the life in a small town is decelerated. To spread this idea, posters and flyers were distributed in the town that explicated Berchings' understanding of slow[9]: "that we are decelerated – not slow, just less hectic" (Klaus). The posters were not so much addressed to guests or tourists, but rather to the local population hanging "in every restaurant [. . . and] in the schools, so people just keep pointing them out" (Sabine). In this way, Cittaslow is used to enhance local place attachment and redefine slowness as an asset and endogenous resource. At the same time, deceleration serves as a strategy for valorizing the physical center, as evident in the *Slow Spots* project, introduced in 2016/17 by the local civil society: "A 'slow spot' is a place off the beaten path. A place where you can come to rest and let your thoughts 'circle'" (Gemeinsam für Berching, 2016). These places are located either in the historic center or outside in nature, from where they offer a view of the picturesque old town. With *Slow Spots*, image reversal materializes in space. If the old town was seen before as a place where people did not go and did not feel good, it now becomes *a place off the beaten path* in a positive sense.

The foregrounding of positive ascriptions to small towns and Forgotten Spaces in both cases is accompanied by a simultaneous downplaying of negative aspects. Decision-makers in Tõrva and the surrounding Valga County were concerned about the consequences that negative images might have for the region and its inhabitants. Several interviewees mentioned cases where the local "perceiving and interpreting coalition of actors" (Bürk et al., 2012, p. 339) such as teachers, parents, politicians and journalists "all the time told the children that they shouldn't come back" and then wonder why they don't return (Leela). Similarly, in Berching, local actors have observed with great concern that young people are leaving the region: "They go to study and are usually gone" (Klaus), since "they want more action" (Chris) than the small town can offer. In Tõrva, politician Peep has even urged journalists to consider the risk of self-stigmatization: "I have several times written critically and told [them] . . . 'Look, I understand that people today want to read negativity, right, and I understand that we shouldn't sugarcoat artificially', but . . . 'we can lead people to a better way of thinking', because if we say all the time that somebody got stabbed here or robbed here, then what will this person start to think? They will indeed think that it is unsafe". For dealing with negative aspects, he continued: "You shouldn't hide anything, but the question is how much you should enable it". Those who have been openly discussing existing problems might also be perceived as troublemakers, destroying the beautiful image others have worked so hard to create (Plüschke-Altof & Grootens, 2019). This has happened, for example, in cases where attention was raised to the problem of empty and decaying houses in the region. Such open problematization was locally interpreted as enabling negativity and ruining the image of the region "where we have many beautiful houses, too" (Reili). While image reversal presents potential for place marketing and the enhancement of place attachment, it also risks leaving little discursive room to address persistent problems that small towns and Forgotten Spaces are facing.

Making Forgotten Spaces visible internally and externally: scale jumping

Both small towns also engage in scale jumping, thereby trying to shift spatial and temporal scales with the aim of making themselves more visible. In order to escape "Valga County's negative image" (Peep), Tõrva intends to shift established scales by connecting to Mulgi cultural heritage. Scale jumping and shifting has also been a prominent strategy in other areas of Valga County. Whereas Otepää has successfully branded itself as an active sport and holiday destination (Leetmaa et al., 2015) that "categorically rejects being represented as part of Valga County" (Peep), the area around Valga city is attempting to build a new image based on the ancient Livonian cultural heritage of the region (Egert and Kaarel). A vivid example of the attempt to jump temporal and spatial scales and thus reach visibility was the so-called "big name debate". When Tõrva town amalgamated with its municipalities in 2017, some lo-cal decision-makers proposed to name the joint municipality South Mulgimaa. For Peep, as one of the main proponents of this name, it would indicate a revival of the Mulgi tradition and would have the potential to elevate the region from "the periphery to the center of Estonia", thus, to "become strong enough to escape the negative flow of Valga County". Locals describe the Mulgi heritage as the "proud" past of a "wealthy" region, which included the southern part of Viljandi and north-ern part of Valga counties, built by "hard-working" and "well-educated" people (Egert, Imbi, Kaarel and Piret).

To escape the negative image of Valga County and Tõrva's invisibility today, local decision-makers try to connect with the Mulgi heritage of the past. Next to jumping temporal scales, this discursive strategy also jumps across spatial scales. First, it connects Tõrva to Viljandi County, known for its Mulgi heritage which is nationally more (positively) visible than in Tõrva and Valga County. The "Mulgimaa topic" is thereby perceived as an opportunity to "distinguish oneself" and be "immediately visible to everybody," because "90% of Estonians know about Mulgimaa," but "no one knows where Tõrva is" (Egert, Merike, Peep). Second, it grows visibility on higher spatial scales. Nationally, an image built on the Mulgi heritage links Tõrva to other heritage culture regions in Estonia that are eligible for specific regional development funds. Internationally, it would connect the small town to the UNESCO-recognized cul-tural heritage of Setomaa and Kihnu areas (Plüschke-Altof & Grootens, 2019). Next to increasing visibility and access to additional development funds, scale jumping via the Mulgi cultural heritage is seen as a potential competitive advantage in a situation of regional competitiveness. Cultural worker Piret, for example, reported how peo-ple from other regions asked her "what are you whining, you actually have a brand. You have Mulgimaa, which people can identify immediately: wealth, richness, a little penny-pinching, a bit of humor here and there."

While this strategy seems promising for external communication, its success was limited internally. Mirroring the critical literature on the authenticity and commod-ification of heritage culture (Annist, 2013; Kavaratzis & Ashworth, 2015), the name proposal, South Mulgimaa, did not gain enough supporters in the end. The main reason for this was that locals felt disconnected from Mulgi heritage, which was heavily suppressed during Soviet times. Several informants explained that "Mulgi language used to be forbidden" and "our wealthy farmers" were "marked as Kulaks[10] and sent to Siberia" (Egert, Gregor, Kaarel, and Piret). As a result of this "disrupted continuity" (Egert, Kaarel), an image built on Mulgi heritage seemed "too historical" or "frozen in time" (Reili), disconnected from the "everyday life" (Eneli) of the residents and their experiences "on the streets" (Merike).

In Berching, scale jumping is closely connected to the image reversal as Cittaslow manifests across temporal and spatial scales. Here, the furthest leap goes directly to the global level, if only because the network describes itself as global, even in local debates. After the city council's decision to apply for membership, the local newspaper described Cittaslow as a "'global engine' for sustainability in municipal decision-making processes and in terms of citizen participation, for regionality and for people to feel comfortable in the region" (Karg, 2012). The emphasis on the global already suggests discursive scale jumping, with it seeming a kind of honor to be part of a worldwide network. In this context, Cittaslow membership also acts as a label that stands for global recognition of local qualities. Furthermore, the network offers the possibility of international and Germany-wide cooperation. Meetings with Cittaslow representatives are highly appreciated by the local authorities, because they can learn a lot from similar small towns without being in competition with each other. There, new ideas are born again and again on how Cittaslow can be filled with life (Klaus). Networking on a supra-regional and even international level seems to be at least as interesting, if not more interesting, for the Cittaslow member towns than cooperation with surrounding towns (Sept, 2018, p. 232).

In this sense, the jump to the global scale was accompanied by hopes of improvement in the local situation, giving more power to redevelopment measures such as redesigning public spaces or supporting local products. In addition to the general global, Cittaslow is discursively and practically associated with Italy and the romantic images of Italian small towns, which creates the impression that German member cities are playing in the same league. Asked what is special about Cittaslow in Berching, respondents refer to Italian imaginaries: "Well, certainly, first of all, that it comes from Italy, and there you have the idea of pretty little towns" (Sabine), "Cittaslow is an award, and it comes from Italy" (Tina), and, "it would be great if people in Italy then also know Berching" (Alma). This way, Cittaslow membership links image reversal and scale jumping: through discursive descriptions, narratives and posters in public space, the image of a decelerated place is created that is worth visiting and offers its residents a high quality of life. Thus, in the case of Berching, image making is aimed at external recognition, such as by guests or subsidies, and at its own residents, with a particular focus on enhancing the qualities of the historic old town. At the same time, the Cittaslow label serves as international recognition for local efforts and attests to a quality of place that sets Berching apart from surrounding places making it something special. In terms of internal impact, there was a certain pride among local actors and residents in being recognized by an international association. This is particularly interesting in light of the fact that the label has not gained any major recognition in Germany to date, nor are there any direct benefits associated with Cittaslow membership.

Conclusion

The aim of this chapter was to discuss the discursive dimension of Forgotten Spaces in the case of small towns. To do so, we linked the debates on forgotten and invisible spaces to those on peripheralization. The research on discursive peripheralization, in particular, helps to widen the notion of Forgotten Spaces to the discursive level as an often overlooked aspect in discussions on regional development. The two cases convey the importance of negative images and invisibility that comes along with the peripheralization of Forgotten Spaces in two ways. First, the discursive dimension affects regional development by influencing the decision to leave or stay, visit and invest in places, and thereby strengthening processes of oblivion. Second, the discursive dimension strongly figures in coping mechanisms of Forgotten Spaces, where local decision-makers address material and immaterial difficulties – be it peripheralization, invisibility, out-migration or urban decay – with the help of discursive strategies. The example of two small towns in Germany and Estonia show image reversal and scale jumping as common discursive strategies despite their different sociohistorical contexts. While the coping strategy in the German town is based on a membership in the international network Cittaslow, the Estonian town addresses national and international audiences by showcasing its Mulgi cultural heritage. Despite focusing on different aspects, we argue that both cases illustrate the importance that local decision-makers ascribe to the discursive dimension and image making as a central way of coping.

The empirical cases discuss in more detail if and how Forgotten Spaces can be made visible, and with what consequences. The dynamics unfolding in each case make clear that in a context of a simultaneous peripheralization of small towns and neoliberalization of regional policy, image making has not only potentials but also pitfalls. Among the potentials are the use of positive images for place promotion to strengthen regional development and cope with peripheralization, achieving visibility on and accessing support from different scales, for example, through networking and cooperation outside their own region. Image making can also help to enhance social capital and place attachment by boosting the pride and participation of locals, even though the translation needs to be studied in more depth (Willet, 2020). However, all of these potentials are simultaneously offset by potential pitfalls. By using positive images for place promotion, discursive strategies may quickly tip over into sugarcoating. As a result, they could leave little discursive room to address (and solve) existing material difficulties which continue to intensify. While going up to a supraregional scale can raise visibility, it also entails the risk of feeding regional competitiveness, which can result in a situation where forgotten and peripheralized spaces compete with each other for scarce resources, while the larger political problem of missing state support for regional development remains unchanged (Bristow, 2010). Images must also be filled with meaning in order to not degenerate into a hollow image leading to local nonacceptance, as the Estonian case showed.

In conclusion, we emphasize the importance of considering the discursive dimension in academic and political discussions on regional development, as it has the potential to influence place development, both positively and negatively. In our cases and other Forgotten Spaces, local decision-makers are acknowledging the power of images and visibility and, as a result, actively incorporate image making as a coping strategy. Our explorative discussion on the advantages and pitfalls of discursive strategies also marks the ground for future research endeavors focusing on the way discursive strategies are received internally and externally and the entanglement between structural and discursive peripheralization contributing to the success or failure of such communication strategies. Taking into consideration the dynamics of image making in forgotten and peripheralized spaces also has practical implications. Thus, we recommend local decision-makers to beware of the potential pitfalls before actively applying discursive strategies. Our final recommendation is that both, scientific discourse and spatial development practice, that is, funding programs and policies, increasingly consider and address the specific needs and challenges of small towns to overcome their oblivion, which is intensified by the structural attention gap they have experienced.

Acknowledgments

The research presented here received funding from the People Program (Marie Curie Actions) of the European Union's Seventh Framework Programme FP7/2007–2013/ under REA grant agreement n°607022 "Socio-economic and Political Responses to Regional Polarization in Central and Eastern Europe," and the German Research Foundation (DFG) graduate school "Innovation Society Today" at Technical University Berlin, grant agreement n° 163866004/GRK 1672. The collaboration between the two authors began as part of a visiting fellowship at the Leibniz Institute for Research on Society and Space in Erkner, Germany, in summer 2019. Our special thanks go to Vitória Fank Spohr for her assistance with the bibliography and formatting, and to Bradley Loewen for his proofreading.

Notes

1 Ph.D., Lecturer for Qualitative Methods, School of Economics and Business Administration, University of Tartu and Senior Researcher in Environmental Sociology, School of Natural Sciences and Health, Tallinn University, Estonia, email: pluschke@ut.ee (ORCID 0000–0002-4153–1540).
2 Ph.D., Professor for Participative Spatial Development and Community Organizing, Munich University of Applied Sciences, Germany, email: ariane.sept@hm.edu (ORCID 0000–0002-8691–1950).
3 International small-town network: www.cittaslow.org/
4 Under the concept of invisible places, acoustic ecology and soundscapes of urban environments are also discussed. However, we explicitly do not refer to this branch of research here.
5 Fifteen interviews for the Tõrva case, thirteen for the Berching case.
6 To ensure anonymity of our interviewees, their names have been changed. For the same reason, we only indicate their fields of activity, without naming the concrete functions they fulfill.
7 The terms kolkhoz and sovhoz refer to collective and state farms, which were the prominent form of agricultural organization in the Soviet Union.
8 Membership is not accompanied by financial support, but on the contrary towns pay an admission fee and an annual membership fee.

9   In Berching, as in other German Cittaslow towns, the term "slow" is mostly used in its original English to indicate that this does not mean slow in the literal sense ("langsam"). The correct English translation would be "slow does not mean slow," which, however, does not reflect the specific meaning.
10 The term "Kulak" was used in the Soviet regime to describe peasants with property/ land ownership who were, according to Marxist-Leninist ideologies, considered class enemies. During the Soviet deportations from Estonia, so-called kulaks were deported to remote areas, most prominently Siberia. The two largest waves of deportations occurred in June 1941 and March 1949.

References

Annist, A. (2013). Heterotopia and hegemony: Power and culture in Setomaa. *Journal of Baltic Studies*, *44*(2), 249–269. https://doi.org/10.1080/01629778.2013.775853

Annist, A. (2017). Emigration and the changing meaning of Estonian rural life. In T. Tammaru (Ed.), *EHDR 2016/2017: Estonia at the age of migration*. Foundation Estonian Cooperation Assembly. https://2017.inimareng.ee/en/estonias-cultural-changes-in-an-open-world/emigration-and-the-changing-meaning-of-estonian-rural-life/

Bristow, G. (2010). Resilient regions: Re-'place'ing regional competitiveness. *Cambridge Journal of Regions, Economy and Society*, *3*(1), 153–167. https://doi.org/10.1093/cjres/rsp030

Bürk, T., Kühn, M., & Sommer, H. (2012). Stigmatisation of Cities: The vulnerability of local identities. *Raumforschung und Raumordnung*, *70*, 337–347. https://doi.org/10.1007/s13147-012-0160-4

Christmann, G. (2017). Analysing changes in discursive constructions of rural areas in the context of demographic change: Towards counterpoints in the dominant discourse on "dying villages". *Comparative Population Studies*, *41*(3–4), 359–378. https://doi.org/10.12765/CPoS-2017-03

Cittaslow. (n.d.a). *Association*, Retrieved March 8, 2022, from www.cittaslow.org/content/association

Cittaslow. (n.d.b). *How to become: Certification*, Retrieved March 8, 2022, from www.cittaslow.org/content/how-become

Elsheshtawy, Y. (2008). Transitory sites: Mapping Dubai's 'forgotten' urban spaces. *International Journal of Urban and Regional Research*, *32*(4), 968–988. https://doi.org/10.1111/j.1468-2427.2008.00819.x

Elwood, S. (2006). Beyond cooptation or resistance: Urban spatial politics, community organizations, and GIS-based spatial narratives. *Annals of the Association of American Geographers*, *96*(2): 323–341. https://doi.org/10.1111/j.1467-8306.2006.00480.x

Ernwein, M. (2014). Framing urban gardening and agriculture: On space, scale and the public. *Geoforum*, *56*: 77–86. https://doi.org/10.1016/j.geoforum.2014.06.016

Esfanjary, E., & Alikhani, A. (2021). Recognition of Saheh as forgotten space of Esfahan historic city [Abstract]. *Journal of Architecture in Hot and Dry Climate*, *8*(12), 1–23. http://smb.yazd.ac.ir/article_2139.html?lang=en

Gemeinsam für Berching. (2016). *Berchinger "slow spots"*, Retrieved March 7, 2022, from www.gemeinsam-fuer-berching.de/slow_spots_berching

GENESIS-Online Datenbank. (2016). Bevölkerung: Gemeinden, stichtage [Data set]. *Bavarian State Office for Statistics*. www.statistikdaten.bayern.de/

Görmar, F., & Lang, T. (2019). Acting peripheries: An introduction. *ACME: An International Journal for Critical Geographies*, *18*(2), 486–495

Grootens, G. M. (2019). *Leadership of peripheral places: A comparative study of leadership processes in Estonian and Dutch Peripheral Places*. Tartu: Tartu University Press.

Halfacree, K. (2006). From dropping out to leading on? British counter-cultural back-to-the-land in a changing rurality. *Progress in Human Geography*, *30*(3), 309–336. https://doi.org/10.1191%2F0309132506ph609oa

Kährik, A., Leetmaa, K., & Tammaru, T. (2012). Residential decision-making and satisfaction among new suburbanites in the Tallinn urban region, Estonia. *Cities*, *29*(1), 49–58. https://doi.org/10.1016/j.cities.2011.07.005

Karg, A. (2012, March 1). Sulzstadt wird noch lebenswerter. *Donaukurier*. https://bit.ly/3MurASx

Kauppinen, K. (2013). Welcome to the end of the world! Resignifying periphery under the new economy: A nexus analytical view of a tourist website. *Journal of Multicultural Discourses*, *9*(1), 1–19. https://doi.org/hjxw

Kašková, M., & Chromý, P. (2014). Regional product labelling as part of the region formation process: The case of Czechia. *AUC Geographica*, *49*(2), 87–98. https://doi.org/10.14712/23361980.2014.18

Kavaratzis, M., & Ashworth, G. (2015). Hijacking culture: The disconnection between place culture and place brands. *Town Planning Review*, *86*(2), 155–176. https://doi.org/10.3828/tpr.2015.10

Knoblauch, H. (2005). Focused ethnography. *Forum Qualitative Sozialforschung/Forum Qualitative Social Research*, *6*(3), Article 44. https://doi.org/10.17169/fqs-6.3.20

Kühn, M. (2015). Peripheralization: Theoretical concepts explaining socio-spatial inequalities. *European Planning Studies*, *23*(2), 1–12. https://doi.org/10.1080/09654313.2013.862518

Kühn, M., & Lang, T. (2017). Metropolisierung und peripherisierung in Europa: Eine Einführung. *Europa Regional*, *2015*(4), 2–14. www.ssoar.info/ssoar/handle/document/53587

Kühn, M., & Weck, S. (2012). Peripherisierung – Prozesse, probleme und strategien in Mittelstädten. *DisP – The Planning Review*, *48*(2), 14–26. https://doi.org/10.1080/02513625.2012.721600

Lang, T., Burneika, D., Noorkõiv, R., Plüschke-Altof, B., Pociūtė-Sereikienė, G., & Sechi, G. (2021). Socio-spatial polarisation and policy responses: Perspectives for regional development in the Baltic States. *European Urban and Regional Studies*, *29*(1), 21–44. https://doi.org/10.1177%2F09697764211023553

Leetmaa, K., Kriszan, A., Nuga, M., & Burdack, J. (2015). Strategies to cope with shrinkage in the lower end of the urban hierarchy in Estonia and Central Germany. *European Planning Studies*, *23*(1), 147–165. https://doi.org/10.1080/09654313.2013.820100

Loewen, B., & Schulz, S. (2019). Questioning the convergence of cohesion and innovation policies in Central and Eastern Europe. In T. Lang, & F. Görmar (Eds.), *Regional and local development in times of polarisation* (pp. 121–148). London: Palgrave Macmillan. https://doi.org/10.1007/978-981-13-1190-1_6

Marston, S. A., Jones, J. P., & Woodward, K. (2005). Human geography without scale. *The Transactions of the Institute of British Geographers*, *30*(4), 416–432.

Medvei, Z. (2011). *Bewerten einer kommunalen Nachhaltigkeitsstrategie am Beispiel des CittaSlow Prinzips in der Stadt Berching* [Unpublished bachelor dissertation]. Fachhochschule Frankfurt am Main.

Meyer, F., & Miggelbrink, J. (2013). The subject and the periphery: About discourses, loopings and ascriptions. In A. Fischer-Tahir, & M. Naumann (Eds.), *Peripheralization: The making of spatial dependencies and social injustice* (pp. 207–223). London: Springer. https://doi.org/10.1007/978-3-531-19018-1_10

Mourão, P. R. (2020). *Economia do esquecimento: Rasgando o estreito de Magalhães*. Braga: UMinho Editora. https://doi.org/10.21814/uminho.ed.12

Najjar, L., & Ghadban, S. (2015). In-between forgotten spaces in Palestinian cities: The twin cities of Ramallah and Al-Bireh as a case study. In O. Ozcevik, C. A. Brebbia, S. M. Sener, & S. Ghadban (Eds.), *WIT transactions on ecology and the environment, sustainable development and planning VII* (pp. 811–822). England: WIT Press Southampton. https://doi. org/10.2495/SDP150681

Oyarzún, J. D. D. (2020). Uncertain futures in forgotten places: A study on education policies and students' subjectivities in rural contexts in Chile. *Compare: A Journal of Comparative and International Education, 50*(7), 1047–1063. https://doi.org/10.1080/03057925.2020.1 758923

Paasi, A. (2013). Regional planning and the mobilization of 'regional identity': From bounded spaces to relational complexity. *Regional Studies, 47*(8), 1206 –1219. https://doi.org/10.108 0/00343404.2012.661410

Plüschke-Altof, B. (2019). Fighting against or hiding behind an image of peripherality? Response strategies to discursive peripheralization in Rural Estonia. *Journal of Baltic Studies, 50* (2), 233 – 250. https://doi.org/10.1080/01629778.2019.1595074

Plüschke-Altof, B., & Grootens, M. (2019). Leading through image making? On the limits of emphasising agency in structurally disadvantaged rural places. In T. Lang, & F. Görmar (Eds.), *Regional and local development in times of polarisation* (pp. 319–341). New York: Palgrave Macmillan. https://doi.org/10.1007/978-981-13-1190-1_13

Plüschke-Altof, B., Loewen, B., & Leetmaa, K. (2020). Increasing regional polarisation in Estonia. In H. Sooväli-Sepping (Ed.), *EHDR: Spatial choices for an urbanised society* (pp. 44 – 55). Latvia: Estonian Cooperation Assembly. https://inimareng.ee/en/increasing-regional-polarisation-in-estonia.html

Porsche, L. (2021). Kleinstädte – Förderprogramme und Forschungsinitiativen. In A. Steinführer, L. Porsche, & M. Sondermann (Eds.), *Kompendium Kleinstadtforschung* (pp. 301–313). ARL – Akademie für Raumentwicklung in der Leibniz-Gemeinschaft. http://hdl.handle. net/10419/237045

Porsche, L., Sondermann, M., & Steinführer, A. (2021). Jenseits der Aufmerksamkeitslücke– was wir bisher über Kleinstädte (nicht) wissen. In A. Steinführer, L. Porsche, & M. Sondermann (Eds.), *Kompendium Kleinstadtforschung* (pp. 314–338). ARL – Akademie für Raumentwicklung in der Leibniz-Gemeinschaft. www.ssoar.info/ssoar/handle/ document/75036

Raagmaa, G., & Noorkõiv, R. (2013). *Globaliseeruv Eesti Küla: Avaneva Maailma Arenguvõimalused ja ohud.* Estonia: Eesti Külaliikumine Kodukant.

Ravelli, F. (2005, February 13). La capitale della lentezza. *La Repubblica.* https://ricerca.repubblica.it/repubblica/archivio/repubblica/2005/02/13/la-capitale-della-lentezza.html

Reynolds, W. M. (Ed.). (2017). *Forgotten places: Critical studies in rural education.* New York: Peter Lang.

Rodgers, D. M., Petersen, J., & Sanderson, J. (2016). Commemorating alternative organizations and marginalized spaces: The case of forgotten Finntowns. *Organization, 23*(1), 90–113. https://doi.org/10.1177%2F1350508415605110

Schiemann, S., & Steinführer, A. (2021). In guter Gesellschaft? Sozialstruktur und soziale Beziehungen in Kleinstädten. In A. Steinführer, L. Porsche, & M. Sondermann (Eds.), *Kompendium Kleinstadtforschung* (pp. 209–248). ARL – Akademie für Raumentwicklung in der Leibniz-Gemeinschaft. http://hdl.handle.net/10419/237041

Schober Architekten. (2012). Ein ISEK für Berching: Integriertes Stadtentwicklungskonzept. *Berching Stadt.* https://www.berching.de/pdf/rathaus/isek_berching_internetfassung2012.pdf

Semian, M., & Chromý, P. (2014). Regional identity as a driver or a barrier in the process of regional development: A comparison of selected European experience. *Norsk Geografisk*

Tidsskrift/Norwegian Journal of Geography, 68(5), 263–270. https://doi.org/10.1080/00291 951.2014.961540

Sept, A. (2018). *Entschleunigung in Klein- und Mittelstädten: Cittaslow als soziale Innovation in der Stadtentwicklung.* Lemgo: Dorothea Rohn.

Sept, A. (2021). 'Slowing down' in small and medium-sized towns: Cittaslow in Germany and Italy from a social innovation perspective. *Regional Studies, Regional Science, 8*(1), 259–268. https://doi.org/10.1080/21681376.2021.1919190

Shatkin, G. (2004). Planning to forget: Informal settlements as 'forgotten places' in globalising metro manila. *Urban Studies, 41*(12), 2469–2484. https://doi.org/10.1080 %2F00420980412331297636

Simmel, G. (1995 [1903]). Die Großstädte und das Geistesleben. In R. Kramme, A. Rammstedt, & O. Rammstedt (Eds.), *Georg Simmel Gesamtausgabe Bd. 7: Aufsätze und Abhandlungen 1901–1908, Bd. 1* (pp. 116–131). Frankfurt a.M.: Suhrkamp. (Reprinted from *Die Grossstadt: Vorträge und Aufsätze zur Städteausstellung*, pp. 185–206, by Petermann, T., Ed., 1903, Dresden)

Stadt Berching. (2015). *Städtebauliche Entwicklung der Altstadt von Berching seit 1975* [Brochure]. Berching: Stadt Berching i.d.OPf. https://www.berching.de/pdf/rathaus/40jahre-sbf_berching_rz_net.pdf

Stadt Berching. (n.d.). *Cittaslow.* Retrieved March 7, 2022, from www.berching.de/cittaslow/

Steinführer, A. (2015). 'Landflucht' und 'sterbende Städte': Diskurse über ländliche Schrumpfung in Vergangenheit und Gegenwart. *Geographische Rundschau, 9*, 4–10.

Steinführer, A., Sondermann, M., & Porsche, L. (2021). Kleinstädte als Forschungsgegenstand: Bestimmungsmerkmale, Bedeutungen und Zugänge. In A. Steinführer, L. Porsche, & Sondermann (Eds.), *Kompendium Kleinstadtforschung* (pp. 5–23). ARL – Akademie für Raumentwicklung in der Leibniz-Gemeinschaft. http://hdl.handle.net/10419/237030

Tõrva vald. (2022). *Tutvustus*, Retrieved March 7, 2022, from https://torva.kovtp.ee/tutvustus

Tuvikene, T., Alves, S. N., & Hilbrandt, H. (2017). Strategies for relating diverse cities: A multi-sited individualising comparison of informality in Bafatá, Berlin and Tallinn. *Current Sociology, 65*(2), 276–288. https://doi.org/10.1177/0011392116657298

Valga, M. (2011). *Valgamaa Kuvandi Uuringu Aruanne*, March 9. www.slideserve.com/manjit/valga-maavalitsus

van Neste, S. L. (2020). Place, pipelines and political subjectivities in invisibilized urban peripheries. *Territory, Politics, Governance 8*(4), 461–477. https://doi.org/10.1080/21622671 .2019.1648314

Weck, S., & Beißwenger, S. (2014). Coping with peripheralization: Governance response in two German small cities. *European Planning Studies, 22*(10), 2156–2171. https://doi.org/1 0.1080/09654313.2013.819839

Willett, J. (2020). Challenging peripheralising discourses: Using evolutionary economic geography and, complex systems theory to connect new regional knowledges within the periphery. *Journal of Rural Studies, 73*, 87–96.

Young, D., & Keil, R. (2014). Locating the urban in-between: Tracking the urban politics of infrastructure in Toronto. *International Journal of Urban and Regional Research, 38*(5), 1589–1608. https://doi.org/10.1111/1468-2427.12146

4 Italian inner areas' strategic plans

A textual network analysis of the *Appennino Emiliano* and *Madonie* case studies

*Riccardo De Vita¹, Giuseppe Lucio Gaeta²,
Francesco Silvestri³ and Stefano Ghinoi⁴*

Introduction

The European Union (EU) is a sociopolitical and economic ecosystem character-ized by regional disparities in the labor market, income distribution, productivity and investments, and access to infrastructures (Degl'Innocenti et al., 2018; Petrakos et al., 2005). These disparities are the result of different historical and political trajectories – such as those influencing Eastern European countries before 1989 – and one of the main aims of the Union is to reduce them and promote convergence. In 1988, the European Community introduced the main principles for its cohesion policy, com-prising specific measures for supporting economic development in less-advanced re-gions (Inforegio, 2008). The cohesion policy and its related funds have been created for this objective. While research studies assessed the positive impact of these tools on reducing disparities (e.g., Crescenzi & Giua, 2020), others demonstrated that signifi-cant differences persist across the European regions (e.g., Borsi & Metiu, 2015).

The economic geography literature considers remoteness as one of the elements that might hinder regional economic growth, reducing access to new markets and acquiring new resources and impeding the accumulation of human capital (López-Rodríguez et al., 2007). The remoteness concept is complex (Bocco, 2016); it should not be simply associated with the physical or spatial dimension since it might also concern the economic, cultural, or institutional dimensions (Huskey, 2006; Leven, 1986). Considering this aspect, in 2012, the Italian government developed a new experimental strategy to be realized in the cohesion policy framework to sup-port the national inner areas, that is, the Italian National Strategy for Inner Areas (*Strategia Nazionale per le Aree Interne* – hereafter SNAI). According to the strategy, inner areas are those "at some considerable distance from hubs providing essential services (education, health, and mobility), with a wealth of key environmental and cultural resources of many different kinds". In other words, these areas are charac-terized by a remoteness that "derives from their lower accessibility to citizenship services" (Barca et al., 2014, p. 7).

For each of the 72 pilot areas identified by the SNAI, a local development strat-egy had to be developed and presented in a document. In line with the cohesion

DOI: 10.4324/9781003256281-7

policy multilevel governance and participatory approach, these documents were codesigned by a team of experts contracted by the national government and local authorities.[5] In addition, following the territorial place-based approach, actions and tools for improving the local population's well-being were designed starting from places' main features and local communities' needs. In sum, the SNAI encouraged local participation in codesigning place-based policies (Barca, 2009).

Concepts and ideas used in the locally developed strategic documents are vital for understanding the contents and potential outcomes of the SNAI strategy (Shanahan et al., 2011; Stoustrup, 2022). As pointed out by Thomas (2014, p. 236), "a word may be defined by its context in usage"; therefore, over recent years, scholars used text analysis techniques to investigate the strategic documents produced in the SNAI formulation. For example, Mantegazzi et al. (2021) explore the coherence between tourism strategies developed in SNAI areas and the SNAI policy framework and guidelines. Punziano & Urso (2016), instead, find that local strategies have a geographical pattern (i.e., those produced by closer areas tend to be similar) even if their content relies on categories and meanings that are highly influenced by the central government's guidelines and formats (i.e., a framing effect is at work). Our study aims to contribute to this stream of literature by investigating the SNAI strategic documents produced by two inner areas, that is, *Appennino Emiliano*, located in the North of Italy, and *Madonie*, in the South. Our focus is on analyzing the concepts included in the documents, their importance, and their co-occurrence. The main novelty of the study is its methodological approach that allows detecting network patterns among the concepts. Understanding how concepts are semantically related is critical for evaluators and policymakers. It enables exploring the dominant knowledge discourse and determining which themes are more central in the discourse, what are peripheral, and if certain themes are introduced and discussed with others that concentrate on different aspects. In this vein, this study provides a novel analytical perspective that has never been used before for studying the Italian SNAI.

The chapter is organized as follows. "The European Community (EC)/European Union (EU) cohesion policy" provides a brief historical overview of the European Community (EC)/European Union (EU) structural funds and regional development policy that allows understanding the SNAI framework. "The Italian Strategy for Inner Areas (SNAI)" presents the main features of the SNAI, highlighting its experimental nature and the novelty of its approach to define and implement local strategies. "*Appennino Emiliano* and *Madonie* – a comparative case study" presents the two Italian inner areas considered by our comparative study and outlines their main features and differences. "Method" provides an overview of the textual data and the method used for analyzing them, while findings are shown and discussed in "Results" and "Discussion". Finally, last section concludes the chapter.

The European Community (EC)/European Union (EU) cohesion policy

Ensuring countries' harmonious development and reducing regional disparities has been one of the priority objectives of the European community since the Treaty of Rome (1957). Nevertheless, the Community's efforts were initially mainly devoted to the promotion of efficiency-oriented policies and efforts aimed at fostering trade and the mobility of production factors among member countries (financed through the European Social Fund – ESF) and ensuring food security through the improvement and coordination of the agricultural production (Common Agricultural Policy – CAP – and European Agricultural Guidance and Guarantee Fund – EAGGF). In addition, common support for investments was granted through the European Investment Bank (EIB).

The Community's concern for tackling regional imbalance issues emerged in the mid of the 1960s[6] and was sped up at the beginning of the 1970s. Indeed, after the publication of the Werner plan on building the economic and monetary union (which happened in 1970), the Member States became increasingly aware of the need for policy coordination to tackle the negative effects that the possible unification could determine on the regions left behind. At the same time, the Community realized that a new common regional policy could provide tangible benefits to two new members, namely Ireland and the UK. Indeed, it could support the extremely poor regions of Ireland (Barry, 2003) and reduce the wide regional disparities within the UK (Gudgin, 1995), counterbalancing the heavy English financial contribution to the common budget (the UK was a minor CAP recipient).

In 1974, the Community established its regional policy instrument, that is, the European Regional Development Fund, to finance investments in small industrial, handicraft, or service activities creating new jobs, and in infrastructures, especially in mountain and farming areas (Regulation 724/1975). These investments were allocated based on countries fixed quotas and national authorities decisions. In other words, a genuinely European regional policy perspective was missing (Hall, 2014).

The Community enlargement in the 1980s – Greece (1981), Spain, and Portugal (1986) – widened the already existing regional disparities, making the need for a common regional policy more evident. In 1985, after the urban pilot projects carried out in Naples (Italy) and Belfast (Ireland), the Communities Council established the Integrated Mediterranean Programmes (IMP; Regulation 2088/1985) to help fragile Mediterranean regions cope with issues determined by the enlargement. The IMP was the first multi-annual large-scale strategy tackling regional development issues by promoting dialogue among regional, national, community-level authorities and societal bodies (e.g., organized interests, firms, and individuals). It represented a valuable experimental test of the innovative approach to regional policy that began to take shape from the end of the '80s.

Indeed, the 1986 Single Act devoted one specific section to social cohesion in the Community. During the period 1989–1993, the Commission proposed to double the previous structural investment budget, reaching 69 billion ECU, which represents 25% of the EU budget and 0.3% of the total GDP (Goulet, 2008). At the same time, it promoted a significant reform of the structural funds regulation (Regulation 2052/1988). On the one hand, the funds interventions were integrated under a common policy focused on five specific objectives (see Table 4.1). On the other hand, these interventions were set to be: (i) concentrated on the regional areas most in need; (ii) additional to national interventions; and (iii) defined by programs whose conception and implementation required multilevel governance (Hooghe

Table 4.1 Structural funds objectives by programming period (from 1989 to 2020)

1989–1993	1994–1999	2000–2006	2007–2013	2014–2020
Objective 1: Development and structural adjustment of regions whose development is lagging behind	*Objective 1*: Development and structural adjustment of regions whose development is lagging behind	*Objective 1*: Development and structural adjustment of regions whose development is lagging behind	*Objective 1*: Convergence	*Objective 1*: Investment for growth and jobs
Objective 2: Conversion of declining industrial regions	*Objective 2*: Conversion of declining industrial regions	*Objective 2*: Economic and social conversion of areas experiencing structural difficulties	*Objective 2*: Regional competitiveness and employment	*Objective 2*: European territorial cooperation
Objective 3: Combating long-term unemployment and assisting the occupational integration of young people	*Objective 3*: Combating long-term unemployment and assisting the occupational integration of young people	*Objective 3*: Support for adaptation and modernization of the education, training, and employment policy	*Objective 3*: European territorial cooperation	
Objective 4: Adaptation of workers to changes in production systems	*Objective 4*: Adaptation of workers to changes in production systems			
Objective 5a: Acceleration of structural adjustment in agriculture	*Objective 5a*: Acceleration of structural adjustment in agriculture			
Objective 5b: Support for development and structural changes in rural areas	*Objective 5b*: Support for development and structural changes in rural areas			
	Objective 6: Development and structural adjustment in regions with low population density			

et al., 2001), that is, the involvement and responsibility of European, national and local government authorities.

The subsequent revision of the structural funds regulation was carried out in 1993 (Regulation 2081/1993), right after the Maastricht Treaty (signed in 1992), and set up the framework for the funds intervention over 1994–1999. Funds available for the common regional policy were further expanded, reaching 168 billion ECU, that is, approximately 33% of the EU budget and 0.4% of the EU GDP (Goulet, 2008). The new regulation introduced a new cohesion fund to support environmental and infrastructure projects to be realized in less developed countries, where it was impossible to finance massive investments while keeping public deficit and debt in line with the Maastricht criteria. This regulation added innovative regional policy goals (see the recap in Table 4.1), but, on the whole, it left unaltered parts of the objectives set up in 1987.

At the beginning of the 2000s, a new massive enlargement involved 10 countries with a level of economic development well under the EU average (Hungary, Poland, Estonia, Czech Republic, Slovenia, Slovakia, Lithuania, Latvia, Malta, and Cyprus). This implied a new structural funds strategy set up by the 1997 "Agenda 2000" communication. Its content was implemented by the new structural funds regulation (Regulation 1260/1999) that presented the three priorities reported in the third column of Table 4.1. Overall, 213 billion euros were financed for the EU15, plus 21.7 billion for the new Member States. This meant approximately 33% of the EU budget and 0.4% of the GDP.

The following structural funds programming period (2007–2013) was marked by significant changes which were mainly led by the debate on the EU priorities that followed the so-called Lisbon Agenda or Lisbon Strategy action and development plan approved by the European Council in 2000 (European Council conclusion, March 23 and 24, 2000). This plan promoted the idea that Europe had to enhance its competitiveness by focusing on knowledge-driven innovation and entrepreneurship. The integration of this orientation in the EU regional policy raised some issues. For example, some scholars noted that the competitive objective required a focus on sectoral policies instead of regional policies (Hall, 2014). In line with this debate, and considering the EU enlargement that included Romania and Bulgaria in 2007, the new design of structural funds intervention was based on the three objectives reported in column 4 of Table 4.1 (Regulation 1083/2006). Overall, the funds spent in this period were approximately €347 billion, representing 35.7% of the EU budget and 0.38% of the EU total GDP.

Article 174 of the Lisbon Treaty (which was signed in 2007) relaunched the importance of the EU regional policy to promote the Union's harmonious development and to strengthen economic and social cohesion. The Treaty also mentioned the territorial dimension of cohesion. The idea behind territorial cohesion is that the Community regional policies had to pay greater attention to spatial factors. In this perspective, addressing issues requires going beyond the potential isolation imposed by administrative boundaries; instead, local endogenous potentials and exogenous factors, such as the development and concentration of economic activities in neighboring places, are complementary. This suggested enhancing profound knowledge of territories, relying on a functional approach when planning their development, and promoting cooperation between different places.

In this framework, the Europe 2020 10-year strategy proposed by the Commission and approved by the European Council in March 2010 (European Council conclusion, March 25 and 26, 2010) set the new strategic goal to support smart (i.e., knowledge and innovation-based), sustainable (i.e., environment-friendly and efficient), and inclusive (i.e., able to foster economic, social, and territorial cohesion) growth. The 2014–2020 cohesion policy implied the two main goals reported in the last column of Table 4.1. Funds supporting the actions planned to achieve these objectives amounted to approximately €352 billion (European Commission, 2014). The new regulation for the European structural and investment funds (Regulation 1303/2013) introduced a Common Support Framework (CSF) that aligned the strategy and the policy tools by translating the objectives into 11 operative thematic priorities. The interventions planning was based on Partnership Agreements prepared by the Member States in collaboration with central and local government bodies and economic and social partners and approved by the EU Commission. These agreements illustrate how and where funds are going to be spent. The SNAI was included in the Partnership Agreement between Italy and the European Commission to coordinate the EU structural funds during the 2014–2020 programming.

The Italian Strategy for Inner Areas (SNAI)

The SNAI preliminary activities started in 2012 with the support of the National Ministry for Territorial Cohesion. They were focused on mapping the Italian national territory to classify municipalities according to their distance from essential services (i.e., railway stations, secondary schools, hospitals, and specialist medical centers). The rationale of this approach was straightforward: bringing into the political debate the peripheral and ultra-peripheral areas where living conditions are difficult due to the lack of access to primary services (Cotella & Vitale Brovarone, 2020). Such mapping demonstrated that 60% of the Italian territory, 51% of the municipalities, and 23% of the population were, on average, more than 20 minutes – of a car, train, or bus ride – away from the services mentioned above (Strategia Aree Interne, 2018). Moreover, these areas were suffering from depopulation and aging problems, both the result and the source of a progressive rarefaction and reduction of services. These areas were labeled as inner areas.

During a process that initially included 1,081 municipalities (out of the 4,000 having the inner area status), 72 inter-municipal pilot areas were selected, covering 16.7% of the national territory and 3.5% of the Italian population. These perimeters were then officially confirmed by regional governments. Once the pilot areas were selected, the municipalities in these territories had to identify a "spokesperson" among the mayors in charge. This "spokesperson" had to act as a link with the regional and the national institutions and entrust a local institution (a municipality or a Union of municipalities) for technical assistance.

The selected areas included, on average, 15 municipalities with an average of 29,000 inhabitants; they range from 3 municipalities (Tesino area in the Autonomous

Province of Trento) to 34 municipalities (Upper Lake Como and Lario Valley areas in the Lombardy region).

The main novelty of SNAI was the place-based approach (Barca et al., 2012) adopted for defining and implementing local strategies. This approach assumes that the knowledge and the resources needed to overcome marginality are available in the inner areas. Nonetheless, marginal areas are often subject to lock-in effects and the adverse consequences of extractive institutions' actions (Pezzi & Urso, 2017; Urso et al., 2019; Acemoglu, 2005). This criticism also concerns the bottom-up approach, which was long assumed by the European Commission as an ideal tool to encourage the emergence of local interests (Sabatier, 1986) and is still central in appreciated development programs such as Leader.

Therefore, the SNAI concentrates on valorizing local knowledge and forcing changes in areas subject to socioeconomic lock-in through the national guidelines and the intervention of external experts. The latter is requested to work with local communities and stakeholders to design a strategy for the area, integrate services and local development, and stimulate a debate on the actions financed by national and European funds. In this vein, the role of the experts was intended to support the emergence of endogenous change dynamics, breaking vicious lock-in type cycles characterizing marginal areas (Mantegazzi et al., 2021; Urso et al., 2019) and, at the same time, creating the conditions for enabling networking processes.

The importance of networking between all the aforementioned actors has been highlighted by recent studies. By looking at the partnership network developed by local farmers to create a "green community", the work of Basile and Cavallo (2020) highlights that supply chains can be redesigned to offer more opportunities to young people and address the depopulation problem in inner areas. Cerquetti and Cutrini (2021) use the social capital lens to investigate cooperation and inclusiveness in implementing local initiatives in Central Italy's inner areas. Their results confirm that bonding ties support short-term community resilience, but resilience and resilience adaptability are possible because of bridging ties in the long run. Finally, Napoli and Petino (2020) apply network theory to map multiple relationships between public and private actors in a Southern Italy inner area. They find that local actors underestimate the beneficial effects of networking activities and tend to establish relationships based on short-term convenience.

Some scholars have criticized the SNAI approach (see, for example, Rossitti et al., 2021; Vendemmia et al., 2021) mixing the bottom-up and top-down policy design. Nevertheless, theSNAI has been confirmed by all the Italian governments from 2012 to present and has caught the interest of the European Commission, which decided to include the support for inner areas as a priority of the Financial Framework 2021–2027.

Appennino Emiliano and *Madonie* – a comparative case study

In this study, we focus on two of the 72 SNAI pilot areas: the *Appennino Emiliano* and the *Madonie*. These two areas are comparable in terms of geomorphological configuration. They are both middle-high mountain areas with peaks rounding 2,000 meters, are rich in springs and waters, and report relevant geological emergencies. A further element of similarity is that they designed their strategy in the same period (2016–2018), being the first area to start this process in their regions.

At the same time, these two areas present some significant differences. First, is about size. The *Appennino Emiliano* counts 7 municipalities and 33,000 inhabitants. In comparison, *Madonie* is made up of 21 municipalities and has 63,400 residents (ISTAT, 2021).

Second, these areas can be considered archetypal of the main cleavage affecting the Italian context, that is, the North-South economic divide. The *Appennino Emiliano* is a pretty wealthy area in a developed Northern region (*Emilia-Romagna*), albeit in a demographic crisis, characterized by the manufacturing of high-value-added agri-food products. Instead, the *Madonie* is a low-income area in *Sicily*, one of the country's Southern regions. Consequently, *Madonie* is involved in the objective 1 of the EU cohesion policy (see "The European Community (EC)/European Union (EU) cohesion policy" and Table 4.1), while *Appennino Emiliano* is not. In addition, from an institutional perspective, the main difference between these areas is that *Madonie*'s Region, *Sicily*, has a special status in Italy, with autonomous legislative and financial powers. Instead, the *Appennino Emiliano* is located in *Emilia-Romagna*, that is, a region with ordinary statute.

Given these similarities and differences between the two areas, it makes sense to explore whether and how the themes and words included in the locally developed strategy documents reflect these common characteristics and dissimilarities.

Method

Addressing the objectives of the study required specific methodological procedures. One document presenting the ultimate local development strategy has been identified for each of the two inner areas under investigation. The document *La montagna del latte: stili di vita salutari e comunità intraprendenti nell'Appennino Emiliani* was considered for the *Appennino Emiliano*, while the document *Madonie resilienti: Laboratorio di futuro* was used for the *Madonie*.[7] Before the data analysis, the documents were edited, and tables and figures were removed to capture only complete text sections.

To process the above data, we relied on textual network analysis, which combines Social Network Analysis (SNA) and Content Analysis (CA). SNA is a well-established approach for studying social relationships and network structures by using concepts and methods from network theory (Prell, 2012); networks are made by nodes and the edges connecting them, and different structures can emerge from different types of networks. CA is applied for analyzing qualitative (textual) data using quantitative techniques to assess the presence of meanings according to the language patterns and structures existing in the text (Carley, 1990). These approaches can be combined for mapping and analyzing the relationships between words and concepts in a text, which can be seen as network nodes. According to Segev (2020, p. 2), textual network analysis "focuses on the network of words appearing together in the text" and is based "on the principle that combinations of words appearing together have unique meanings". This type of analysis follows a precise structure:

first, once identified a research question, it is necessary to define the corpus (text data) to be studied; second, researchers must decide the main approach for including or excluding network actors (i.e., words) and mapping relationships; third, the list of words should be converted into a network; fourth, researchers should decide for the type of analysis to be run; finally, results can be interpreted.

Data have been analyzed using Leximancer (Smith & Humphreys, 2006). This software has been chosen for its capacity to automatically perform conceptual analyses, retrieving concepts in a text, and relational analysis, mapping the relationship between such concepts. Leximancer has recently been used to explore strategy and policymaking at different regional levels, for example, entrepreneurship (Moyle et al., 2020) and environmental sustainability (Ghinoi et al., 2021). In some studies, Leximancer is used to identify and explore specific concepts of interest to the researchers (e.g., Herington & van de Fliert, 2018) through an approach called "profiling". Instead, in this study, the concept identification phase is entirely automated. In other words, the concepts generated from Leximancer are based on seed words found in the documents, not input received from the researchers. We reviewed the concept lists initially produced by Leximancer for both the areas under scrutiny to avoid duplications and inconsistency. For example, we separated words included in the same concepts due to their common root while they represent different ideas (e.g., *comunità* = community and *comunicazione* = communication).

Two conceptual maps, one for each of the cases under investigation, have been produced, representing the most recurring concepts (dots on the maps) and their co-occurrence (lines). Concepts are grouped into themes, visualized as heat-mapped bubbles; hot colors (red and orange) refer to relevant concepts and themes, while cool colors (blue and green) are associated with the least relevant concepts and themes. Themes represent clusters of concepts that often appear together in the same portion of text. The size of the bubbles is the result of the number of themes identified by the software and does not carry a specific meaning. Themes are visualized as circles so that to identify which concepts are associated with the different themes.

Results

Figures 4.1 and 4.2 provide the conceptual maps visualizing the links between the concepts that emerge from the strategic documents of the two areas under scrutiny. The output presented in the figures shows three similarities between the content of the two documents.

First, both areas strategies reveal a focus on the local territory (*territorio*) and the supply (*offerta*) of public services (*servizi*). This finding aligns with the idea that the critical element characterizing the SNAI is its focus on the territorial dimension (Barca et al., 2014) and that inner areas are defined by their limited access to essential citizenship services (Carrosio, 2016).

Second, in both documents, the local territory (territorio) is linked with economic-related themes: *sviluppo* (development), *lavoro* (labor/work), *offerta* (supply of goods and services), *risorse* (resources), and *imprese* (enterprises). Entrepreneurship and job creation are fundamental for the survival of inner areas, which

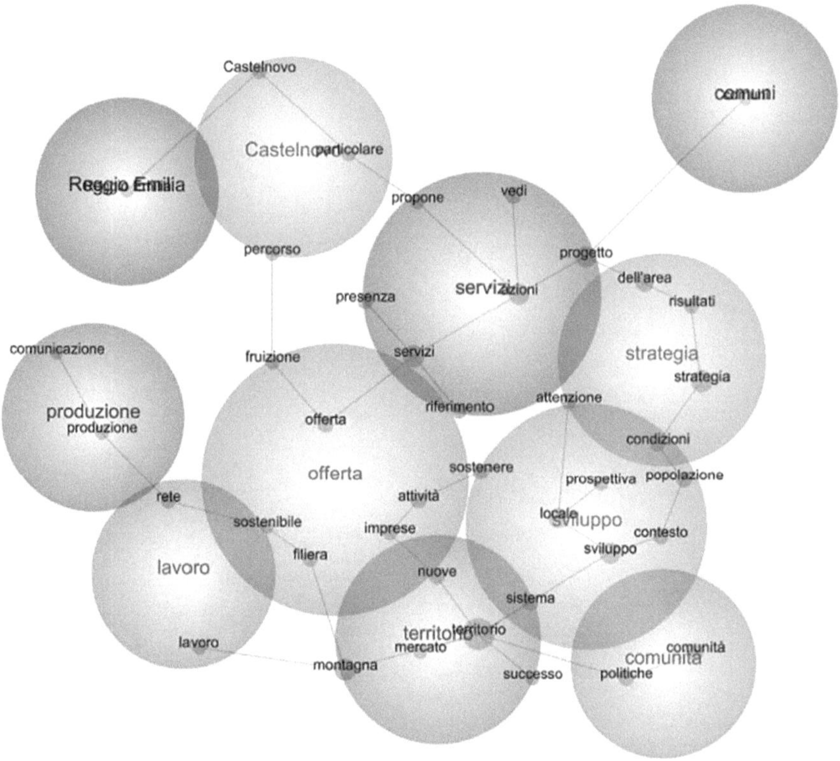

Figure 4.1 The *Appennino Emiliano* conceptual map

are not able to attract specialized and creative workers and, in general, are characterized by pervasive informal work and a high incidence of retired individuals (Compagnucci & Morettini, 2020; Mariotti et al., 2023). In this vein, the most recent literature has highlighted that community enterprises and cooperatives play a pivotal role in these areas (Sanna & De Bernardo, 2015; Mastronardi & Romagnoli, 2020). Apparently, the SNAI does not recognize a specific role for these actors (Borzaga & Zandonai, 2015). This is true for the strategic documents analyzed in this study: concepts related to the cooperative ecosystem do not appear in Figures 4.1 and 4.2.

Nevertheless, one concept – often associated with the idea of cooperation and cooperatives – emerges in these graphs: *comunità* (community). While this concept is somewhat peripheral in *Appennino Emiliano*'s strategy, *Madonie*'s strategy is included in the *territorio* theme and is more central. It is worth noting that the *Appennino Emiliano* is where, at the beginning of the 2000s, the Community Cooperatives were created for the first time. In the subsequent years, these cooperatives represented a model taken up in many of the country's inner areas. The fact that cooperatives are not so central in the strategy of this place reveals that they are now considered an institution wholly embedded in the local fabric, which no longer requires particular

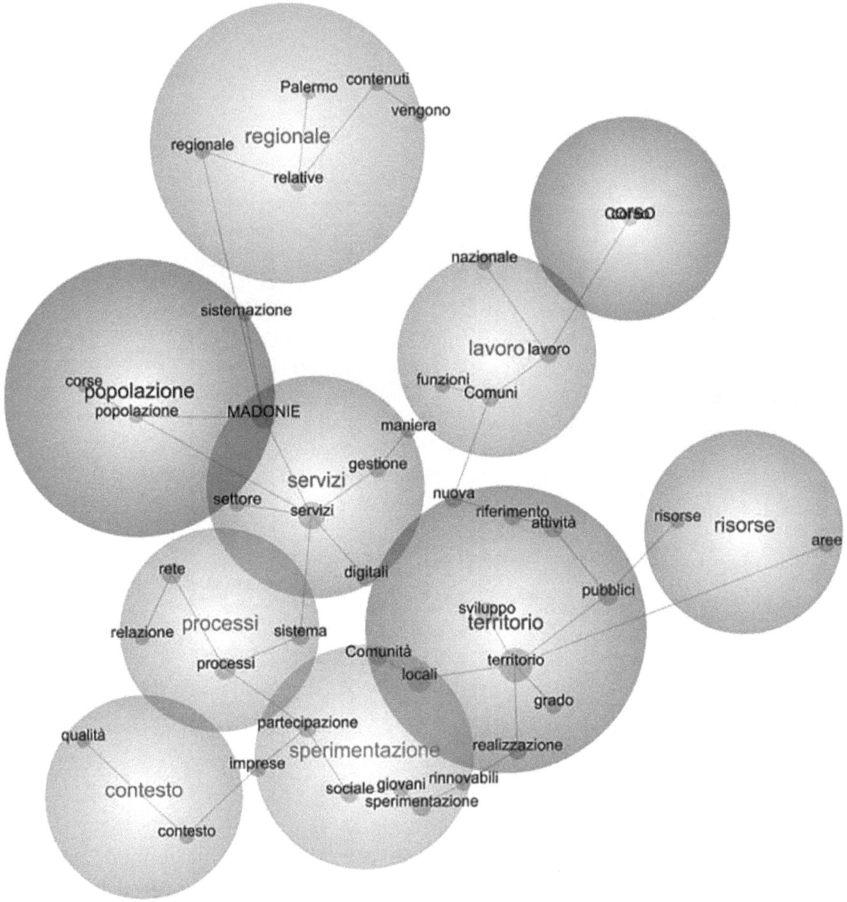

Figure 4.2 The *Madonie* conceptual map

policies. Instead, in *Madonie*, strengthening the presence of social and business relationships at the community level is considered crucial.

Third, the concepts associated with provincial- and regional-level institutions
appear peripheral in both documents. In the case of *Appennino Emiliano*, Reggio
Emilia (the province's chief town and administrative center) is peripheral and connects with only one theme: *Castelnovo*. This is the territory's main town center –
with around 10,000 inhabitants – the only one with essential services such as a
hospital, care homes, and high schools. In the case of *Madonie*, the central theme
identified by the concept regionale (regional) includes *Palermo*, the capital of the
Sicily region where *Madonie* is located that is the political and administrative center
of the entire region. This finding supports the idea that the local, territorial dimension has great importance in the strategy. Higher institutional levels, such as provincial or regional governments, are still considered in the discussion – because of their

role in managing and transferring national and European financial resources – but they seem to be noncentral. This result is aligned with the main findings by Urso (2016), who investigated the relationship between central and peripheral nodes (i.e., territories), observing that cities and inner areas are more separated than expected. This suggests that opportunities are missed to strengthen local economies and address people's needs.

Fourth, concepts such as actions, activities, and projects appear to be central in the strategic documents of both territories. This is not surprising, because these are expected to be focused on the descriptions of what will be carried out during the implementation phase.[8]

Discussion

Our analysis confirms most of the previous findings by the literature on inner areas (Cotella & Vitale Brovarone, 2020; Pezzi & Urso, 2017; Urso, 2016): the focus on local territory and public services, which distinguish the SNAI policy from other development policies; the link between the local territory and economic-related aspects; the (lack of) relationships between central and peripheral territories. Despite the socioeconomic differences between the two case studies, the documents analyzed present a common background focusing on demographic conditions, environmental maintenance, and territorial capital. At the same time, differences emerge when considering networking. Networking is fundamental in inner areas; it creates synergies between local actors that ease the provision of services and create economic opportunities (Borghi, 2017). While networks might be local development drivers, our findings suggest that the definition and interpretation of networking activities can differ according to the preconditions characterizing a territory. Indeed, in the *Appennino Emiliano* graph (Figure 4.1), rete (*network*) is linked to produzione (*production*), sostenibile (*sustainable*), comunicazione (*communication*), and filiera (*supply chain*). In other words, networking seems to have a clear business-oriented focus. Instead, in the *Madonie's* strategy, rete (*network*) is associated with relazione (relationship) and processi (processes), which suggests that networking is perceived as a social process for creating opportunities without a business-related approach. This is coherent with the idea that the interconnected systems of local actors in Southern inner areas need to be strongly supported because they are not as mature as those in Northern inner areas where networks are already concentrating on elements pertaining to economic activities.

Conclusion

In the European cohesion policy framework, the SNAI presents elements of innovativeness that have received attention from scholars and policy practitioners in Italy and Europe. On the one hand, it focuses and defines remote areas by looking at their distance from hubs providing essential citizenship services. On the other hand, it proposes an innovative approach combining bottom-up (e.g., engagement of local authorities and actors in designing the areas development strategy) and top-down features (e.g., national selection of the areas to be involved, national guidelines, involvement of external experts selected by the national government) to design these areas local development strategies. Therefore, it leverages multilevel co-decision to identify effective locally drafted place-based strategies. The documents illustrating these strategies are particularly valuable because they provide an overview of how local development is conceived in each area.

This chapter proposed a quantitative textual examination of the SNAI strategic documents produced by two Italian inner areas that are highly homogenous in terms of geomorphic features and remoteness but highly heterogeneous from the socioeconomic point of view.

The analysis suggests that the local development strategies include elements related to the top-down and bottom-up approaches. On the one hand, they focus on elements that represent a feature of the SNAI framework setting, such as local territory, the supply of public services, and local economy-related themes. Such a focus can be considered as the effect of the top-down framing of local strategies triggered by the national SNAI guidelines and supported by the involvement of nonlocal experts in the codesigning process. At the same time, the strategies investigated reveal evident differences. The main issue is the heterogeneous interpretation of the role that networking might play in triggering development. In the *Appennino Emiliano* strategy, promoting networks is mainly interpreted as an instrument to strengthen business activities. Instead, the *Madonie* strategy is conceived more generally as a tool for creating new opportunities and supporting social engagement.

The coexistence of these two lines, of which our analysis provides some evidence, reflects the SNAI expectations and suggests that the strategies developed locally propose place-based solutions framed in a general orientation that might overcome lock-in policy design issues. The ex post evaluation of the interventions that will be implemented in the future will tell us whether the strategies developed in this way will be effective in stimulating local development.

Notes

1   Ph.D., Professor, Head of School, School of Business, Operations and Strategy, University of Greenwich, United Kingdom, email: r.devita@gre.ac.uk.
2   Ph.D., Associate Professor, Department of Human and Social Sciences, University of Naples L'Orientale, Italy, email: glgaeta@unior.it (ORCID: 0000–0001–7994–292X).
3   Ph.D., Assistant Professor (tenure track), Department of Communication and Economics, University of Modena and Reggio Emilia and CiMET, Italy, email: francesco.silvestri@ unimore.it (ORCID: 0000–0002–5698–5959).
4   Ph.D., Senior Lecturer, School of Business, Operations and Strategy, University of Greenwich, United Kingdom, email: S.Ghinoi@greenwich.ac.uk (ORCID ID: 0000–0002–9857–47369).
5   Namely, municipalities, both autonomous and associated in a second-level local body, that is, the Union of municipalities.
6   See the memorandum SEC (65) 1170, 1 May 1965, and the recommendation COM(69) 950, 15 October 1969, both focused on regional policy.
7   The *Appennino Emiliano* document is available here: www.agenziacoesione.gov.it/ strategia-nazionale-aree-interne/regione-emilia-romagna-aree-interne/appennino-emiliano/ [link tested on 15 September 2022]. The *Madonie* document is available here:

www.agenziacoesione.gov.it/strategia-nazionale-aree-interne/regione-sicilia/madonie/ [link tested on 15 September 2022].

8 The SNAI procedure is organized in three progressive steps, each defined by the presentation of a strategic document. The first is the "Draft" describing the area, the main well-being problems, and the local and external resources to be activated. The second one is the "Preliminary Strategy", where the backbone idea for future development of the area and the action plan is defined. Finally, the "Ultimate strategy", where the specific projects to be implemented in the following three years (phases, agents, financing source, beneficiaries) are presented.

References

Acemoglu, D. (2005). Institutions as the fundamental cause of long-run growth. In P. Aghion, & S. Durlauf (Eds.), *Handbook of Economic Growth*. Amsterdam: Elsevier.

Barca, F. (2009). An agenda for a reformed cohesion policy. A place-based approach to meeting European Union challenges and expectations. In *Independent Report Prepared at the Request of Danuta Hübner*. Bruxelles: Commissioner for Regional Policy, European Parlament.

Barca, F., Casavola, P., & Lucatelli, S. (2014). A strategy for inner areas in Italy: Definition, objectives, tools and governance. *Materiali Uval*. www.agenziacoesione.gov.it/wp-content/uploads/2020/07/MUVAL_31_Aree_interne_ENG.pdf

Barca, F., McCann, P., & Rodríguez-Pose, A. (2012). The case for regional development intervention: Place-based versus place-neutral approaches. *Journal of Regional Science*, *52*(1), 134–152.

Barry, F. (2003). Irish economic development over three decades of EU membership. *Czech Journal of Economics and Finance*, *53*, 9–10.

Basile, G., & Cavallo, A. (2020). Rural Identity, Authenticity, and Sustainability in Italian Inner Areas. *Sustainability*, *12*, 1272.

Bocco, G. (2016). Remoteness and remote places. A geographic perspective. *Geoforum*, 77, 178–181.

Borghi, E. (2017). *Piccole Italie: le aree interne e la questione territoriale*. Rome: Donzelli Editore.

Borsi, M. T., & Metiu, N. (2015). The evolution of economic convergence in the European Union. *Empirical Economics*, *48*(2), 657–681.

Borzaga, C., & Zandonai, F. (2015). Oltre la narrazione, fuori dagli schemi: I processi generativi delle imprese di comunità. *Rivista Impresa Sociale*, *5*, 1–7.

Carley, K. M. (1990). Content analysis. In R. A. Asher, & J. M. Y. Simpson (Eds.), *The encyclopedia of language and linguistic* (pp. 725–730). Edinburgh: Pergamon Press.

Carrosio, G. (2016). A place-based perspective for welfare recalibration in the Italian inner peripheries: The case of the Italian strategy for inner areas. *Sociologia e Politiche Sociali*, *19*(3), 50–64.

Cerquetti, M., & Cutrini, E. (2021). The role of social ties for culture-led development in inner areas. The case of the 2016–2017 Central Italy Earthquake. *European Planning Studies*, *29*(3), 556–579.

Compagnucci, F., & Morettini, G. (2020). Improving resilience at the local level: The location of essential services within inner areas. Three case studies in the Italian Marche region. *Regional Science Policy and Practice*, *12*(5), 761–786.

Cotella, G., & Vitale Brovarone, E. (2020). The Italian national strategy for inner areas: A place-based approach to regional development. In J. Bański (Ed.), *Dilemmas of regional and local development*. London: Routledge.

Crescenzi, R., & Giua, M. (2020). One or many cohesion policies of the European Union? On the differential economic impacts of cohesion policy across member states. *Regional Studies*, *54*(1), 10–20.

Degl'Innocenti, M., Matousek, R., & Tzeremes, N. G. (2018). Financial centres' competitiveness and economic convergence: Evidence from the European Union regions. *Environment and Planning A, 50*(1), 133–156.

European Commission (2014). *An introduction to EU Cohesion Policy 2014–2020.* https://ec.europa.eu/regional_policy/sources/docgener/informat/basic/basic_2014_en.pdf [checked on 22 june 2022].

Ghinoi, S., De Vita, R., & Silvestri, F. (2021). Local policymakers' attitudes towards climate change: A multi-method case study. *Social Networks.* http://dx.doi.org/10.1016/j.socnet.2021.09.001

Goulet, R. (2008). EU cohesion policy 1988–2008: Investing in Europe's future. *European Commission Regional Policy DG, 26.*

Gudgin, G. (1995). Regional problems and policy in the UK. *Oxford Review of Economic Policy, 11*(2), 18–63.

Hall, R. (2014). The development of regional policy in the process of European integration: An overview. In G. Bischof (Ed.), *Regional economic development compared: EU-Europe and the American South* (pp. 13–33). Innsbruck: Open Edition Books.

Herington, M. J., & van de Fliert, E. (2018). Positive deviance in theory and practice: A conceptual review. *Deviant Behavior, 39*(5), 664–678.

Hooghe, L., Marks, G., & Marks, G. W. (2001). *Multi-level governance and European integration.* Rowman & Littlefield.

Huskey, L. (2006). Limits to growth: Remote regions, remote institutions. *Annals of Regional Science, 40*(1), 147–155.

Inforegio (2008). EU cohesion policy 1988–2008: Investing in Europe's future. *European Commission, Regional Policy DG, 26.* https://ec.europa.eu/regional_policy/sources/docgener/panorama/pdf/mag26/mag26_en.pdf

ISTAT. (2021). Demografia in cifre. *Dataset.* https://demo.istat.it/index.php

Leven, C. (1986). A note on the economics of remoteness. In E. Bylund, & U. Wiberg (Ed.), *Regional dynamics of socio-economic change: The experiences and prospects in sparsely populated areas* (pp. 80–86). Umea and CERUM.

López-Rodríguez, J., Faíña, J. A., & López-Rodríguez, J. (2007). Human capital accumulation and geography: Empirical evidence from the European Union. *Regional Studies, 41*(2), 217–234.

Mantegazzi, D., Pezzi, M. G., & Punziano, G. (2021). Tourism planning and tourism development in the Italian inner areas: Assessing coherence in policy-making strategies. In M. Ferrante, O. Fritz, & Ö. Öner (Eds.), *Regional science perspectives on tourism and hospitality* (pp. 447–475). London: Springer.

Mariotti, I., Akhavan, M., & Rossi, F. (2023). The preferred location of coworking spaces in Italy: An empirical investigation in urban and peripheral areas. *European Planning Studies, 31*(2), 467–489. http://dx.doi.org/10.1080/09654313.2021.1895080.

Mastronardi, L., & Romagnoli, L. (2020). Community-based cooperatives: A new business model for the development of Italian inner areas. *Sustainability, 12*(5), 2082.

Moyle, C. L., Moyle, B., & Burgers, H. (2020). Entrepreneurial strategies and tourism industry growth. *Tourism Management Perspectives, 35*, 100708.

Napoli, M. D., Petino, G. (2020). The resilient potential of some Sicilian inner areas. *Cuadernos Geográficos, 59*(1), 279–298.

Petrakos, G., Rodríguez-Pose, A., & Rovolis, A. (2005). Growth, integration, and regional disparities in the European Union. *Environment and Planning A, 37*(10), 1837–1855.

Pezzi, M. G., & Urso, G. (2017). Coping with peripherality: Local resilience between policies and practices. Editorial note. *Italian Journal of Planning Practice, 7*(1), 1–23.

Prell, C. (2012). *Social network analysis: History, theory & methodology*. Thousand Oaks: SAGE.

Punziano, G., & Urso, G. (2016). Local development strategies for inner areas in Italy. A comparative analysis based on plan documents. *Italian Journal of Planning Practice*, *6*(1), 76–109.

Rossitti, M., Dell'Ovo, M., Oppio, A., & Torrieri, F. (2021). The Italian national strategy for inner areas (SNAI): A critical analysis of the indicator grid. *Sustainability*, *13*, 6927.

Sabatier, P. A. (1986). Top-down and bottom-up approaches to implementation research: A critical analysis and suggested synthesis. *Journal of Public Policy*, *6*(1), 21–48.

Sanna, F., & De Bernardo, V. (2015). *Sviluppo locale e Cooperazione Sociale. Beni Comuni, Territorio, Risorse e Potenzialità da Connettere e Rilanciare*. Rome: Ecra.

Segev, E. (2020). Textual network analysis: Detecting prevailing themes and biases in international news and social media. *Sociology Compass*, *14*, e12779.

Shanahan, E. A., Jones, M. D., & McBeth, M. K. (2011). Policy narratives and policy processes. *Policy Studies Journal*, *39*(3), 535–561.

Smith, A. E., & Humphreys, M. S. (2006). Evaluation of unsupervised semantic mapping of natural language with leximancer concept mapping. *Behavior Research Methods*, *38*(2), 262–279.

Stoustrup, S. W. (2022). The re-coding of rural development rationality: Tracing EU governmentality and Europeanisation at the local level. *European Planning Studies*, *30*(12), 2474–2491. http://dx.doi.org/10.1080/09654313.2021.2009776.

Strategia Aree Interne. (2018). *Relazione annuale sulla Strategia Nazionale per le Aree Interne*. www.agenziacoesione.gov.it/wp-content/uploads/2020/07/Relazione_CIPE_ARINT_311218.pdf.

Thomas, D. A. (2014). Searching for significance in unstructured data: Text mining with leximancer. *European Educational Research Journal*, *13*(2), 235–256.

Urso, G. (2016). Polycentric development policies: A reflection on the Italian "national strategy for inner areas". *Procedia – Social and Behavioral Sciences*, *223*, 456–461.

Urso, G., Modica, M., & Faggian, A. (2019). Resilience and sectoral composition change of italian inner areas in response to the great recession. *Sustainability*, *11*(9), 2679.

Vendemmia, B., Pucci, P., & Beria, P. (2021). An institutional periphery in discussion. Rethinking the inner areas in Italy. *Applied Geography*, *135*, 102537.

5   Engaging with forgotten places

Applying a multifaceted
understanding of place in an analysis
of two Danish cases

Ina Drejer[1] and Lea Holst Laursen[2]

Introduction

Since its introduction in 2009 (Foray et al., 2009), smart specialization as a place-based approach to regional development has been positioned as the European response to the need for increased regional cohesion (e.g., Kroll, 2015; McCann & Ortega-Argilés, 2015). Yet, prior studies have shown that it can prove challenging for less developed regions to benefit from smart specialization due to both institutional and capacity-related weaknesses (Marques & Morgan, 2018; McCann & Ortega-Argilés, 2015). Based on the assumption that a key issue associated with these challenges involves identifying and leveraging place-specific development potentials, this chapter presents two case studies of local development initiatives in North Denmark, which illustrate both the promise and the peril linked to place-specific development.

Taking smart specialization as our starting point, we explore the notion of place specificity in more detail, with a particular emphasis on how an integrated perspective on place and place specificity can enable the development of efficient, tailor-made policies for reducing the gap between prosperous places and those struggling with population decline and job losses.

We apply a multifaceted understanding of place, where we analyze place as defined by the interplay between materialities, actors, and narratives. These three dimensions form the character of a given place and can serve as anchors for truly place-specific local development approaches.

Smart specialization strategies and policies are typically applied at the administrative and regional levels; however, regions can be quite diverse internally in terms of their economic activity and population composition (Pugh, 2018). In this chapter, the emphasis is on development initiatives on the smaller geographical and administrative scale of the Danish municipalities that are inspired by (but not full-fledged examples of) smart specialization policies. Smaller locations may have an advantage when compared with larger regions when it comes to engaging in interactive and consensus-based processes that represent a core aspect of smart specialization strategies (Foray et al., 2012), as passionate individuals representing different types of actors may have more specific local knowledge and greater commitment to their local, rather than broader regional, communities. Furthermore, the distance between

DOI: 10.4324/9781003256281-8

decision-makers and stakeholders is smaller in lower-level territories than in large-scale regions.

We introduce two very different local development initiatives from North Denmark to illustrate how a broad approach to place-specific development has the potential to facilitate local, bottom-up processes in disadvantaged remote areas. Denmark is a small and relatively cohesive country, with a less prominent problem of forgotten remote areas than in other countries. Nonetheless, although "remote" may have a different connotation in Denmark than in other countries, certain areas of Denmark face challenges in relation to issues such as shifting demographics, low population densities, low tax bases, and thin labor markets. The two cases exemplify different meanings of "remote." Indeed, one is located in the outermost periphery of Denmark, whereas the other is "squeezed" due to being located between two large cities. The case of the squeezed location in particular reveals how challenges associated with promoting place-specific development can occur when the physical setting of a place is not leveraged by an actor-based place identity and the subjective interpretations of actors' ties to places. In combination, the two cases show that the extent to which key actors identify themselves as bound to a place is particularly relevant with regard to retaining successful activities within the target area, which remains a concern in disadvantaged places (Foray, 2015).

The starting point: smart specialization and place

Foray et al.'s (2009) original theoretical introduction to smart specialization focuses on explaining the key processes that characterize smart specialization and distinguishing the concept from classical (i.e., Ricardian) relative economic specialization. Smart specialization is a strategy for diversification into related areas. The approach is based on learning through entrepreneurial processes of discovery that can result in the identification of promising areas of future specialization. Rather than being industry-focused, smart specialization should prioritize research and development (R&D) and innovation specialization (Foray et al., 2009; Foray et al., 2012).

Smart specialization has rapidly gained political momentum in Europe, with smart specialization strategies forming the foundation for investments by the European Regional Development Fund during the programming period 2014–2020 (Capello & Kroll, 2016) and remaining so during the programming period 2021–2027.

Despite frequent references in the smart specialization literature to the place-specific nature of the approach, discussions concerning the notion of region and place, including what it means to be place-specific, remain sparse in the smart specialization theory and conceptualization. Estensoro and Larrea (2016) emphasize how regions are not homogeneous at the territorial scale when it comes to implementing regional smart specialization strategies. In addition, subregional governments can play important roles due to their closeness to the various types of actors, which allows them to understand what is occurring in the area as well as to identify intangible place-specific assets. These intangible place-specific assets relate to the meaning that actors ascribe to a given place. In turn, this meaning determines the sense of attachment that actors have to a place and the entrepreneurial activities pursued there by different types of actors (e.g., Kalantaridis et al., 2019; Pancholi et al., 2019). This is particularly relevant in rural and remote regions, where the potential for innovation-led job creation is likely to relate to innovation in a more broad sense. Such an interpretation also incorporates social innovation, which is heavily dependent on the "social, cultural and institutional characteristics of the place" (Morgan, 2013, p. 105), rather than the more widely acknowledged concept of industrial innovation. However, basing development strategies and policies on these characteristics of place not only requires a broader understanding of innovation that is not necessarily strongly associated with R&D, but also requires a broadened understanding of place and a reconceptualization of place specificity in relation to smart specialization-inspired policies (Hassink, 2020).

A multifaceted understanding of place: materialities, actors, and narratives

Place is a complex, multilayered, and multipurpose notion (Harvey, 1993; Thrift, 1999). Thus, several interrelated categorizations of place have been introduced in an effort to reduce the complexity of the concept and highlight the different aspects associated with conceptualizing the multiplicity of place (e.g., Agnew, 1987; Agnew & Duncan, 1989; Canter, 1977; Cresswell, 2004). The shared (simplified) message of these categorizations is that place can be understood as simultaneously being (i) a geographic setting, (ii) a set of social interactions, and (iii) an experienced entity with a subjective meaning for actors. The common denominator among these aspects is that place is an assemblage of experienced, physical, and social interactions constituted by material things, flows, and connections (Dovey, 2010). Accordingly, place is not a static and fixed entity; rather, it is something that is "constantly in the making" (Jóhannesson & Bærenholdt, 2008, p. 156), being produced and reproduced over time. As a result, places are "constantly performed, dreamt, negotiated, mediated, built and demolished" (Ren, 2009, p. 47).[3]

To operationalize this multifaceted understanding of place in a context that is based on a smart specialization logic and in line with the aforementioned complexities of place, we synthesize place into the interplay between: (1) materialities, (2) actors, and (3) narratives, with these three dimensions covering the tripartition of place.

First, we consider place as an assemblage of materialities situated in a specific location (Pred, 1984). Here, the focus is on the physical aspects of place, as every place has physical characteristics, is located at a specific set of geographical coordinates, and is defined by a specific set of attributes (e.g., buildings, infrastructure, public space). Yet, a physical place can manifest at different scales depending on the demarcation of that specific place, ranging from larger regional scales to very local and specific contexts (Burns & Kahn, 2005; Kahn, 2005; Herod, 2011). Moreover, within one larger geographical setting – for example, an administrative region – smaller geographies (i.e., municipalities, towns, villages, and public spaces) are situated. Thus, there are places within places, just as there are places surrounding places. This means that place specificity (in terms of both the material and physical aspects) can be addressed at multiple scales, across scales, and as something derived from both inside and outside the boundaries of place.

Second, we argue that places are cultural compositions formed through social reproduction, being human products (Harvey, 1993; Pred, 1984) that are made and remade by actors over time (Urry, 2007). This dimension comes close to the focus of economic geographers on place as being defined by actors and their interactions. From this perspective, places represent the product of the actors in place, their skills and capabilities, and the relationships between actors and locations. More specifically, places are interconnected by the actors "in place," their movements, and their interrelations, meaning that the identity of a given place is constructed and continuously developed by people (Cresswell, 2004; Dale & Berg, 2013). This renders place a dynamic entity shaped by human actions and experiences (Ringgaard, 2010; Vestby, 2009). In other words, it is an "inextricably intertwined knot of spatiality and sociality" (Dovey, 2010, p. 6). When considering the roles of actors, the role of power is important with regard to who determines the character of a place (Arnstein, 1969). This is highly relevant to smart specialization-inspired processes, as the dominant regulatory power is not necessarily perfectly aligned with the trendsetting local/regional stakeholders.

Third, the perception and experience of place are individualized in what we refer to as "place narratives." This understanding of place is related to what many scholars term a "sense of place," which reflects the subjective meanings, memories, performances, conceptions, and emotional aspects of a given place (Larsen & Laursen, 2012). It is about the felt sense of quality related to a specific place, which is also referred to as "the local 'structure of feeling'" (Agnew, 1987, p. 28). In this chapter, we define the narrative of a given place as the person-dependent conceptualization of that place as affected by the aforementioned materialities as well as the cultural and social processes that occur between actors – this implies that a shared locality can have different meanings for different actors (Urry & Larsen, 2011). The fact that actors experience places differently, as well as the reality that no two places are alike, can benefit a smart specialization-inspired development process, as it is possible to create multiple place narratives and so foster situated economic and cultural development by exploiting different place-specific strongholds.

These three dimensions all contribute to the specific character of a given place. They can serve as anchors for a place-specific development approach that exploits the distinct strongholds of a given place as the catalysts for its development (Laursen, 2012). Importantly, such a place-specific approach is both dependent on and partially shaped by local actors, as place specificity is the result of how different actors (government, business, civil society, etc.) work together in order to construct, form, perform, perceive, and experience places (Laursen, 2021).

Below, we present two empirical case studies from relatively remote locations in North Denmark that exemplify how the deliberate interplay between materialities, actors, and narratives can ignite smart place-specific development processes as well as how weak relationships between place identity and targeted development areas can limit the effects of such processes. The two cases are Thy National Park and Hydrogen Valley, which are located at two different municipalities in North Denmark.

Data and method

The two cases were not chosen as examples of best practice; rather, they represent illustrative examples that offer important learning points concerning place-based development. The case selection was based on the premise that place-based development starts with a specific geographical location. This means that the place specificity of an activity must be assessed in relation to those factors that render the specific place the center of the activity in question.

A combination of research methods were used to gather insights regarding the two cases, including semi-structured open-ended interviews, workshops, site visits, and desk studies. The desk studies were performed at two time points: (1) prior to the interviews and workshops in 2015 and (2) as a follow-up to the realizations of the plans and expectations in 2022. An inductive approach was used to condense the data into overall patterns, which were then evaluated with regard to the three dimensions of place and place specificity.

Eight on-site interviews were conducted between May and August 2015. Moreover, three workshops involving different types of actors, such as politicians, policymakers, business representatives, civil society representatives, and researchers, were also held to gather insights into the cases.

The interviewees and workshop participants were selected based on the need to have representatives from public authorities, businesses, and civil society. There was some self-selection into the workshops, as the invitations were broadly circulated, and the initial recipients were encouraged to disseminate the invitations across their networks. Table 5.1 provides an overview of the different data sources and how they were applied in the analysis.

Place-based development in two Danish cases: analyzing development initiatives through a multifaceted understanding of place

The disparity within Denmark is relatively small when compared with that in other countries when it comes to income, education, health, and social mobility. However, since the 1990s, inequality has increased in Denmark in all these respects, albeit with an uneven geographic distribution (Ministry of Finance, 2020). The wealthiest municipalities are located around the large urban growth centers of Copenhagen and Aarhus, while the poorest municipalities are situated in the more remote areas (Fig. 5.1).

North Denmark is the country's most remote region. Its population of approximately 590,000 is currently increasing, albeit at a lower rate than seen in other parts of the country. Furthermore, this population development is largely driven by growth in the main city of Aalborg and, to a lesser extent, the two neighboring municipalities. This reflects the increased urbanization and centralization taking place within the overall Danish territory, which negatively influences the populations of remote and less populated areas. The remote areas of North Denmark are particularly challenged by job loss and a declining and aging population.

The two empirical cases discussed in this chapter are based in the North Danish municipalities of Thisted and Mariagerfjord. Both municipalities receive targeted

Table 5.1 Types of Data and Their Applications

Type of Data	Application	
Desk research of policy documents, websites, news media, and consultancy reports	Early stage (2015): Informed the selection of cases and interviewees. Helped to prepare interviews and workshops. Desk research was also used to describe and analyze the physical aspects of the place (supplementing the site visits).	Late stage (2022): Allowed to follow-up on the development and realization of plans. Moreover, added updated data.
Interviews and site visits	Eight interviews were conducted, four for each case. For Thy National Park, the interviewees were two municipal planners, the secretariat director of the national park, and a business forum director. For Hydrogen Valley, the interviewees were a business developer at the business park that is the physical center of Hydrogen Valley, a technical manager of a firm located in the business park, a municipal planner, and an executive from the municipality. Transcriptions of the interviews were analyzed through the lenses of materialities, actors, and narratives.	
Workshops	Three workshops were held in 2015 to validate the findings and add further details and perspectives to the early-stage desk research and interviews. The workshops also fulfilled a specific function in terms of testing the extent to which the participants identified with the narratives discovered through the desk studies and interviews.	

subsidies from the central Danish government due to their challenging conditions.[4] Moreover, in the Danish context, they are among the "forgotten places" with regard to the national growth and development agenda. Figure 5.2 illustrates some of these challenges, including the relatively low tax bases (which, as labor market participation rates are higher than both the national and regional averages, can be seen as an indicator of thin labor markets), the high age-determined expenditure needs, and the low population densities in the two municipalities.

The first case, Hydrogen Valley, is situated in Mariagerfjord, where it is squeezed between two large cities (see Figure 5.1). It is this "squeezed-ness" that has caused the area to be forgotten, as the two adjacent cities tend to attract economic activity and population away from Mariagerfjord (see Figure 5.3).[5]

The second case, Thy National Park, is located in the outermost periphery of both North Denmark and the Danish territory (see Figure 5.1). For many years, the area of Thy was forgotten in the national agenda, but even though Thy still struggles with a declining population (see Figure 5.4), it has become a hot spot in recent years for people who enjoy the qualities of its landscape.

Whereas Hydrogen Valley is an example of the desire to promote technology-based development, Thy National Park is representative of a development approach that embraces a broader concept of territorial development that focuses on "local

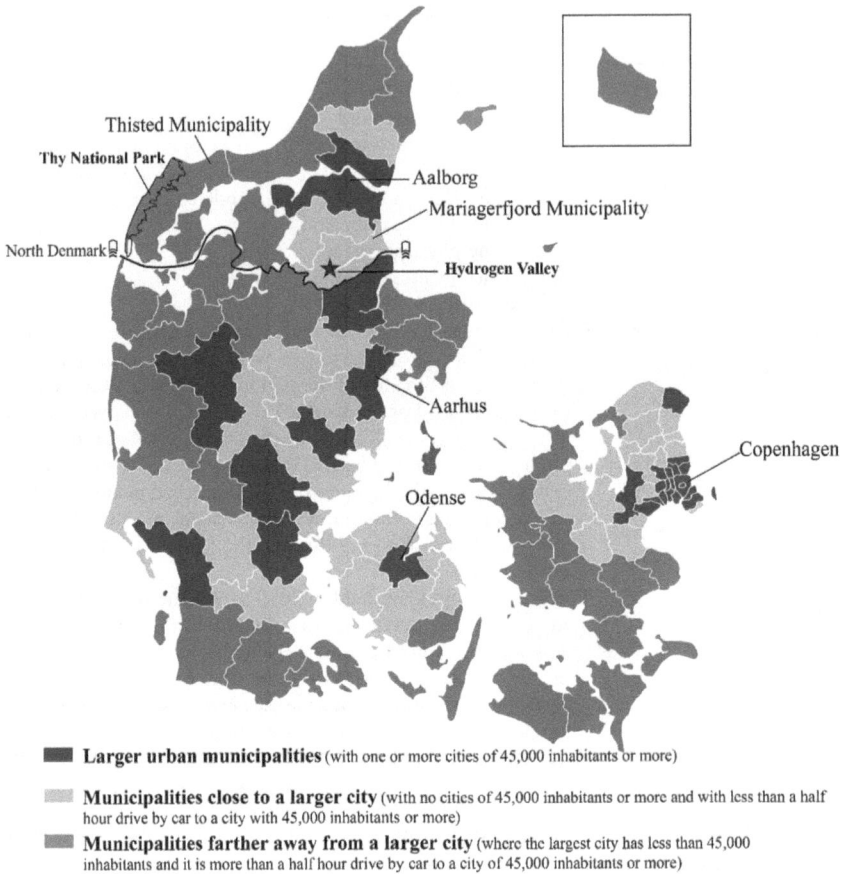

Figure 5.1 Map of the Danish municipalities

Source: Authors' own illustration, where the division of the municipalities into the three categories follows the division made by the Ministry of the Interior and Housing (2021b)

untapped, intangible potentials" (Capello & Kroll, 2016, p. 1401). Such an approach is particularly relevant to remote regions that are struggling with depopulation.

Hydrogen Valley

Hydrogen Valley is located in a relatively rural municipality with a population of around 42,000. The two main university cities of Mainland Denmark, Aalborg and Aarhus, are within an hour drive (see Figure 5.1).

The physical center of Hydrogen Valley is a business park that was established in 2002. The initial plan was to base the profile of the business park on a project regarding energy and materials technology conducted in cooperation with Aalborg University; however, when this project fell through, the presence within

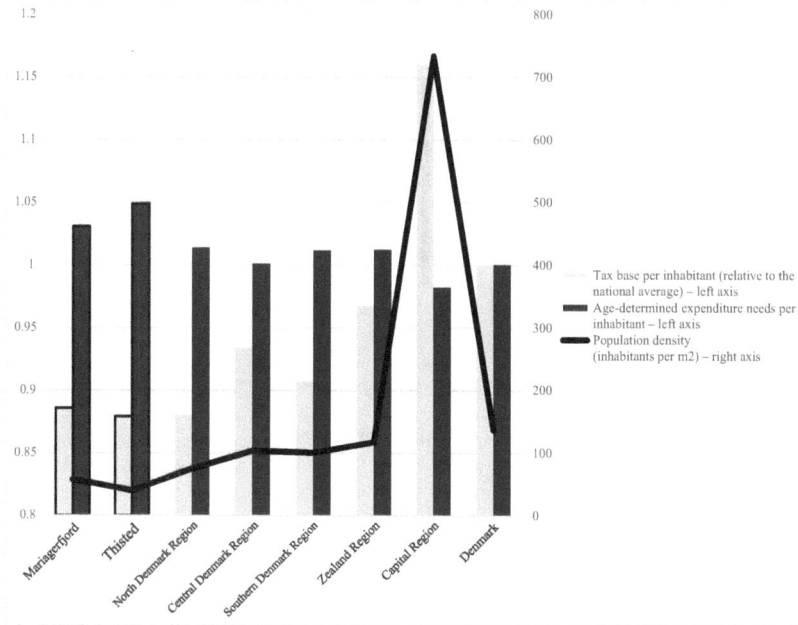

Figure 5.2 Tax base and age-determined expenditure needs per inhabitant relative to the national average (left axis) and population density (right axis)

Source: Ministry of the Interior and Housing (2021a), www.statistikbanken.dk, www.regioner.dk, www.rn.dk

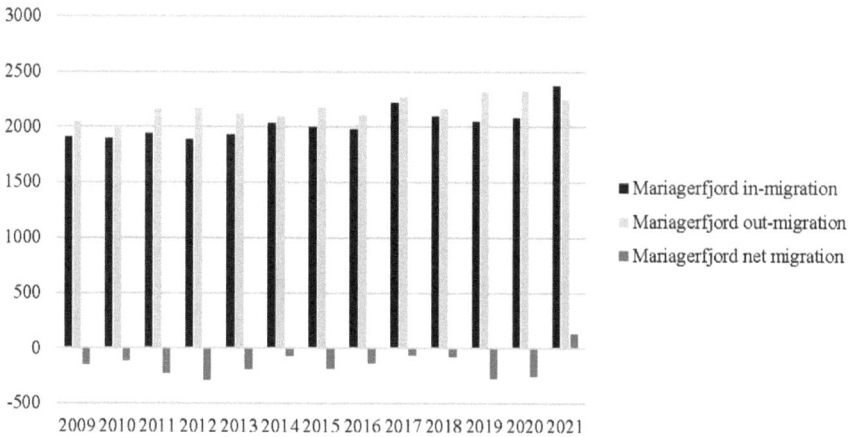

Figure 5.3 In-, Out-, and net migration in Mariagerfjord municipality

Source: www.statistikbanken.dk

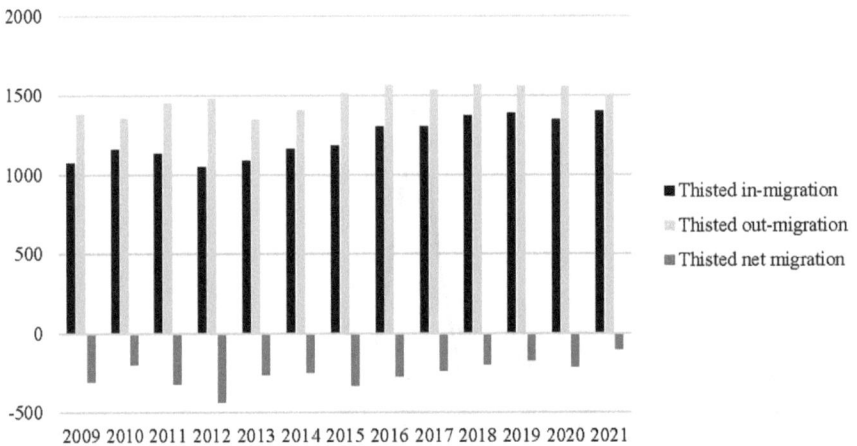

Figure 5.4 In-, Out-, and net migration in Thisted municipality

Source: www.statistikbanken.dk

the municipality of Denmark's largest hydrogen-consuming company, Sintex, was viewed by the municipal authorities as a good alternative for developing a clear profile around hydrogen at the business park. Consequently, the Hydrogen Valley Knowledge & Business Center was established as a nonprofit knowledge and business development center tasked with transforming Danish climate visions into actions, with a particular focus on green gasses such as hydrogen and biogas. In addition, the municipal authorities also decided to dedicate a nearby industrial area to companies working with hydrogen in an industrial context.

The municipal and regional authorities funded the acquisition and development of project competencies related to hydrogen and green gasses within the Hydrogen Valley organization. Furthermore, in 2008, the authorities played an active role in attracting a small company focused on developing fuel cell backup power solutions for communications networks to Hydrogen Valley. This company was subsequently acquired by Ballard Power Systems, a multinational company, in 2010. Ballard has maintained its plant within Hydrogen Valley since then, and in the late 2010s, it expanded into the production of fuel cells for buses and the maritime sector. Despite considerable growth following the move to Hydrogen Valley, Ballard's local plant has remained relatively small, employing around 130 people as of mid-2022.[6]

As an indirect effect of the construction of Hydrogen Valley, a range of local suppliers have acquired competencies in working with hydrogen. Despite this, there have been no reports of the creation or attraction of new companies as a direct consequence of Hydrogen Valley.[7] At present, Ballard is the only tenant of the business park that has hydrogen solutions as its main area of business. Two tenant firms provide services related to renewable energy; however, these are micro-companies with only satellite offices in Hydrogen Valley.

Around 2010, the municipal authorities proved instrumental in encouraging a utility company to establish a local facility for hydrogen production. Yet, following a change in its strategic focus, this utility company sold its hydrogen production plant in 2018 to a hydrogen refueling station network operator.[8]

Since 2015, Hydrogen Valley has become increasingly invisible within municipal policy documents. Nevertheless, it has been successful in attracting publicly funded projects, often in collaboration with partners located outside the municipality and region. The most prestigious of these was the €15 million HyBalance project, an EU Horizon 2020 collaboration between Hydrogen Valley and partners such as Air Liquide, a French multinational industrial gas and chemical company, and Centrica, an international energy trading company. The aim of the HyBalance project was to document the technical viability of large-scale hydrogen production to store energy from renewable sources. It ran from 2015 to 2020, and in 2018, the HyBalance plant was inaugurated as one of Europe's largest hydrogen-producing plants. The plant was considered a success, and HyBalance continued to operate under the remote management of Air Liquide after the completion of the project. As of 2022, Hydrogen Valley remains active in national and international projects related to, for example, power-to-X solutions. The most recent addition is a test center for fuel cells.

In conclusion, Hydrogen Valley is a successful project generator that has exhibited a strong capability to attract high-level international collaboration partners. It is marketed as a green energy cluster, although it remains dependent on public funding to develop new hydrogen-related activities. Additionally, there is no documented spin-off activity or evidence of attracting private businesses with considerable job-generating effects. This indicates that business-driven entrepreneurial discovery activities around Hydrogen Valley remain lacking.

Analyzing Hydrogen Valley through the lenses of materialities, actors, and narratives

The three dimensions of place differ in terms of their importance in the case of Hydrogen Valley. With regard to **materialities**, the business park itself can be considered the heart of Hydrogen Valley; however, aside from the handful of staff employed in the Hydrogen Valley secretariat, only one tenant firm (i.e., Ballard Power Systems) is dedicated to hydrogen. Recently, the HyBalance plant, which is located five kilometers from the business park, has been added as a physical manifestation of the area's focus on hydrogen. Yet, except for the presence of Sintex, there were no built structures of particular relevance to hydrogen when the idea of Hydrogen Valley was born.

Turning to the **actors** involved in the creation of Hydrogen Valley, the municipal authorities were the main driving actors behind the development, together with a local bank, local politicians, and researchers from Aalborg University. Although Hydrogen Valley was the first of what are now several European hydrogen valleys commonly presented as examples of how smart specialization strategies can "bring life to rural areas" (Biebuyck, 2021), there is little evidence of learning through entrepreneurial processes of discovery related to the initiative, and Mariagerfjord has not developed a strong actor-based identity as a place associated with hydrogen-based activities.

In addition to the limited and local top-down actor involvement in Hydrogen Valley, there are some indications of a weak sense of place-specific belonging among the productive actors involved in the initiative. This is illustrated by, for example, the fact that several employees and top managers from the focal company (i.e., Ballard) commute into the municipality, some over long distances. Moreover, the HyBalance project mainly involves international and other nonlocal actors, such as Air Liquide, which oversees the operation of the plant from a distance, with no employees being registered in Mariagerfjord. To date, it has proven difficult to build and retain a "critical mass" of activities that would encourage further development in and around Hydrogen Valley. It offers facilities and project development competencies on favorable terms, although there are no wider place-specific ties able to negate the attractiveness of the two major cities that squeeze Mariagerfjord. Despite efforts to discursively construct the municipality as a hydrogen hub, the intended **narrative** never caught on, and as of early 2022, efforts to discursively construct Mariagerfjord as a green energy or hydrogen hub appear to have died out.

Thy National Park

Thy National Park, which was founded in 2008 as the first national park in Denmark, is a local territorial development effort centered on place-based landscape characteristics and actor capabilities. It is situated in the periphery of Denmark in Thisted municipality, which encompasses a 55-kilometer coastal stretch containing a variety of landscapes, including a unique dune and moor landscape.

The overarching purpose of Thy National Park is to preserve, strengthen, and develop the unique nature and landscapes found within it. Its secondary aim is to generate profits for local communities by utilizing the national park area to, for example, produce local food products and encourage tourism activities, in addition to strengthening the availability of outdoor activities. The promotion of businesses within the national park represents only a small part of its purpose, although the national park framework has inspired a range of stakeholders to use Thy National Park for the purpose of business development.

Shaped by the extraordinarily strong winds and rough coastal conditions in Thy, the landscapes in the national park are unique, and several other initiatives related to the area's specific landscape characteristics have appeared alongside the establishment of Thy National Park. In the coastal village of Klitmøller and adjacent areas, for example, the distinctive water, wind, and shore conditions have led to the area being known as "Cold Hawaii," a development that has transformed the previously tired fishing village into not only a surfers' paradise but also a micro hot spot for entrepreneurial activities. Another notable initiative that exploits the unique landscape's potential is the Østerild's large-scale wind turbine test center.

In recent years, new types of place-specific innovations related to the interplay between foodstuffs and tourism and experience economies have emerged. Local entrepreneurs have successfully exploited the national park framework in a commercial way through actively applying the national park's local identity and/ or physical locality − over the years, a total of 38 small companies have been granted permission to use the national park's logo in connection with their food and nonfood products (Nationalpark Thy, 2020, 2021). With regard to tourism, overnight stays in the area increased by approximately 22% from 2017 to 2021 (Visit Denmark, 2022), with the national park playing a key role in attracting international nature tourists (Thisted Municipality, 2020). Moreover, a number of small companies have emerged throughout the municipality that use values associated with the national park in their branding, including sustainability, respecting nature, utilizing local inputs, and promoting the local way of life. These companies include high-end local product-based restaurants (associated with the New Nordic food trend), ecologically branded clothing firms, recreation and therapy activity centers involving nature (e.g., surf therapy), and products made from recycled plastic waste left in nature. Several such companies were started by "hipster" newcomers or younger people who were returning to their area of origin after living in larger cities. This trend is especially prominent in the coastal area of Klitmøller (Figure 5.5 provides an illustration of the population growth and associated average age decrease in Klitmøller). Developments such as these have increased the national focus on Thy and restored it as an attractive area in which to live a nature-based lifestyle – that is, a place where people can live "the good life" in harmony with nature.

The principal driving actors involved in Thy National Park include civil stakeholders who have been eager to voluntarily participate in exploiting the park's

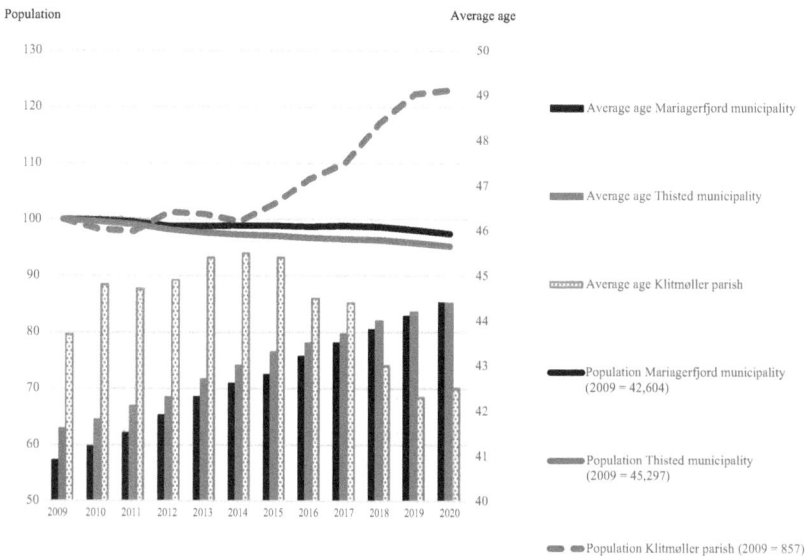

Figure 5.5 Average age and population in Mariagerfjord and Thisted municipalities and Klitmøller Parish (Population Index 2009 = 100)

Source: www.statistikbanken.dk

potential, with the growth of local businesses having largely occurred as a result of a bottom-up approach. The distinction between civil society and local business is blurred here – indeed, the two are interrelated because what began as voluntary community projects have, in some cases, grown into the livelihoods of local citizens. For example, small companies have been set up to allow locals to make a living out of foodstuffs from the national park or by using the national park for experience-related activities.

The local national park secretariat plays an important role in Thy National Park, handling daily operations and management within the park itself. It does not serve as the performing body with regard to the national park; rather, it acts as a developer of nature that is responsible for coordinating efforts as well as a developer and promoter of the national park brand. In addition, the local national park secretariat acts as a boundary-spanning moderator, fostering meaningful collaborations among stakeholders with different interests in an effort to develop the local area.

Thy National Park is explicitly mentioned in municipal strategies and planning documents, and it represents an important potential contributor to growth and development due to its intended key role in relation to settlement, tourism, and the branding of the municipality (Thisted Municipality, 2018). It is also included in the local business forum's efforts to attract new businesses and settlers to the area (e.g., the *Fra Bybo til Thybo* ["From Townie to Thy-Dweller"] project initiated in 2018) as well as in efforts to support local entrepreneurial stakeholders by providing counseling, courses, and business development activities.

As a result, the national park today represents a framework that is actively used by local authorities as a brand for the area. The municipality explicitly states that Thy National Park plays a key role in attracting tourists and settlement to the area, and further, that there exists the potential to use nature as an active element in village development, climate adaptation, and tourism (Thisted Municipality, 2020). The observed trends support this statement – despite a general population decline within the municipality, the population of Klitmøller increased by 16% between 2014 and 2020 (see Figure 5.5), thereby serving as the main driver of the 4% population increase seen in the coastal towns of Thisted municipality between 2016 and 2020 (Thisted Municipality, 2020). Furthermore, there has been an increase in young families settling in the most rural parts of the municipality (Thisted Municipality, 2020).[9]

Analyzing Thy National Park through the lenses of materialities, actors, and narratives

In the case of Thy National Park, the **materialities** of place play a crucial role, enabling the establishment of the national park itself and the different business initiatives within in, with the entrepreneurial processes being dependent on the local geographic specificities. The establishment of the national park and other place-based initiatives that leverage the area's landscape potential has created a new narrative for Thisted municipality, with the landscape playing a major role in the current process of transformation. Indeed, Thisted municipality is currently being reconceptualized from being almost forgotten to being recognized for its local strongholds. This development is in line with a general trend that can be observed in Denmark, whereby the negative perception of the Danish periphery, which followed in the wake of neoliberal planning approaches to urban development during the 1990s, is being disputed. While the public and political debate around the turn of the millennium generally had a negative tone, equating remote areas with decaying villages full of run-down and unsaleable houses rented to poor and socially marginalized citizens, the rhetoric is gradually changing. Indeed, the narrative of the Danish periphery being a "Rotten Banana"[10] has at least partially developed to include the qualities and place-specific potential of some of Denmark's peripheral areas.

The territorial framing of Thy National Park as *one* national park has contributed to the creation of a strong, united conceptualization – a demarcated geographic area that has been given a (new) role by using nature as its connective tissue, underpinning a regional identity that allows for local place-specific development. Therefore, the national park framework enhances the **narrative** of place-based potentials, which in turn enhances the joint conceptualization of place. A strong sense of place has developed among the local citizens, local authorities, and visitors, as stated by the former head of the local business forum. This has changed the collective mindset and transformed into business potential. This business development potential is strongly based on intangible resources and narratives characterized by nature- and environment-related values.[11] This accords with the work of Sörvik et al. (2019), who argue that there is potential for sparsely populated areas to exploit the opportunities generated by the sustainable "valorization of natural resources" (p. 1078). Efforts in this regard were rewarded in early 2022, when Thy was included as number 27 on *The New York Times'* list of "52 Places for a Changed World."[12]

The collaboration among enterprising local stakeholders, local authorities, and the national park secretariat has leveraged the area's potential, transforming something that primarily began as a governmental nature preservation strategy into a place-based business initiative. Thy National Park acts as a platform for gathering different **actors**, and the place-specific development is characterized by a network approach that deliberately brings together different stakeholders and creates meaningful collaborations. This approach is based on a local culture characterized by a strong local drive and a will to develop the community.[13] Moreover, this case illustrates how local governmental policies can support local entrepreneurial activities, thereby indicating how the top-down and bottom-up perspectives can work together. This is an interesting perspective with regard to the challenges facing many lower-tier Danish territories where job creation is sparse; however, to date, the impact in terms of economic and population growth at a municipal level is low and it remains challenging to generate sufficient micro-initiatives to have a major impact that extends beyond the "pockets" of development.

Conclusion

This chapter discusses how a reconceptualization of place can facilitate local, bottom-up development processes in disadvantaged remote areas. Tailor-made smart specialization strategies for struggling places must generally address challenges associated with a weak technology base in order to identify paths for related diversification. If the existing technology base is weak, it can be tempting to focus on complex areas unrelated to existing economic strengths (Deegan et al., 2021); however, doing so undermines the place specificity of the strategy. This chapter proposes an alternative route for struggling places, whereby the notion of smart specialization as a technology- or research and development-based innovation strategy is broadened through paying greater attention to the intangible qualities of places. In addition, this chapter adopts a geographic bottom-up approach that allows the attachment to and perceptions of a place to drive local micro-development activities that may have the potential to attract national attention and generate broader geographic impacts over time. Thus, this chapter focuses on very local development processes without addressing either the relationship between local and regional areas or how regional development processes can embrace – and take advantage of – local differences to ensure coherence between local sub-strategies and an overall regional strategy for supporting development at a wider geographic level.

Although the two case studies presented in this chapter are examples of smart specialization-inspired development processes rather than full-fledged smart specialization policies, the analyses nonetheless contribute to the smart specialization literature by introducing a multifaceted understanding of what it means to be place-specific. This is particularly relevant to "forgotten places," as several studies have identified challenges related to developing and implementing smart specialization strategies in sparsely populated and lagging regions (e.g., Marques & Morgan, 2018; McCann & Ortega-Argilés, 2015; Sörvik et al., 2019).

Smart specialization is a well-established framework for place-based development, and we are not claiming that the importance of place has been overlooked in relation to smart specialization. However, we do argue that smart specialization could be strengthened as a place-based development strategy (not least for remote and forgotten places) by adopting a more exhaustive approach to place specificity within the entrepreneurial discovery processes guiding the subsequent identification and development of distinctive areas of specialization (Foray et al., 2012). This could contribute to generating increased visibility and an enhanced sense of value both locally and with regard to the national growth and development agenda. The two cases reveal the importance of tailoring development to the specific context and basing it on existing potentials, rather than attempting to force the attachment of a particular capability or feature to the place in question. Place specificity can vary, with the three dimensions of materiality, actor-based cultural composition, and narratives of place not necessarily being equally pronounced. Thus, it is important to identify the place-specific characteristics of a given location when performing the challenging task of identifying and attempting to realize the development potential of forgotten and struggling places.

The findings of this chapter have a number of general implications for development processes and policies in struggling remote places. First, it is crucial to establish a systematic understanding of areas with the greatest development potential by identifying and engaging key actors. The involvement of civil society actors in the process represents a useful starting point for directing attention toward the narratives of place as a component of place-specific development processes. Additionally, attention must also be directed toward elements that can reveal where and how civil society engagement could drive economic development. This implies that the focus within the strategy development process should be broadened to extend beyond the elements usually emphasized in such processes, for example, existing clusters, key sectors, education and research institutions, and capabilities. More intangible elements, such as subjective meanings, conceptions, and emotional aspects, that connect actors to a specific place and can mobilize them to actively contribute to a strategy development process should be included here. The consideration of intangible elements should be combined with a focus on how the physical setting of a place shapes and interacts with the narratives and social processes that exist and occur among actors. As illustrated by the two case studies, this implies a highly relevant link between spatial planning and business development policy. In fact, in both Hydrogen Valley and Thy National Park, the different actors and institutional capacities in place must clearly work together to foster local development. If they do not do so, local and place-specific development cannot occur. This suggests the need for the genuine involvement of actors at different levels in promoting smart local development in remote settings that are often forgotten in terms of the national agenda.

We do not claim to have identified a miracle cure that will eliminate the challenges faced by places located outside urban growth centers. However, local and bottom-up processes based on a multifaceted understanding of place-specific potentials may help to curb the accelerating declines in population and jobs as well as reduce the perception of places being forgotten.

This chapter focuses on those aspects and understandings of place that are particularly valuable when developing and regaining attention for forgotten remote areas. Yet, Denmark is a small and wealthy nation that does not face the same level of challenges when it comes to regional disparities and lagging remote areas as other countries both within and outside the European Union. Hence, further research is required to explore how the proposed broadened approach to place-specific development can benefit places facing greater challenges than the remote areas of Denmark.

Notes

1 Professor (with special responsibilities), Aalborg University Business School, Denmark, email: id@business.aau.dk (ORCID ID 0000–0002–2463–4724).
2 Associate Professor, Department of Architecture, Design and Media Technology, Aalborg University, Denmark, email: llhl@create.aau.dk (ORCID ID 0000–0001–5139–5282).
3 Authors' own translation from the Danish.
4 Since 2017, the Danish government has had a specific fund for municipalities with low tax bases, demographic challenges, increasing elderly populations, structural challenges, and weak job markets.
5 In 2021, we observe positive net migration into Mariagerfjord, which coincides with a substantial decline in the net migration into Aalborg municipality, and more remarkably, with negative net migration into Aarhus municipality. It is too early to say whether this is part of a post-COVID-19 trend that has been observed across several countries, whereby smaller towns and municipalities are gaining inhabitants at the cost of major cities – likely linked to an increase in remote work.

6   See https://virk.dk, the national Danish company register.

7   Temporary exceptions include a university spin-off company developing low-emission methanol fuel cell solutions, which was located in Hydrogen Valley from 2008 to 2013. After growing from 4 to 40 employees over a five-year period, the company outgrew the business park and so relocated to Aalborg in 2013. The industrial area formerly dedicated to companies working with hydrogen is no longer included in the land use plans.

8   Hydrogen refueling stations are still in their infancy in Denmark, with only a handful of stations being available throughout the country.

9   In 2019, birthrates in the countryside were 21% higher than those in the remainder of the municipality (Thisted Municipality, 2020).

10 This term was invented by Connie Hedegaard, former minister of the environment, with reference to Faludi's "Blue Banana" conception of the European growth region (e.g., Faludi & Van der Valk, 1994) albeit with a negative connotation. The area covers the peripheral regions of Denmark, taking the shape of a banana starting from north of Jutland, running along the western part of Jutland, and covering the southern part of Jutland, southern Funen, and the islands in the south-eastern part of Denmark.

11 Parallels can be drawn with the emergence of neolocalism as a reaction to the destruction of modern America's traditional bonds with the community (Shortridge, 1996). Neolocalism appeals to narratives concerning the sustainability of the environment and local economies, and it is associated with, for example, place-based branding. The concept is mainly used in analyses of the craft beer industry ("the geography of beer") (e.g., Gatrell et al., 2018).

12 The 2022 list focuses on sustainability, the climate crisis, and over-tourism (New York Times, 2022).

13 Thy has a long history of bottom-up activities, such as the Thy Camp social experiment initiated in 1970, which can be seen as North Denmark's version of Freetown Christiania in Copenhagen. It also has a Nordic Folkecenter for Renewable Energy founded in 1983.

References

Agnew, J. A. (1987). *Place and politics: The geographical mediation of state and society*. Crows Nest: Allen & Unwin.

Agnew, J. A., & Duncan, J. S. (Eds.) (1989). *The power of place: Bringing together geographical and sociological imaginations*. Boston, MA: Unwin Hyman.

Arnstein, S. R. (1969). A ladder of citizen participation. *Journal of the American Institute of Planners, 35*(4), 216–224.

Biebuyck, B. (2021, February 23). Hydrogen valleys driving growth and jobs. *The European Files*. www.europeanfiles.eu/energy/hydrogen-valleys-driving-growth-and-jobs

Burns, C. J., & Kahn, A. (2005). *Site matters: Design concepts, histories, and strategies*. London: Routledge.

Canter, D. (1977). *The psychology of place*. New York: Architectural Press.

Capello, R., & Kroll, H. (2016). From theory to practice in smart specialization strategy: Emerging limits and possible future trajectories. *European Planning Studies, 24*(8), 1393–1406. https://doi.org/10.1080/09654313.2016.1156058

Cresswell, T. (2004). *Place: A short introduction*. Hoboken: Blackwell Publishing.

Dale, B., & Berg, N. G. (2013). Hva er stedsidentitet, og hvordan fanger vi den opp? In A. Førde, B. Kramvig, N. G. Berg, & B. Dale (Eds.), *Å finne sted: Metodologiske perspektiver i stedsanalyser* (pp. 23–41). Oslo: Fagbokforlaget.

Deegan, J., Broekel, T., & Fitjar, R. D. (2021). Searching through the haystack: The relatedness and complexity of priorities in smart specialization strategies. *Economic Geography, 97*(5), 497–520. https://doi.org/10.1080/00130095.2021.1967739

Dovey, K. (2010). *Becoming places: Urbanism/architecture/identity/power*. London: Routledge.

Estensoro, M., & Larrea, M. (2016). Overcoming policy making problems in smart specialization strategies: Engaging subregional governments. *European Planning Studies*, *24*, 1319–1335. https://doi.org/10.1080/09654313.2016.1174670

Faludi, A., & Van der Valk, A. J. (1994). *Rule and order: Dutch planning doctrine in the twentieth century*. Boston: Kluwer Academic Publishers.

Foray, D. (2015). *Smart specialization. Opportunities and challenges for regional innovation policy*. London and New York: Routledge.

Foray, D., David, P. A., & Hall, B. H. (2009). Smart specialization: The concept. In European Commission, Directorate-General for Research and Innovation (Ed.), *Knowledge for growth: Prospects for science, technology and innovation* (pp. 20–24). European Union Publications Office. https://data.europa.eu/doi/10.2777/47564

Foray, D., Goddard, J., Beldarrain, X. G., Landabaso, M., McCann, P., Morgan, K., Nauwelaers, C., & Ortega-Argilés, R. (2012). *Guide to research and innovation strategies for smart specializations (RIS 3)*. Brussels: European Commission. https://s3platform.jrc.ec.europa.eu/en/w/guide-on-research-and-innovation-strategies-for-smart-specialisation-ris3-guide-

Gatrell, J., Reid, N., &. Steiger, T. L. (2018). Branding spaces: Place, region, sustainability and the American craft beer industry. *Applied Geography*, *90*, 360–370. https://doi.org/10.1016/j.apgeog.2017.02.012

Harvey, D. (1993). From space to place and back again: Reflections on the condition of post-modernity. In J. Bird, B. Curtis, T. Putman, G. Robertson, & L. Ticker (Eds.), *Mapping the futures – Local cultures, global change* (pp. 3–29). London: Routledge.

Hassink, R. (2020). Advancing place-based regional innovation policies. In M. González-López, & B. T. Asheim (Eds.), *Regions and innovation policies in Europe: Learning from the margins* (pp. 30–45). Cheltenham: Edward Elgar.

Herod, A. (2011). *Scale*. London: Routledge.

Jóhannesson, G. T., & Bærenholdt, J. O. (2008). Enacting places through the connections of tourism. In J. O. Bærenholdt, & B. Granås (Eds.), *Mobility and place: Enacting Northern European peripheries* (pp. 155–166). Farnham: Ashgate.

Kahn, A. (2005). Defining urban sites. In C. J. Burns, & A. Kahn (Eds.), *Site matters: Design concepts, histories, and strategies* (pp. 281–296). London: Routledge.

Kalantaridis, C., Bika, Z., & Millard, D. (2019). Migration, meaning(s) of place and implications for rural innovation policy. *Regional Studies*, *53*(12), 1657–1668. https://doi.org/10.1080/00343404.2019.1597971

Kroll, H. (2015). Efforts to implement smart specialization in practice – Leading unlikely horses to water. *European Planning Studies*, *23*(10), 2079–2098.

Larsen, J. R. K., & Laursen, L. H. (2012). Family place experience and the making of places in holiday home destinations – A Danish case study. In R. Sharpley, & P. Stone (Eds.), *The contemporary tourist experience: Concepts and consequences* (pp. 181–200). London: Routledge.

Laursen, L. H. (2012). Enhancing the landscape – Architectural installations in the landscape. In V. Andrade, S. Smith, & D. Bendix Lanng (Eds.), *Musings: An urban design anthology* (pp. 102–111). Chicago: Aalborg University Press.

Laursen, L. H. (2021). Entangled networks in place-specific tourism development. In L. Lassen, & L. H. Laursen (Eds.), *Mobilising place management* (pp. 68–90). London: Routledge.

Marques, P., & Morgan, K. (2018). The heroic assumptions of smart specialization: A sympathetic critique of regional innovation policy. In A. Isaksen, R. Martin, & M. Trippl (Eds.), *New avenues for regional innovation systems – Theoretical advances, empirical cases and policy lessons* (pp. 275–293). London: Springer. https://link.springer.com/book/10.1007/978-3-319-71661-9

McCann, P., & Ortega-Argilés, R. (2015). Smart specialization, regional growth and applications to European Union cohesion policy. *Regional Studies*, *49*(8), 1291–1302. https://doi.org/10.1080/00343404.2013.799769

Ministry of Finance. (2020). *Ulighedsredegørelse 2020*. https://fm.dk/media/18359/ulighedsredegoerelsen-2020_web.pdf

Ministry of the Interior and Housing. (2021a). *Kommunal udligning og generelle tilskud 2022*. https://im.dk/Media/637660791586136952/Kommunal%20udligning%20og%20generelle%20tilskud%202022_web.pdf

Ministry of the Interior and Housing. (2021b). *Regional- og landdistrikspolitisk redegørelse 2021*. https://im.dk/publikationer/2021/okt/regional-og-landdistriktspolitisk-redegoerelse-2021

Morgan, K. (2013). The regional state in the era of smart specialization. *Ekonomiaz*, *83*(2), 102–125. https://ideas.repec.org/a/ekz/ekonoz/2013205.html

Nationalpark Thy. (2020, July 21). *Redegørelse for udviklingen i og omkring Nationalpark Thy samt evaluering af indsatsen i planperioden 2016–2022–1. udkast*. https://nationalparkthy.dk/media/279599/redegoerelse-og-evaluering_21072020.pdf

Nationalpark Thy. (2021). *Årsberetning 2021 for Nationalparkfond Thy*. https://nationalparkthy.dk/media/317364/npt-aarsberetning-2021-final-low.pdf

New York Times (2022). *52 places for a changed world*, January 9. www.nytimes.com/interactive/2022/travel/52-places-travel-2022.html#thy-denmark

Pancholi, S., Yigitcanlar, T., & Guaralda, M. (2019). Place making for innovation and knowledge-intensive activities: The Australian experience. *Technological Forecasting and Social Change*, *146*, 616–625. https://doi.org/10.1016/j.techfore.2017.09.014

Pred, A. (1984). Place as historically contingent process: Structuration and the time-geography of becoming places. *Annals of the Association of American Geographers*, *74*(2), 279–297. www.jstor.org/stable/2569284

Pugh, R. (2018). Questioning the implementation of smart specialization: Regional innovation policy and semi-autonomous regions. *Environment and Planning C: Politics and Space*, *36*(3), 530–574. https://doi.org/10.1177%2F2399654417717069

Ren, C. (2009). Destinationen som sted: Forsøg på en rationel konceptualisering. *Nord Nytt*, *106/107*, 35–51.

Ringgaard, D. (2010). *Stedssans*. Aarhus: Aarhus Universitetsforlag.

Shortridge, J. R. (1996). Keeping tabs on Kansas: Reflections of regionally based field study. *Journal of Cultural Geography*, *21*, 45–59. https://doi.org/10.1080/08873639609478344

Sörvik, J., Teräs, J., Dubois, A., & Pertoldi, M. (2019). Smart specialization in sparsely populated areas: Challenges, opportunities and new openings. *Regional Studies*, *53*(7), 1070–1080. https://doi.org/10.1080/00343404.2018.1530752

Thisted Municipality. (2018). *Kommuneplan 2017–2029*. https://thisted.viewer.dkplan.niras.dk/plan/40#/12827

Thisted Municipality. (2020). *Fysisk udviklingsplan for Thisted Kommune – Planstrategi 2020*. https://thisted.viewer.dkplan.niras.dk/media/1309225/Planstrategi-2020-Forudsaetningsredegoerelse-FINAL.pdf

Thrift, N. (1999). The place of complexity. *Theory, Culture & Society*, *16*(3), 31–69. https://doi.org/10.1177/02632769922050610

Urry, J. (2007). *Mobilities*. New York: Polity Press.

Urry, J., & Larsen, J. (2011). *The tourist gaze 3.0*. New York: Sage Publications.

Vestby, G. M. (2009). Stedsutvikling i Eidfjord – Sosiokulturell stedsanalyse. *NIBR Report 2009:22*. Norsk Institut for by-og regionforskning. https://oda.oslomet.no/oda-xmlui/handle/20.500.12199/5633?show=full

Visit Denmark. (2022, March). *Kommunal overnatningsstatistik*. www.visitdenmark.dk/corporate/videncenter/turismen-i-dit-omraade

6 Revitalizing Forgotten Spaces through local leadership and social entrepreneurial ecosystems

The case of Muszyna commune

Marta Gancarczyk[1], Jacek Gancarczyk[2] and Marek Reichel[3]

Introduction

Regions feature polarization and uneven growth not only from the interregional perspective but also internally. Internal regional polarization is underresearched and often ignored in regional cohesion policy. Consequently, we predominantly deal with a conjuncture of less developed, peripheral, and forgotten places (Loewen & Schulz, 2019; Broadhurst et al., 2021). These places are heterogeneous in terms of characteristics and antecedents of their disadvantageous position (David, 2021). However, they also demonstrate some common characteristics, such as weak social and economic collaboration and lower levels of entrepreneurship and human resource competence (Asheim, 2019; Hassink et al., 2019). The distinctive feature of forgotten places is that they are often abandoned, excluded, or neglected in development strategies, planning, and policy measures (Gilmore, 2008; Rogerson, 1995). This can also coincide with their lost identity, low self-recognition, and inability to recognize and exploit the opportunities for breaking the unfavorable path (Shatkin, 2004).

Forgotten Spaces often emerge as regional microstructures – subregional territorial units with lower economic development and institutional voids (Kroehn et al., 2013; Asheim, 2019; Hassink et al., 2019). Understanding how these microstructures evolve to break decline paths represents a gap in regional development studies (David, 2021). Identifying the mechanisms that lead to resurgence and industrial path renewal or creation is therefore important both from theoretical and policy angles (Hassink et al., 2019).

Solutions to weak internal potential are proposed as top-down and external solutions, based on European Union (EU), national and regional cohesion policies (González-López et al., 2019). However, this external perspective must be matched with the place-based internal strategy of local actors, including local government, entrepreneurs, educational institutions, the nonprofit sector, and the local community at large (Thompson et al., 2018; Gancarczyk et al., 2021a).

This research aims to identify the mechanisms of resurgence and industrial path renewal of a formerly forgotten and underdeveloped territory by exploring the case of the Muszyna commune in the Malopolska region of Southern Poland. The commune belongs to one of the industrial specializations of the region, that is, tourism

DOI: 10.4324/9781003256281-9

and health resorts (MRDO, 2015; MRGO, 2015), as well as extraction and distribution of mineral water. However, throughout the economic and political transformation of Poland, economic performance and public support were inferior in this territory compared to other communes with similar specialization in Malopolska (Statistics Poland, Regional Statistics, 2021). The current revitalization and successful development of Muszyna over 2004–2020 can be described as bottom-up and based on local leadership that formed a social entrepreneurial ecosystem (SEE) in this territory. The country-level or regional policies were effective in exploiting external opportunities, rather than directly driving this resurgence (Thompson et al., 2018; Gancarczyk et al., 2021a).

We adopted a longitudinal case study method of the Muszyna commune in the multi-scalar context of the EU, national, and regional cohesion policies after Poland's EU accession in 2004. Primary and secondary data sources were used. That is, the primary data was obtained from interviews with local government representatives and officials, while the secondary data was drawn from public statistics, reports, local and regional government records, and strategic and programmatic documents. As a theoretical background, we integrated the concepts of coevolution (Gong & Hassink, 2019; Gancarczyk et al., 2023) and industrial path dynamics (Asheim, 2019; Hassink et al., 2019), as well as SEE (Thompson et al., 2000; Thompson et al., 2018; Villegas-Mateos & Vázquez-Maguirre, 2020; Stam, 2015; Acs et al., 2017; Wurth, Stam & Spigel, 2021).

This research has provided theoretical and policy-relevant contributions. First, it contributes to the literature on entrepreneurial ecosystems, in particular on social entrepreneurial ecosystems, by extending the knowledge of how these systems emerge through bottom-up and place-based leadership to produce local development (Thompson et al., 2018; Broadhurst et al., 2021). Our study emphasizes how leaders cocreate entrepreneurial communities (Van de Ven, 1993; Wurth et al., 2021) through process approach, namely, by implementing sets of related projects (Lowe & Feldman, 2017). Second, the chapter adds to the path literature and coevolutionary strand in regional studies, by broadening the knowledge of how the interactions of local agents generate an industrial path renewal (Hassink et al., 2019) (Asheim, 2019). The recent study by Gancarczyk et al. (2023) has identified types of internal and external processes driving the interactions between coevolving populations to raise transformation and a new regional path configuration. This study focuses on an in-depth explanation of internal, place-based processes leading to a territorial path renewal (Hassink et al., 2019; Pushkarskaya et al., 2021). Third, the study is informative for local policymakers. It provides knowledge of the drivers and barriers in industrial path renewal and of the mechanisms underlying territorial resurgence, as framed by the concept of the social entrepreneurial ecosystem (Feldman & Lowe, 2018).

Literature review

The coevolutionary mechanisms and industrial path transformation

Territorial development is conditioned by complex and multi-scalar mechanisms, that is, processes at regional, national, and international scales that produce industrial path transformation toward sustainable growth of communities (Gong et al., 2022).

Processes are conjunctures of decisions and actions by relevant agents in the time perspective and represent the primary unit of analysis in the coevolutionary perspective of regional studies (Gong & Hassink, 2019). The coevolutionary approach assumes that the transformation processes stem from the interactions of agents rather than from only one group of entities that independently reinforce their decisions (Gancarczyk et al., 2023; Benner, 2021). Recognizing the value of local government vision and leadership, this view emphasizes that policymakers' decisions and actions are the result of complex interactions, that is, mutual influences with other actors, such as industry and nonprofit organizations, in multi-scalar contexts (Gancarczyk et al., 2021a, 2021b).

Since evolutionary mechanisms are recurrent processes that produce territorial industrial transformation, their identification and description ensure scripts or benchmarks that can be adopted in other spatial contexts. Furthermore, the continuous nature of processes often results in the development of formal and informal institutions, such as rules, regulations, habits, norms, and organizations (Benner, 2021; Williamson, 2000; Zukauskaite et al., 2017). This, in turn, reaffirms and institutionalizes local development processes as repetitive and potentially pursued by other actors in the absence of the leaders who pioneered them in a given community (Ostrom, 1986; Ostrom, 2010). From the theoretical angle, the identification of territorial development mechanisms allows for analytical generalization based on qualitative methods in particular spatial contexts (Gancarczyk et al., 2023). In practical terms, the identification of transformation processes informs development policy (Gancarczyk et al., 2021a, 2021b).

The coevolutionary processes require more empirical evidence in different spatial contexts, in particular, in the subregional and less-develop unit of the Central and East European (CEE) countries after their accession to the EU (Klincewicz et al., 2021). The coevolution process can be described as the stream of interlocking decisions and actions of local populations marked by their structural changes (Ter Wal & Boschma, 2011). The resulting transformation can bring either the decline of the existing path, the renewal and further growth of the path, or the creation of a completely new path (Hassink et al., 2019; Asheim, 2019). Consequently, we formulate the first research question regarding the dynamics of evolution of the Polish peripheral commune of Muszyna after the country's accession to the EU.

RQ1. *What were the dynamics of the evolution of the Muszyna commune after 2004 toward its path transformation?*

Structural changes in peripheral territories are driven by multi-scalar, internal and external conditions (Isaksen et al., 2019). External drivers can include actors and factors, such as organizations, policies, and economic trends at regional, national, and international levels. Internal actors might include local government, industry, nonprofit organizations, and industrial and social leaders. Internal factors can be represented by local entrepreneurial dynamics and development policies (Gong et al., 2022). Therefore, we pose the second research question.

RQ2. *What were the external and internal drivers of the dynamics of the territorial path in the Muszyna commune?*

Social entrepreneurial ecosystems and local place-based leadership

SEEs are derived from the core concept of entrepreneurial ecosystems (EEs) and provide a conceptual canvas to understand the processes that lead to the transformation of the local path (Spigel & Harrison, 2018). They enable a comprehensive understanding of territorial conditions, that is, actors and factors, and their functioning as a system that can produce a progressive structural change.

EEs comprise interrelations among industrial, social, public, and institutional actors and factors that are outcome-oriented to generate development of territorial units (Stam, 2015; Mason & Brown, 2014; Isenberg, 2010; Stam & Spigel, 2016; Brown & Mason, 2017). The EE outcomes were originally defined as the productive entrepreneurship of high-growth commercial companies and innovative companies. However, other studies also proposed other outcomes, including increase in regional product value, wealth, and overall socioeconomic development (Wurth et al., 2021).

Working as a system of interlocking actors and factors, EEs also represent governance modes, whereby governance denotes sets of informal and formal institutions (rules, habits) that regulate a system, such as EE, and affect its economic efficiency (Colombo et al., 2019; Wurth et al., 2021). Namely, the relationships and interactions among EE actors and factors produce rules of the game that both constrain the actions and enable predicable collaboration and goal attainment (Bendickson et al., 2021). However, in the longer period, institutions and resulting governance are dynamic, since EE participants perceive and also change their interests and objectives differently, producing new institutions (Lowe & Feldman, 2017; Bessagnet et al., 2021).

EE actors and factors can be derived from a variety of industrial, social, public, and institutional dimensions that require a specification. Based on the ontological approach, universal dimensions should be identified, either as necessary and sufficient, or as possibly broad and comprehensive (Wurth et al., 2021; Stam & Van de Ven, 2021). The dimensions considered could be institutional, financial, human and social capital, tangible infrastructure, and research and development infrastructure (Stam & Van de Ven, 2021; Stam, 2015). However, considering the complexity and heterogeneity of territorial units, there is a threat of a one-size-fits-all approach in policy or a lack of parsimony in research (Mason & Brown, 2014). Therefore, an epistemological perspective can be a solution, focusing on the process of EE emergence and evolution, and on select, place-based, and theory-driven spheres (Wurth et al., 2021; Spigel, 2017; Spigel & Harrison, 2018; Spigel, 2022). This results in the identification of different configurations of EE governance rather than its one type (Gancarczyk & Konopa, 2021), and also in the emergence of EE types, such as start-up ecosystems or social entrepreneurial ecosystems (Wurth et al., 2021; Thompson et al., 2000; Thompson et al., 2018).

The SEEs are conceptualized in the same way as EE in terms of possible dimensions within which actors participate in development processes, but are differentiated by the types of lead actors and expected outcomes (Thompson et al., 2000; Thompson et al., 2018; Villegas-Mateos & Vázquez-Maguirre, 2020). The animators of processes within SEEs are often social and public stakeholders, such as social entrepreneurs, local government, and nonprofit organizations (Demil, 2020). The type of active leadership affects the expected outcomes of their actions, which go beyond profit making toward territorial socioeconomic development and social objectives, acknowledging economic efficiency (Tiwari et al., 2022; Thompson et al., 2000).

Given the epistemological view, SEE emerges and evolves to attain different levels of fulfillment (Wurth et al., 2021; Brown & Mason, 2017; Spigel & Harrison, 2018). However, it is still underresearched what causes the emergence and dynamics of SEE to produce results (Tiwari et al., 2022; Kroehn et al., 2013), especially in the context of peripheral subregional structures in CEE countries (Loewen & Schulz, 2019; Wojnicka-Sycz, 2020; Klincewicz et al., 2021; Dziemianowicz et al., 2018). The existing literature suggests local leadership and bottom-up interactions as driving forces for the emergence of SEE (Feldman & Lowe, 2018; David, 2021; Broadhurst et al., 2021; Kroehn et al., 2013). SEEs are created from the bottom-up rather than through external forces, such as central government intervention or targeted policy instruments (Thompson et al., 2018; Feldman & Lowe, 2018).

They are also dynamic and can transform from inception to maturity (Mason & Brown, 2014), which is achieved through place-based interactions and establishing the rules of the game, acknowledging a multi-scalar context (Chen & Hassink, 2020) (Pushkarskaya et al., 2021). Local leaders cocreate SEE and territorial development rather than individually impose objectives and measures (Thompson et al., 2018). Consequently, we can assume coevolutionary processes that frame SEE institutions that constrain a collective action (Feldman & Lowe, 2018; Spigel & Harrison, 2018). Recognizing the importance of place leadership performed by concrete actors, institutions are necessary to enable the system to act in the absence of particular leaders, as well as to enhance a new leadership through adequate mechanisms (Yeung, 2019; Williamson, 2000). The embryonic and advanced SEEs differ in the number of actors and their relationships, the development of their institutional structure, and the availability of funding (Brown & Mason, 2017). These systemic qualities produce higher levels of entrepreneurship and territorial path upgrading. The above considerations and a research gap lead to the third research question.

RQ3.   *What were the mechanisms of local development in Muszyna? How factors and actors interplayed to produce SEE and to accomplish the advancement of the territorial path?*

RQ3 explores the mechanisms of local development as coevolutionary and outcome-oriented processes, that is, the processes generating SEE and a progressive change (Yeung, 2019; Bessagnet et al., 2021; Spigel & Harrison, 2018). There are possible interactions, conjunctures, and mutual reinforcement among these processes, when their actors could interact (Hedström & Ylikoski, 2010), such as (i) the development of local strategy gathering local government, industrial, and social actors; (ii) local events (i.e., festivals, competitions gathering local government, industrial, and social actors); and (iii) regional committees and councils giving a platform for regional and local governments, as well as business associations (Gancarczyk et al., 2021b).

Research methods

The process approach and the complexity of the actors and factors considered in the evolution of territorial units justify the adoption of the case study method (Yin, 2018; Silverman, 2015; Piekkari & Welch, 2018). Process and qualitative perspectives are also recommended at the early stage of EE and SEE research to explore microcausalities and achieve analytical rather than statistical generalization (Spigel & Harrison, 2018; Wurth et al., 2021).

Our case study is longitudinal and focuses on the period from 2004, the year of Poland's accession to the EU and the decentralization of regional policies, up to the present. Case selection criteria were based on Muszyna characteristics as a peripheral and less developed territorial unit that underwent a successful transformation. Therefore, analytical generalization can apply to spatial units with similar properties (Yin, 2018; Hassink, 2019). First, the commune featured considerable territorial development and a renewal of the industrial path in the referred period. Second, the commune is peripheral and it started the path to the present resurgence as one of the least developed and forgotten territorial units of its parent county of Nowy Sącz and the Malopolska region of Southern Poland. Regarding its industrial profile as a tourism and health resort, both economic performance and territorial brand were minor before the EU accession compared to other communes with similar specializations. Typically, to peripheral regions, Muszyna suffered from institutional voids and low social and industrial activity (Reichel et al., 2021). Third, this case is representative of local leadership mechanisms as determinants of the emergence of SEE and territorial transformation in the face of external opportunities but low internal capabilities (Ma & Hassink, 2014).

The challenge in process-based and SEE research is to reveal past decisions and actions due to retrospection bias. However, past processes and local actors' decisions and actions can be detected through their outcomes as artifacts (O'Shea et al., 2021). Our approach focuses on how local leaders cocreate SEE and local development in interaction and collaboration with other local actors (Van de Ven, 1993; Kroehn et al., 2013; Feldman & Lowe, 2018). From this point of view, evolutionary processes and SEEs are embodied in the documents of implemented projects and their effects (O'Shea et al., 2021).

The artifacts will be studied based on data triangulation from secondary and primary sources (Piekkari & Welch, 2018; Silverman, 2015). Primary sources included interviews with local government representatives and officials held from January 2022 to April 2022. The interviews were held with key respondents, namely the Mayor of Muszyna and two officials responsible for economic issues and image promotion. The Mayor of Muszyna demonstrates over 30 years of experience in supervising local government, including his responsibilities in Muszyna since 2009. Six on-site visits were conducted in Muszyna to implement the interviews and discussions with residents and tourists. Additionally, one telephone interview was held with the Mayor of Muszyna in September 2022 in order to complement the lacking information and clarify ambiguities. The referred officials have over 10 years of experience in the area of basic infrastructure, natural environment preservation, and image promotion in the studied commune. The interviews were semi-structured and lasted for a total of six hours. They were held at the local government site in three rounds; approximately two hours with the head of the local government and four hours with the officials. The interviewer used recording and took notes, which were transcribed into written material just after the interview (Piekkari & Welch, 2018).

To ensure triangulation, secondary evidence was collected, including participant observation, public statistics, commune records, public research on the development of the Malopolska region, as well as press releases and internet sources related to Muszyna activities and projects (Silverman, 2015; Wright et al., 2020). Participant observation was performed by one of the authors who have been involved in the cyclical research on the Malopolska local government performance and the resulting 14 commune rankings since 2008. The rankings used surveys and interviews with residents and tourists, besides a secondary data analysis, which additionally increased the stock of knowledge. The participant observation consisted of collecting data and secondary sources from the local government (records and semi-structured interviews) (Piekkari & Welch, 2018). This long-term experience enabled the validation of evidence and conclusions related to the particular case of the Muszyna commune (Wright et al., 2020). The secondary sources related to Muszyna accomplished 49 items, including the commune's records, reports, and strategic programmatic documents, books, journal articles, and strategic programmatic documents of Muszyna and the Malopolska region. These items covered around 3,000 normalized pages. The notes from the interviews and participant observation amounted to around 100 normalized pages.

The coding themes were driven by the theoretical framework of this research and by the experience from participant observation made during the ranking-oriented investigations (Locke et al., 2022). The coding themes revolved around three research questions that were paraphrased and specified by the interviewer during direct interactions with the respondents. These thematic blocks included the Muszyna development phases with a focus on the post-EU accession period (RQ1); internal and external drivers of the commune's path toward progressive transformation (RQ2); and the mechanisms of local development, including collaborative practices and experience, development projects, and community involvement (RQ3). The material from thematic blocks was organized into separate folders, each one containing the notes from the interviews and participant observation, as well as notes and data from written secondary sources. The coding was manual, with the use of paraphrasing and direct quotes from the interviews and secondary sources. Primary and secondary data were coded by three independent researchers, then compared and discussed to resolve inconsistencies (Yin, 2018).

To address three research questions, the research procedure included the following phases. Phase 1 focused on the dynamics of evolution of Muszyna commune after 2004 toward its current path transformation. This question resulted in the description of local development dynamics in terms of economic and social indicators, as well as development policy in the multi-scalar context of the region, country, and the EU (Gross, 2009; Murmann, 2013; Yeung, 2019). Phase 2 explored the external and internal actors and factors of the territorial path dynamics in the Muszyna commune in the referred period. Phase 3 sought to identify the mechanisms of local development in Muszyna. In particular, we observed how factors and actors interacted to produce SEE and to advance the territorial path. We investigated processes that raise structural change, such as elaborating and implementing local development strategy, enterprise growth to increase local wealth, or activities of nonprofit organizations that produce social effects (Langley et al., 2013; Garud et al., 2020). Phase 4 aimed to obtain analytical generalization in the form of a theoretical framework corroborated in this investigation (Yeung, 2019; Hassink, 2019). After addressing the research questions, we synthesized conclusions and elaborated a descriptive model of a transformation of peripheral and less-developed territorial unit (Hedström & Ylikoski, 2010). Synthesis was achieved through iterative reflection on the results given by triangulation from various data sources (Silverman, 2015).

Results

The dynamics and drivers of the evolution of the Muszyna commune and its industrial path

Historical outlook and pre-accession period

Muszyna as a commune represents the level of smallest administrative units in Poland, covering 14,144 hectares with a population of 11,000 inhabitants in the town of Muszyna (5,000 population) and surrounding rural areas (Local Data Bank, Statistics Poland, 2022). In 1930, the town of Muszyna was officially registered as a spa and wellness destination valued for mineral water extraction, and gained countrywide recognition as a tourism destination. Before the Second World War, the location became a member of the Association of Polish Spas, which ensured a strong growth impulse. A vigorous investment in spa and tourism infrastructures, such as hotels, facilities and mineral water balnearia, attracted growing interest from visitors and ensured business and labor opportunities for citizens. Muszyna became a popular and fashionable location for Polish political, cultural, and business elites after Poland became an independent state in 1918, and successfully competed with neighboring health and tourism locations of Krynica-Zdroj and Zegiestow (Gancarz, 1995).

This golden period of industrial growth and local brand establishment was broken by the Second World War, when the resort underwent a complete devastation and robbery. Recovery of the core tourism and spa activity started only at the end of 20th century (Gancarz, 1995). However, by the end of the 20th century, the restoration and development efforts were hindered by the communist political and economic regime, preventing private enterprise and economic freedom. Instead of a local private initiative, large state-owned entities were established, which governed tourism and resort activities in a heavily centralized and uniform way, with no opportunity for place-based differentiation and unique branding.

> Centralized and inefficient financing and even a reinforced distribution of visitors (e.g., workers were forced to choose particular locations for their vacations) neglected Muszyna in favor of other health and tourism resorts, such as Krynica-Zdroj.
>
> (Mayor of Muszyna)

Muszyna turned into a forgotten place as a peripheral and underdeveloped administrative unit, featuring a decline in the industrial path of its tourism and spa specialization. Located in the distant border area near Slovakia's frontiers, the commune was overshadowed by its dynamically growing neighbor spas of Krynica-Zdroj i Zegiestow.

> Decaying infrastructure and low accessibility to transport discouraged tourists and visitors. These inferior conditions were accompanied by low incomes of the population and local government, weak social and economic collaborations, and low levels of education and entrepreneurial activity.
>
> (Mayor of Muszyna)

These internal weaknesses prevented the exploitation of opportunities for independent governance and sustainable growth after Poland's transformation to a democratic society and market economy in 1990. The underdeveloped and peripheral communes faced challenges of self-sustained and bottom-up rather than central governance. However, they lacked both the ability to perform democracy in action (Putnam, 1992; Lowe & Feldman, 2017; Feldman & Lowe, 2018) and the ability to pursue a progressive industrial path. Muszyna, like many other Polish low-income communes, was forced to support its budget by selling formerly state-owned land property. Currently, this is a path-dependent factor that undermines further investment in tourism and spa infrastructure.

> Development plans require dynamic investment in tourism and spa attractions for which land property is a crucial basis. Now, it demands repurchasing the previously divested property from private owners, which represents a considerable barrier in the planned undertakings.
>
> (Mayor of Muszyna)

After Poland's administrative reform in 1998, Muszyna was included on the borders of the Malopolska region (Figure 6.1), a medium performer in the EU rankings of regional competitiveness and innovativeness (RIS, 2012, 2016, 2017, 2019; ERCI, 2010, 2013, 2016, 2019).

Since its restoration after the countries administrative reform in 1998, the region has experienced a high internal polarization, evident at the county level (the medium subregional unit), but, in particular, at the level of communes (the smallest subregional units) (MRGO, 2005). After 1998, growth focused on Kraków, which was the capital of Malopolska and the sixth largest concentration of business services in the world (OECD, 2019).

Post-EU-accession dynamics of territorial and industrial development

After Poland's EU accession in 2004, Muszyna faced challenges of low internal capability, ncreasingly polarized regional structure, and competition from locations with similar industrial specialization. However, the important opportunities were

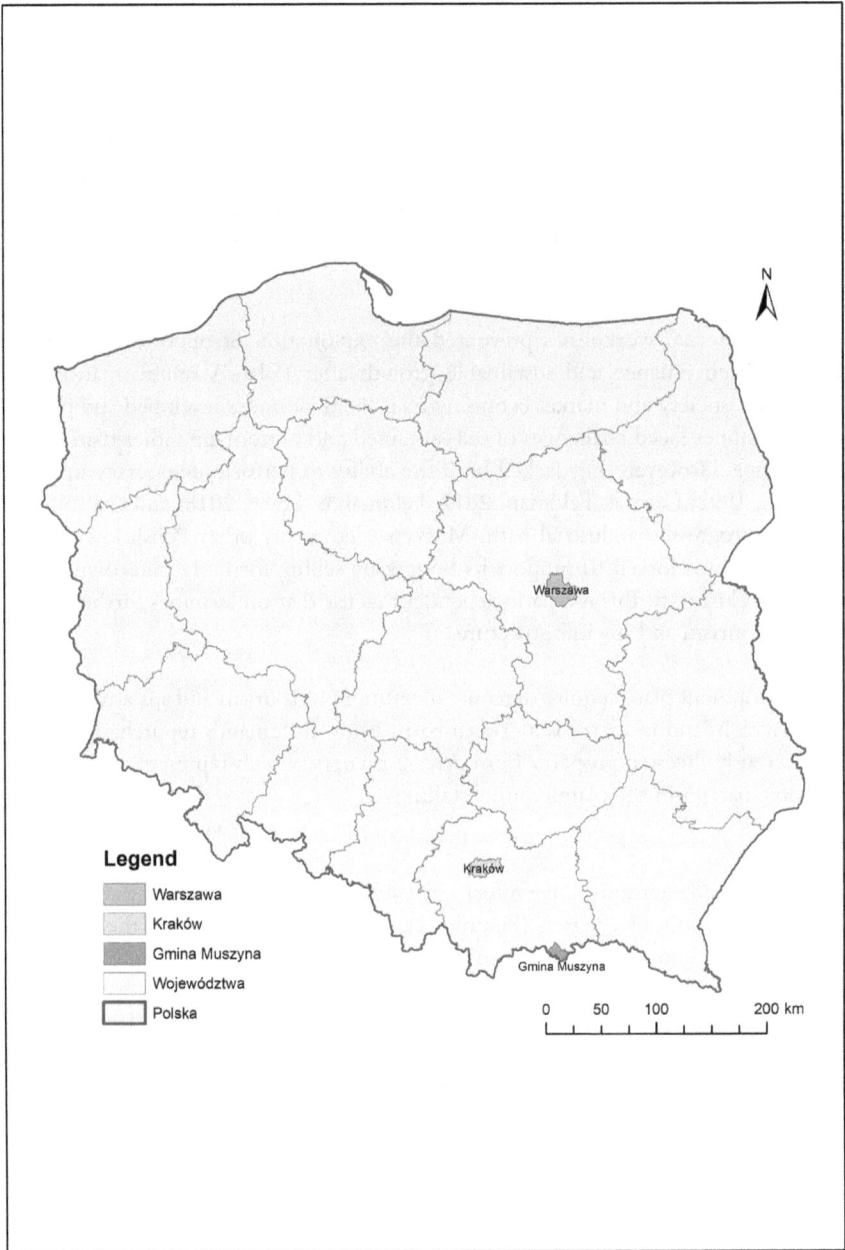

Figure 6.1 The location of Muszyna vis-à-vis Malopolska and Poland

decentralized regional and local policies and development strategies, as well as the infusion of EU structural funds. Last but not least, the location demonstrated natural tourism and landscape spa endowments, and a recognized brand of mineral water (MC (Muszyna Commune), 2012, 2020).

The external opportunities were similar for all communes with adjacent specializations in Malopolska; however, the leading tourism and spa destinations excelled in internal capabilities compared to Muszyna. Muszyna not only suffered from a destroyed and neglected tourism infrastructure but also from a relatively lower recognition and investment than other competitor destinations in the region. This made the citizens and local government feel abandoned and forgotten by regional and central planners, thus undermining their sense of identity and recognition as a historically attractive resort. Given these conditions, Muszyna recorded unprecedented growth in the post-accession period.

DEVELOPMENT OF TANGIBLE INFRASTRUCTURES

The development of tangible infrastructures represents one of the main responsibilities of the local government to ensure the quality of life. For Muszyna, these infrastructures are also crucial given its industrial specialization and attractiveness for tourists, visitors, and patients of spas and health resorts. Investment in material infrastructures were made to improve the local economy and quality of life, such as waste, water, and sewage systems, and to preserve the natural environment, such as preventing air pollution and protecting biodiversity (Figure 6.2) (Ministry of Finance, 2014). Nevertheless, important elements of the material basis for tourism development go beyond the responsibilities of the local government and should be ensured by the central government.

[T]o alleviate the transport exclusion in our commune, we expect the central government to build a high-speed road to the A4 highway, a high-speed rail to Krakow, a system of interlocking connections among tourism and spa locations, and panoramic tourist trains. . . . These are the conditions necessary for

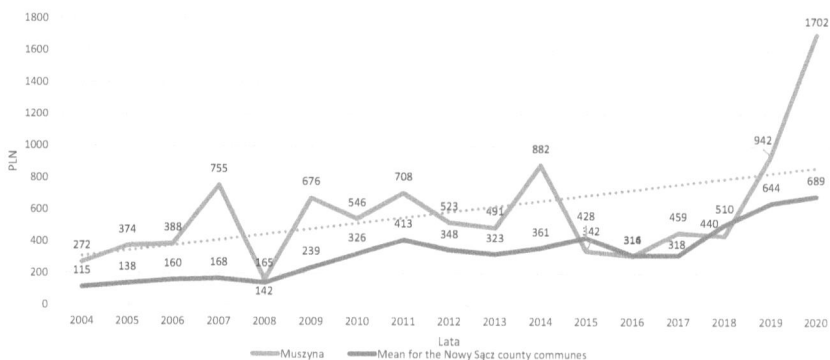

Figure 6.2 Expenditures per capita on the commune's economy and preservation of the natural environment in Muszyna 2004–2020

the development of tourism in our commune and the entire county. Naturally, we need to consider environmentally friendly technologies, such as public transport and electric power and hydrogen-based means of transportation.

(Mayor of Muszyna)

In addition to direct expenditures, the local government has been developing complementary legislative and subsidy-based incentives for environmental protection.

Our board has been considering a ban on the use of non-ecological energy sources, in particular, for house heating, and concurrent 10-year subsidies for the removal of non-ecological heaters. We would like to follow the example of the Alpine countries and Krakow.

(Mayor of Muszyna)

INTANGIBLE INFRASTRUCTURE AS IMAGE BUILDING

The local image building represents a crucial intangible asset of the tourism and spa territory, and Muszyna shapes its profile as attractive due to the beauty of the landscape and the preservation of the natural environment. The expenditures on the promotion of local brands per capita (Figure 6.3) illustrate the scale of the initiatives that affect both visitors and investors (Reichel et al., 2021). Although Muszyna's trend is declining in absolute terms, spending is higher relative to other spas in the region.

Not so long ago, Muszyna was a transit location, passed by tourists on their way to Krynica-Zdroj. Now, this is increasingly a primary destination, while Krynica-Zdroj has been turing to a one-day stop.

(Member of the Board of Muszyna)

SOCIAL CAPITAL AND ENTREPRENEURSHIP

The joint efforts of local communities are strongly dependent on social capital that builds both commercial and social entrepreneurship. After 2004, the starting point for Muszyna's social capital was lower, but the density of nonprofit organizations and citizens' activity considerably increased during the period under study (Figure 6.4).

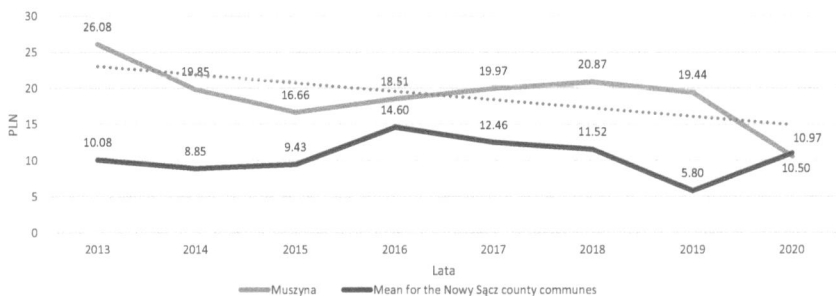

Figure 6.3 Expenditures on image promotion per capita in 2013–2020

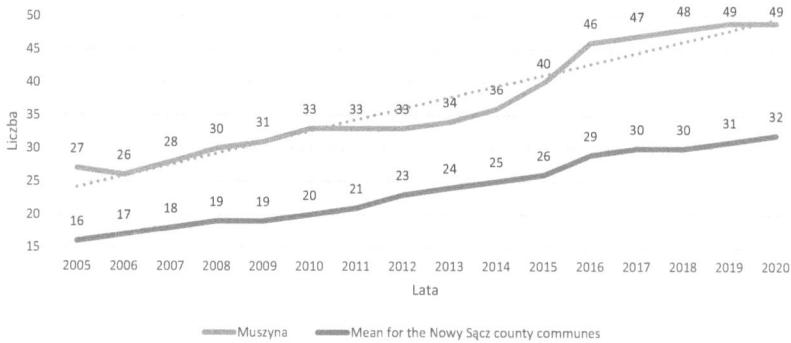

Figure 6.4 Foundations, associations, and social organizations per 10,000 inhabitants of Muszyna in 2005–2020

The statistics reported below are also confirmed through the interviews with the residents, who appreciated the activity of charitable, cultural, and social organizations and their projects targeted at the local community.[4] In Poland, the collaboration between public administration and nonprofit and nongovernment organizations (foundations, associations, and social organizations) is legally bounded (Polish Journal of Laws, 1990, 2003). This regulation is based on the principle of subsidiarity, which may delegate broad responsibilities to bottom-up collective action.

> Nonprofit community initiatives are primarily based on a detailed and accurate understanding of local needs and are better targeted in terms of objectives and measures.
>
> (A Muszyna commune official)

Following the legal obligation, Muszyna authorities collaborate with nonprofit organizations based on annual and formalized action plans, which makes this relationship systematic and institutionalized.

Social capital building and social entrepreneurial activity are associated with business activity and commercial entrepreneurship in Muszyna, as reflected in the registered enterprises per 10,000 citizens (Figure 6.5).

The positive trend of entrepreneurial activity recorded in Figure 6.4 is further supported by the consistent surplus of business births over failures in 2009–2020 (Local Data Bank, Statistics Poland, 2022). Furthermore, we deal with productive entrepreneurship that generates income for the owners and tax revenues for the budget of the Muszyna commune (Figure 6.6).

In 2019–2020, the decline in corporate tax revenues was due to the COVID-19 pandemic, which had a particularly severe impact on tourism and spa businesses.

THE WEALTH OF COMMUNE AND ITS CITIZENS

The progress reported in infrastructural and socioeconomic dimensions raised the results in terms of the wealth of the commune as administrative unit and, most

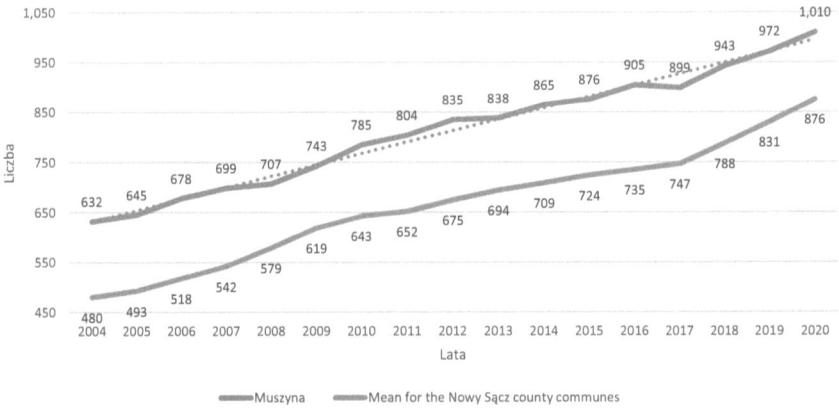

Figure 6.5 Registered enterprises in Muszyna per 10,000 citizens during 2004–2020

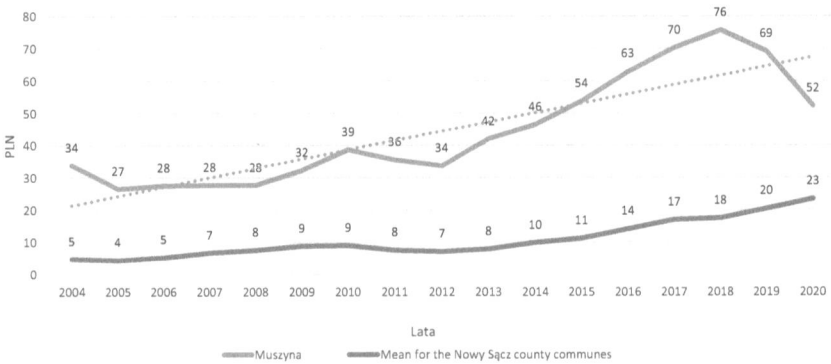

Figure 6.6 Revenues from corporate income tax per capita in Muszyna in 2004–2020

importantly, its inhabitants. Besides the evidence from the statistics given below, the improvement of the citizens' wealth has also been reported by their opinions reflected in the interviews in 2017, 2018, and 2019.[5] The unemployment rate, which was approximately 10% at the start of the post-accession period, was systematically dropping down until 2020 to approximately 3% (Local Data Bank, Statistics Poland, 2022). Related indirect evidence of increasing wealth is revenue from personal income tax per capita (Figure 6.7).

The growing income of the population contributed to the commune's budget and resulted in its operating surplus, as a basis for accessing external funds and loans (Reichel et al., 2016). The latter indicate the ability to implement planned investments, which was positive during the considered period, despite the natural decline from the crises 2007–2009 and the recent coronavirus pandemic (Reichel et al., 2021). The ability to source external funds was proved, among others, by the

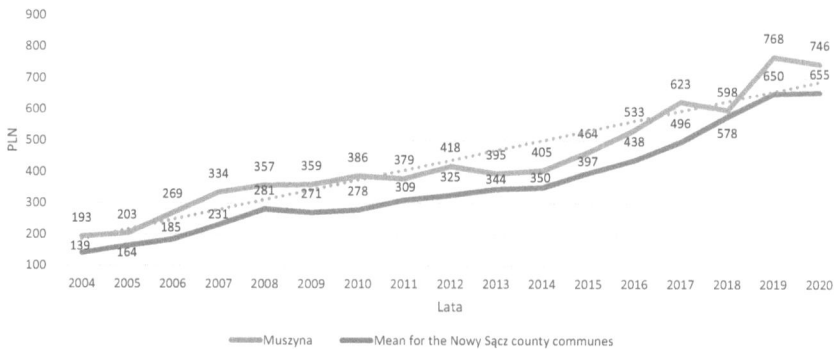

Figure 6.7 Revenues from personal income tax per capita in Muszyna in 2004–2020

amount of the structural funds, ranging from 42 million PLN in 2008 to 1466 million PLN in 2013 to 1256 million PLN in 2020 (Reichel et al., 2021).

Socioeconomic improvement was recently confirmed by the inclusion of the commune in the Nowy Sącz County Functional Area, which is an association of administrative units with coherent socioeconomic and spatial characteristics and thus functionally relate to one another. Inclusion into the core functional areas of the county shows the increased cohesion of Muszyna development versus the earlier exclusion and peripheral status.

The mechanisms of local and industrial development – an analytical generalization

Strategic place-based leadership in exploiting internal potential and external opportunities

Despite the inferior conditions at the start of the post-accession period, Muszyna demonstrated a long-term positive dynamics, evolving as a socioeconomic structure toward a progressive and sustainable renewal of its industrial path and wealth. This has been achieved by exploitation of the external opportunities mentioned above, such as decentralized regional and local development policies and EU funds, and the internal potential of natural endowments such as spa and wellness. Development processes are driven by people who undertake actions, projects, and initiatives. However, these were a sort of passive assets that should be activated or those that should be created first. Muszyna progressed to establish a social entrepreneurial ecosystem in the dimensions of tangible and intangible infrastructures, social capital and entrepreneurship, as well as overall economic performance and citizen wealth. What were the mechanisms, that is, key outcome-related processes that led to this structural transformation of territorial path?

Since processes are conjunctures of decisions and actions of particular actors, we also need to acknowledge the key actors initiating these processes. In the case of Muszyna, local place-based leadership performed by two mayors supported by their boards and teams of local government officials played these major roles. The studied period includes the terms of two mayors who governed the commune from 2004 to

2009 and from 2010 until the present. It is important to note the legitimacy of the mayor's position in the Polish public administration system, as they are elected by direct vote by all citizens. The two leaders referred marked two phases of Muszyna development and initiated the mechanisms for local coordinated action involving other actors, such as enterprises and nongovernmental organizations.

The first post-accession mayor (2004–2009) laid foundations for crucial tangible infrastructures for tourism and spa activity based on the structural funds absorption. The structural funds distribution is a competitive process among local governments based on investment plans. Therefore, the winning communes needed to prove both the relevance and feasibility of their projects. The orientation to basic infrastructures and horizontal investment rather than vertical support and industrial specializations was typical of this EU programming period in Poland (MRGO, 2005).

The second development period was marked by the complementary election of the current Mayor (since 2010) after the death of its predecessor in the road accident. The current leadership distinguishes by dynamic investment and activities that not only comprise basic tangible infrastructures but also tangibles of the natural environment. In addition, intangibles became the focus, including territorial image, social capital, and entrepreneurship. Looking from the multi-scalar perspective, the period 2013–2020 was marked by vertical, country, and regional policies for smart specializations (MRGO, 2015). Since the introduction of innovation strategies in Malopolska, the area of creative and leisure industries, including tourism, has been highlighted as a regional specialization. This also affected the focus of local governments on their specialization profiles, uniquely adopted by Muszyna (MC (Muszyna Commune), 2012, 2020). Consequently, the commune has renewed its industrial path to become a recognizable and branded spa and wellness for tourists, guests, and patients, as well as a favorable location for the quality of life for its residents. The empirical corroboration of these outcomes can be found in the interview material investigating the tourists' perceptions of the attractiveness of the Muszyna spa and wellness.[6]

The two leadership phases feature a strategic approach that goes beyond the Mayor's one-term perspective, and a consistent view of building the location brand on a prior investment in basic infrastructure. The important mechanism for leadership was the process of setting up and implementing the local development strategy. Although not reinforced by law, this mechanism was adopted by the local government of Muszyna as a practical governance tool. The commune strategy is a process led by the Mayor and engaging the community, such as enterprises, regular citizens, and nongovernment stakeholders.

> The activities are iterative and involve the drafting of proposals, consulting, amending, redrafting, and reconsulting, until the ultimate approval.
> (A Muszyna county official)

This process can be treated as a development mechanism, being recurrent (periodically created and redrafted) and outcome-oriented. The latter not only comprises the artifact but also a formal strategic plan and action agenda.

The [commune's] strategy also represents a motivating and integrating tool for the local community and an advantage in seeking external investment and funding.

(A Muszyna county official)

The strategic plans for 2013–2020 and 2021–2027 (MC (Muszyna Commune), 2012, 2020) are complementary in setting out such priorities as development of internal and external transport and communication infrastructure, tourism and spa facilities, acknowledging natural environment preservation, and strengthening the territorial image. Compared to most local strategies, Muszyna's plans are unique in emphasizing local human and social capital by promoting health care, education, cultural heritage, and fostering community social and commercial entrepreneurship.

A project-based venturing in the social entrepreneurial ecosystem of Muszyna

The local leadership has become an animator of the undertakings, that is, the social project-based venturing to develop the Muszyna SEE for territorial and industrial development (Table 6.1). Local government-led initiatives and projects should not be treated as one-time events, but as continuous and outcome-related processes, which are the mechanisms of Muszyna development. Within these processes, the local government managed to liaise with social and industry stakeholders turning this accumulated experience to institutions, that is, rules and routines for collective action. Table 6.1 presents how the selected projects in 2014–2020 involved stakeholders, developed particular dimensions of the SEE and related institutions of collective action, and how they contributed to the development of the territorial and industrial path.

The projects demonstrate a consistent development pathway, from building basic and tangible infrastructures and only indirectly targeting intangible assets (e.g., water and sewage system), to more advanced investments tailored at industrial specialization and quality of life (e.g., water sports and recreation facilities), to creative and sophisticated instruments directed at local differentiation (e.g., thematic gardens). Muszyna boasts the largest thematic Bible story garden in Poland (1,2 ha), which is one of four such landscape architectures in Poland (MC (Muszyna Commune), 2022a). Sensory gardens appeal to all senses with a variety of shapes, colors, sounds, and descents. Greek- and Roman-style gardens, also called Magic or Love Gardens, attract with sophisticated cultural reminiscences and enhance a relaxing atmosphere among tourists and guests (MC (Muszyna Commune), 2021, 2022a).

In addition, we can observe the widening and diversifying stakeholder groups in these initiatives. Basic infrastructure projects featured limited diversity and scope, where the local government engaged necessary subcontracting enterprises and landowners contributed their property in exchange for public compensation. However, advanced sports and recreation projects required a thorough and professional expertise of sports experts and organizations, as well as educational institutions (MC (Muszyna Commune), 2022b). Even a wider and more diversified representation was gathered by innovative and visionary projects of thematic gardens and creative

Table 6.1 A project-based venturing in Muszyna SEE (selected projects)

Project description (all projects implemented in 2014–2020)	Local stakeholder involvement	SEE dimensions and institutions	Outcomes for territorial and/or industrial path
Water-sewage system renovation; basic infrastructure project; total investment of 73 million PLN (38 million from EU funds)	Local government, enterprises as contractors, citizens providing necessary access to land property	Economic and Social Dimensions – directly: basic infrastructure; indirectly: intangible infrastructure – the commune's image as promoting ecology and quality of life; Institutional Dimension: rules and routines of negotiating access to land property for public purposes	Territorial development for quality of life; basic infrastructure for industrial path renewal in tourism and spa
A ring road for Muszyna town; transport and communication infrastructure; total investment 30 million PLN (23,5 million PLN from EU funds)	Local government, enterprises as contractors, citizens providing necessary access to land property	Economic and Social Dimensions – directly: basic infrastructure for quality of life and tourism movement; indirectly: intangible infrastructure – the commune's image for quality of life; Institutional Dimension: rules and routines of negotiating access to land property for public purposes	Territorial development for quality of life; basic infrastructure for industrial path renewal in tourism and spa
Center for Water Sports and Recreation Zapopradzie, *SledLand* (toboggan run); *Hiking and Biking Trails*; new and advanced tourism and sports infrastructures	Local government, enterprises, local sports associations and organizations, educational institutions landscape architects	Cultural and social dimensions: advanced and tailored tangible infrastructure for differentiation in industrial specialization; image and social capital building; Economic Dimension: market attraction of tourists and visitors; Institutional Dimension: rules and routines of coordinating the interests, creativity, and capabilities of a large group of stakeholders	Industrial path renewal in tourism and spa; territorial development for quality of life, health, and social needs
Thematic gardens (sensory, Bible stories, Greek- and Roman-style gardens); creative landscape architecture *Renovation of the Old Castle*; *Renovation of the Old Town of Muszyna* (total investment 21,5 million, 13 mln from EU funds); conservation of artifacts and landscape architecture	Local government, enterprises, local cultural associations and organizations, educational institutions, artists, and landscape architects	Cultural and Social Dimensions: intangible infrastructure for differentiation image, cultural heritage preservation, and social capital building; Economic Dimension: market attraction of tourists and visitors; Institutional Dimension: rules and routines of coordinating the interests, creativity, and capabilities of a large group of stakeholders	Industrial path renewal in tourism and spa; territorial development for quality of life, human, and social needs

Source: Own elaboration based on the interviews with Muszyna commune's officials and the commune's records.

landscape architectures. Besides those responsible for the tangible side of construction, the contributors included experts and organizations in culture, fine arts, and architecture. The local government leader acted as a hub and animator for these entities (MC (Muszyna Commune), 2022b, 2022c).

The increasing complexity and the ability to address higher-order needs in the projects were also associated with the development and creation of SEE dimensions. These progressed from a predominantly economic dimension (e.g., tangible infrastructure projects) to social and cultural dimensions (sport and recreation facilities, thematic gardens), and finally to the institutional dimension (Table 6.1). The latter component is a learning outcome from the projects, which raised experience, rules, and routines that became conducive to further collective action. For instance, institutions negotiating access to land property for public purposes turned to rules and routines, that is, institutions framing future undertakings. Coordinating the interests, creativity, and capabilities of a large group of stakeholders in cultural heritage projects produced a comprehensive understanding of the related rules and routines for similar future activities.

Our research has revealed three interrelated routines derived from the local government's experience in implementing projects and involving the community. These practices can be informative as micro-causalities of the bottom-up collective action for revitalizing Forgotten Spaces. They also form an accelerating and snowball effect for local community involvement and the building of SEE.

The first routine embraces mission-oriented social entrepreneurship of local government and those social organizations that expose strong ties with local authorities. These strong ties form a hub of initiatives to launch and implement the development projects. The hub's activities also include the dissemination of the project idea to the community through information, advocacy, and public consultation activities. "The Muszyna Key Association," is an example of a strong-tie organization, which is a nonprofit cultural and educational organization that is active among both young and aged people, and with influential reputation as a supporter of disadvantaged groups. Another strong initiative is formed by "The Circle of Tourist Guides" who are offered trainings about the attractions of Muszyna at the local government office, and thus act as local ambassadors for tourists and local community. The Academy of Applied Sciences in Nowy Sącz has been involved in the strategy development processes, both with its faculty and students, who have contributed with research-backed analyses and development proposals. A dozen or so sports clubs, such as football, volleyball, basketball, tennis, chess, and bridge clubs, are also strongly linked to the local government initiatives. At the stage of launching and implementing the project, these strong-tie organizations support the local government's initiatives with their advocacy, persuasion, and communication to citizens. Moreover, before a project starts, the local government will open community consultations, where residents can provide their feedback and evaluate – accept or reject the project proposal. The hub organizations are often the first to encourage this public evaluation.

The second routine exemplifies the local government and local community negotiation skills and ability to find an agreement for development projects. The development largely depends on infrastructural projects or projects for which a material infrastructure and the availability of land property are prerequisites. For most of Polish local governments, the buyout of land property from private owners or obtaining their allowance for a neighboring investment represents one of the biggest challenges. The Mayor of Muszyna distinguishes two types of negotiating procedures and relevant practices. The first type is associated with tourism investments, which are convincing for citizens who recognize the opportunities for their own benefits. The second type refers to hard investments, such as road building, when negotiations are difficult since citizens are concerned about their comfort of living and a possible decrease of the value of their own land property. Besides negotiating skills, the harder negotiations are supported with social processes.

> A social pressure loop uses the earlier communication and advocacy activities of local government and the collaborating social organizations, turning all these to a network around the project. As a result, the local community at large puts a pressure on those who prevent the implementation of development projects by pursuing only their individualistic interests.
>
> (The Mayor of Muszyna)

However, this pressure is not a hard one and the local government is very much cautious in using it, so as not to cause disagreement that is detrimental to investment, as observed in other competitor spa and wellness locations.

Ultimately, the third routine has been identified as commercial entrepreneurship that follows as the next step after the earlier referred routine of social entrepreneurship. When the infrastructural, cultural, or sports investment is nearing completion, local residents and businesses recognize their opportunities and start exploiting them by establishing their businesses, and make private investments.

The referred routines or practices have been largely an informal and tacit knowledge of the rules of the game in governing stakeholders within SEE. This knowledge is integrated into the awareness of local government leaders and the experiences of collaborating individuals and organizations rather than formalized. However, formal institutionalization is important to continue development, even in the absence of individual founding leaders (Ostrom, 2010). Codified knowledge is needed to sustain the current SEE and make it less vulnerable to erosion when new, maybe less talented, leaders step in (Ostrom, 1986; Helmke & Levitsky, 2004). The Muszyna SEE is highly dependent on the individual leadership traits of the current Mayor, the experiences of the Board and Office team, as well as enduring collaboration with a group of social stakeholders. The personal authority becomes a kind of informal institution as well, turning to a strong attachment of the local community to this Mayor, as evidenced in his only candidature in the recent election.[7] The collaboration is currently enhanced by legal institutions, such as public procurement, public consultation and collaboration programs (Polish Journal of Laws, 1990, 2003). These formal institutions act as an effective framework for the generation of informal and place-based rules and routines for public action.

The current SEE represents a coherent system that efficiently uses its internal potential and external opportunities, notably investment funds. Membership and collaboration in county-level initiatives, such as the Nowy Sącz County Functional Area, are also relevant and useful. However, both local government leaders and entrepreneurs still consider their community as somehow forgotten by the central government.

> . . . neglected and marginalized in supraregional and international tourism and sports projects, compared to other locations, such as Solina or Duszniki-Zdroj. . . . Tourism demands a systemic support, going beyond local and regional efforts to country-level investment in transport and communication and specialized facilities. Muszyna has established its differentiation among other communes in our tourism county; however, our own efforts are not sufficient and we need unique and courageous investment in recreation, medical, and diagnosis centers, as well as facilities for business tourism, among others.
>
> (Mayor of Muszyna)

Discussion and conclusions

Discussion

This research has implemented the objective of identifying the mechanisms of territorial development of an initially peripheral and underdeveloped territory, based on the Muszyna case study. Based on the empirical findings, we can respond to research questions and derive an analytical generalization regarding revitalizing Forgotten Spaces through SEE building by local place-based leadership.

In response to RQ1 on the dynamics of the territorial path of the initially peripheral and underdeveloped commune, we observe positive dynamics in key dimensions of tangible and intangible infrastructures, social capital, and entrepreneurship, as well as the overall wealth of the administrative unit and its population. This makes the territorial and industrial path of Muszyna unique compared to other low-potential territories and industrial leaders in Malopolska. The unique approach was a combination of the following activities: (i) recalling the historical industrial and place identity through a number of renovations (the old downtown, the castle), (ii) developing of a modern tourism and communication infrastructure, and (iii) developing practices and principles of collective action and social agreement on the development strategies and measures. The competitor locations lacked this unique capability and, despite a more favorable initial conditions, their development was largely undermined by local disagreements with regard to investment and the interests of private land property owners with the community development needs. Therefore, these locations are at a disadvantage with regard to collaboration for development and tourism infrastructure, compared to Muszyna.

Responding to RQ2 regarding the drivers of observed dynamics, this research identified external conditions, such as the country-level decentralization of regional development policies and the availability of the structural funds for investment. These funds were primarily available to Muszyna through regional operational programs to support the infrastructure development in Malopolska (MRGO, 2007, 2014).

Their rationale also stemmed from creative and leisure industries, including tourism, being one of the region's smart specialization area (MRDO, 2015; MRGO, 2015). Although these were important growth impulses, they were not available per se, but required a competition-based applying for funds, in which processes Muszyna excelled. The internal drivers were the potential of the commune in terms of natural endowments and local place-based leadership. The latter was strongly legitimized by an external institution of direct election by the whole population of the commune, and by the personal capabilities of the Mayor and his team of coworkers. The role of local leadership and efficient governance leading to improvements in life quality and touristic attractiveness was confirmed by the interview evidence among the residents and visitors, as reported in the results section. However, besides this secondary data, we would need more qualitative and granular insights from the interviews with enterprises, tourists, and residents to highlight micro-causalities and specify development processes from their perspective.

In RQ3 we explored the mechanisms of local development in Muszyna and how factors and actors interacted to produce SEE and achieve the advancement of the territorial path. The response to RQs requires higher-order reasoning that points to causalities and processes rather than statistically verified determinants, and it will represent an analytical generalization from this research (Hedström & Yliko-ski, 2010) (Figure 6.8).

The mechanisms for local development relevant to Forgotten Spaces start from the recognition of internal potentials of the territory and external opportunities. In the case of Muszyna, the internal potentials primarily included natural endowments (see Figure 6.8, the upper left area). Human and social capital, as well as tangible infrastructures and the territorial image necessary to use these resources, were either passive or undermined assets. The peripheral status and underdevelopment of the commune were not met by the central government support, which continues to be minor in relation to other tourism and spa destinations in the region. Faced with these disadvantages, the local leadership had to both activate passive potentials and at least partially substitute for central government investment to compete with neighboring communes as industrial leaders (see Figure 6.8, left-lower box).

Leadership requires legitimization. In the Muszyna case, it was founded on a formal institution of direct election of the mayor by all citizens, formal and legal institutions

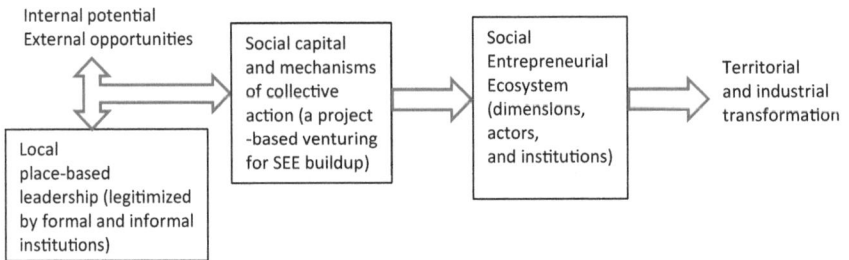

Figure 6.8 Mechanisms for revitalizing forgotten spaces through SEE building by local place-based leadership: an analytical framework

promoting a collaboration between local government and nongovernmental organizations, and an informal institution of personal authority – leadership capabilities of subsequent mayors. Mayors were animators of local social capital for collective action, activating people and their self-organization ability. This was exemplified by project-based venturing for an evolutionary buildup of the local SEE (see Figure 6.8, central boxes). The projects focused on the mechanism of development, growing in complexity, progressing in differentiation, and the density of social participation. The SEE accomplished some place-based dimensions, relevant for this peripheral unit (e.g., Economic, Social, Cultural, and Institutional Dimensions). Within these dimensions, groups of actors under the local government leadership were identified to produce rules and routines for further collective action. The emerging SEE is a mediator between leadership activating local communities and a progressive territorial and industrial transformation (Figure 6.7, area at the left edge area).

The current development of Muszyna SEE features strengths, but also some points for refinement and upgrade. The latter comprises the sustainability issues that might arise in the absence of a talented personal leadership from the mayor and his or her local government team, as well as social collaborators. The current SEE Institutional Dimension features strengths in terms of the accomplished institutions of collaboration, predominantly informal and being a club good of the local government and the most active social leaders. To be sustainable and replicative in other conditions of leadership, the institutional dimension requires a formalization of predominantly informal rules and routines. This can be accomplished through a more pronounced and public recognition of individuals and organizations contributing to the social business venturing in Muszyna. The example includes public recognition of the road renovation funded by Muszyna entrepreneurs associated with the Local Development Initiative (MC (Muszyna Commune), 2022a). This can serve as a means of raising awareness of and motivating participation of broader industrial and social groups in this location.

Implications for theory

This research primarily contributes to the literature on entrepreneurial ecosystems, in particular, to SEE as a particular type of EE. It broadens our knowledge of how SEE emerge through bottom-up and place-based leadership to produce local development (Thompson et al., 2018; Broadhurst et al., 2021). Our study responds to the recent call for more in-depth and presenting conditions and causalities of SEE emergence and dynamics (Wurth et al., 2021). In particular, this research stream seeks to explain what makes for the dynamics of ecosystems, since they are predominantly studied as overly static. EE and SEE are presented as sets of dimensions and relevant resources or abstract relationships (Spigel, 2017; Stam & Van de Ven, 2021). However, it is still unexplained what makes EE operate as a system and how the system evolves to produce territorial and industrial development (Van de Ven, 1993; Wurth et al., 2021). This study is unique in emphasizing local place-based leadership as cocreating social entrepreneurial communities through process approach, that is, by activities and projects that we call a social entrepreneurial venturing (Lowe &

Feldman, 2017; Broadhurst et al., 2021). Furthermore, we present the origins of and identify SEE dimensions that are place-based and relevant to local government units progressing from a peripheral and underdeveloped status (Spigel, 2017; Spigel, 2022). Based on our case study, ecosystem structures can emerge and evolve as project-based. Joint projects initiate and activate actors and resources to produce SEE dimensions and institutions of collective action.

This chapter also adds to the path literature and coevolutionary strand in regional studies (Hassink et al., 2019; Asheim, 2019). It broadens the knowledge of how the interactions of local agents emerge from local leadership and project-based mechanisms of collective action to generate an industrial path renewal (Gancarczyk et al., 2023). We have revealed types of internal and external mechanisms that drive the mutual influences of populations to produce regional and industrial transformation. Current research has identified and described one type of internal mechanism in terms of project-based venturing (Hassink et al., 2019; Pushkarskaya et al., 2021). We also point to institutions as both generating these mechanisms and conducive for them. Formal and legal institutions, for example, the election system that gives legitimacy and legal enforcement of collaboration with social actors, represent a firm framework that enables and constrains leadership and joint activities. They are also providing incentives and sustainability for the SEE. This study contributes by revealing how a unique territorial SEE produces its own internal institutions of collective action. Still, these informal institutions call for a formalization to make them sustainable and reproduce and develop SEE in the absence of the current leaders and established collaborators.

The case of Muszyna points to the fact that the transformation of peripheral and underdeveloped territories can be driven by local leadership and external institutions. This adds to the understanding of coevolutionary processes in the context of the peripheral and Forgotten Spaces with internal institutional voids (Ma & Hassink, 2014). In contexts lacking social capital and internal institutions of collective action, we can hardly expect spontaneous action of homogeneous coevolving local populations (local government, citizens, enterprises, organizations) (Feldman & Lowe, 2018). Therefore, leadership is a crucial instrument to activate bottom-up activities organizing industrial and social actors into a SEE system (David, 2021).

Implications for practice

This study is also informative for local policymakers in peripheral and Forgotten Spaces with institutional voids. It provides the knowledge of how concrete and tailored activities can turn into mechanisms of joint social action and underlie the buildup of a local SEE and territorial resurgence (Feldman & Lowe, 2018). Moreover, the case points to the advantages of local leadership and its underlying institutional conditions (Broadhurst et al., 2021). Besides following formal institutions demanded by law, local leaders can gain awareness and use the value of creating their own internal collaborative rules and routines to complement and specify formal institutions (Zukauskaite et al., 2017). These observations and conclusions are relevant for the transformation of spatial units in CEE countries, and, in particular, for

Forgotten Spaces, which often need to substitute their own SEE with central government intervention (OECD, 2019 (Loewen & Schulz, 2019). Formal and informal institutions interplay and are mutually supportive (Helmke & Levitsky, 2004). The example is development strategy, once formalized as an external institution and required from local governments by Polish law, but currently turned into a formalized internal institution by some communes, including Muszyna.

This study is also relevant for understanding the specificity of SEE in local government units, since it specifies theory and place-based dimensions in this regard, following their evolutionary emergence as Economic, Social, Cultural, and ultimately Institutional Dimensions (Spigel, 2022).

Limitations and future research

Our research is not without limitations, which we acknowledge and indicate how they were tackled. The case study is exploratory in addressing the renewal of a forgotten space from the perspective of SEE and local leadership. Considering its focus, we primarily interviewed the local government leader and its direct coworkers; however, the knowledge is normally dispersed over a wider range of actors such as citizens and enterprises (Piekkari & Welch, 2018; Wright et al., 2020). This deficiency can raise a potential bias, since the primary qualitative sources from the interviews were limited to the mechanisms derived from the reflection and perception of local authorities. The voices from other stakeholders, such as residents and tourists, were limited to the secondary material from the past interviews. In particular, we lack granular and qualitative insights from social entrepreneurs, enterprises, and residents to support or question social venturing mechanisms, rules, and routines in action. We addressed this deficiency by triangulation of data and using secondary research material from participant observation, commune records, and strategic documents, as well as internet sources that describe social initiatives and relevant actors (Boje & Rosile, 2020). Future studies can expand the interview groups to other actors, based on the knowledge of collective mechanisms provided by our case study.

We have described how particular SEE dimensions emerged in the transformation process. The set of dimensions is relevant in the context of a peripheral local unit in a given development phase. However, this set of SEE dimensions cannot be treated as exhaustive. Taking this approach, we follow the view that configurations of SEE dimensions are unique to particular units (Brown & Mason, 2017). Our study complements this place-based approach with the phase of territorial development as an explanatory condition for a set of SEE dimensions (Brown & Mason, 2017). For instance, basic infrastructures in the Economic Dimension are important at the start of transformation, while differentiation-oriented branding activities in Social and Cultural Dimensions appear in the advanced phases of the SEE development. Future studies might focus on the identification of relevant SEE dimensions by adopting a multiple case method in local units that differ in the SEE evolution phase. Consequently, this research calls for future multiple case studies that would match local units at different levels of SEE development and initial economic, social, and institutional conditions.

Notes

1 Ph.D., Hab., Full Professor, Institute of Economics, Finance, and Management, Faculty of Management and Social Communication, Jagiellonian University, Kraków, Poland, email: marta.gancarczyk@uj.edu.pl (ORCID: 0000–0003–2078–9320).
2 Ph.D., Adjunct Professor, Institute of Entrepreneurship, Faculty of Management and Social Communication, Jagiellonian University, Kraków, Poland, email: jacek.gancarczyk@uj.edu.pl (ORCID 0000–0002–5636–1062)
3 Ph.D., Adjunct Professor, Department of Entrepreneurship and Innovation, Faculty of Economic Sciences, Academy of Applied Sciences in Nowy Sącz, Poland, email: mreichel@ans-ns.edu.pl (ORCID: 0000–0003–3358–6768)
4 A secondary interview material collected for the Ranking of the Communes of the Nowy Sącz County in 2018.
5 A secondary interview material collected for the Ranking of the Communes of the Nowy Sącz County in 2017, 2018, and 2019.
6 A secondary interview material collected for the Ranking of the Communes of the Nowy Sącz Sub-Region 2019.
7 Interview with a Muszyna county official.

References

Acs, Z. J., Stam, E., Audretsch, D. B., & O'Connor, A. (2017). The lineages of the entrepreneurial ecosystem approach. *Small Business Economics*, *49*(1), 1–10. https://doi.org/10.1007/s11187-017-9864-8

Asheim, B. T. (2019). Smart specialisation, innovation policy and regional innovation systems: What about new path development in less innovative regions? *Innovation: The European Journal of Social Science Research*, *32*(1), 8–25.

Bendickson, J. S., Irwin, J. G., Cowden, B. J., & McDowell, W. C. (2021). Entrepreneurial ecosystem knowledge spillover in the face of institutional voids: Groups, issues, and actions. *Knowledge Management Research and Practice*, *19*(1), 117–126. https://doi.org/10.1080/14778238.2020.1768810

Benner, M. (2021). Retheorizing industrial – Institutional coevolution: A multidimensional perspective. *Regional Studies*, 1–14.

Bessagnet, A., Crespo, J., & Vicente, J. (2021). Unraveling the multi-scalar and evolutionary forces of entrepreneurial ecosystems: A historical event analysis applied to IoT Valley. *Technovation*, *108*. https://doi.org/10.1016/j.technovation.2021.102329

Boje, D., & Rosile, G. A. (2020). *How to use conversational storytelling interviews for your dissertation*. Cheltenham: Edward Elgar Publishing.

Broadhurst, K., Ferreira, J., & Berkeley, N. (2021). Collaborative leadership and place-based development. *Local Economy*, *36*(2), 149–163.

Brown, R., & Mason, C. (2017). Looking inside the spiky bits: A critical review and conceptualisation of entrepreneurial ecosystems. *Small Business Economics*, *49*(1), 11–30.

Chen, Y., & Hassink, R. (2020). Multi-scalar knowledge bases for new regional industrial path development: Toward a typology. *European Planning Studies*, *28*(12), 2489–2507. https://doi.org/10.1080/09654313.2020.1724265

Colombo, M. G., Dagnino, G. B., Lehmann, E. E., & Salmador, M. (2019). The governance of entrepreneurial ecosystems. *Small Business Economics*, *52*(2), 419–428.

David, L. (2021). *The Different Paths from which Place leadership Can Manifest: A Meta-analysis Using Qualitative Comparative Analysis (QCA)*. Lund: Lund University, Centre for Innovation Research (CIRCLE).

Demil, B. (2020). Reintroducing public actors in entrepreneurial dynamics: A co-evolutionary approach to categorization. *Strategic Entrepreneurship Journal*, *14*(1), 43–65.

Dziemianowicz, W., Łukomska, J., & Ambroziak, A. A. (2018). Location factors in foreign direct investment at the local level: The case of Poland. *Regional Studies, 53*(8), 1183–1192.

European Commission, ERCI (European Regional Competitiveness Index). (2010, 2013, 2016, 2019). https://ec.europa.eu/regional_policy/en/information/maps/regional_competitiveness/ (Access: 01.07.2021).

European Commission, RIS (Regional Innovation Scoreboard). (2012, 2016, 2017, 2019). https://ec.europa.eu/growth/industry/policy/innovation/regional_en/ (Access: 01.07.2021).

Feldman, M., & Lowe, N. (2018). Policy and collective action in place. *Cambridge Journal of Regions, Economy and Society, 11*(2), 335–351.

Gancarczyk, M., & Konopa, S. (2021). Exploring the governance of entrepreneurial ecosystems for productive high growth. *Foresight and STI Governance, 15*(4), 9–21. https://doi.org/10.17323/2500-2597.2021.4.9.21

Gancarczyk, M., Najda-Janoszka, M., Gancarczyk, J., & Hassink, R. (2023). Exploring regional innovation policies and regional industrial transformation from a coevolutionary perspective: The case of Małopolska, Poland. *Economic Geography, 99*(1), 51–80. https://doi.org/10.1080/00130095.2022.2120465

Gancarczyk, M., Ujwary-Gil, A., & González-López, M. (2021a). *Partnerships for regional innovation and development: Implementing smart specialization in Europe.* London: Routledge.

Gancarczyk, M., Ujwary-Gil, A., & González-López, M. (2021b). The expansion of the smart specialization concept and practice. In *Partnerships for regional innovation and development* (pp. 1–18). London: Routledge.

Gancarz, A. (1995). *Społeczność miasta Muszyna w latach 1918–1939.* http://www.almanachmuszyny.pl/spisy/1995/AM1995_09_spolecznosc_miasta_muszyny_w_latach_1918_1939.pdfgancA

Garud, R., Jarzabkowski, P., Langley, A., Tsoukas, H., Van de Ven, A., & Lê, J. (2020). Process research methods: A conversation among leading scholars★. In T. R. Crook, J. Lê, & A. D. Smith (Eds.), *Advancing methodological thought and practice* (Vol. 12, pp. 117–132). Bingley: Emerald Publishing Limited. https://doi.org/10.1108/S1479-838720200000012019

Gilmore, R. W. (2008). Forgotten places and the seeds of grassroots planning. *Engaging Contradictions: Theory, Politics, and Methods of Activist Scholarship*, 31–61.

Gong, H., Binz, C., Hassink, R., & Trippl, M. (2022). Emerging industries: Institutions, legitimacy and system-level agency. *Regional Studies, 56*(4), 523–535.

Gong, H., & Hassink, R. (2019). Co-evolution in contemporary economic geography: Towards a theoretical framework. *Regional Studies, 53*(9), 1344–1355.

González-López, M., Asheim, B. T., & Sánchez-Carreira, M. del C. (2019). *New insights on regional innovation policies.*

Gross, N. (2009). A pragmatist theory of social mechanisms. *American Sociological Review, 74*(3), 358–379.

Hassink, R. (2019). How to decontextualize in economic geography? *Dialogues in Human Geography, 9*(3), 279–282.

Hassink, R., Isaksen, A., & Trippl, M. (2019). Towards a comprehensive understanding of new regional industrial path development. *Regional Studies, 53*(11), 1636–1645.

Hedström, P., & Ylikoski, P. (2010). Causal mechanisms in the social sciences. *Annual Review of Sociology, 36*, 49–67.

Helmke, G., & Levitsky, S. (2004). Informal institutions and comparative politics: A research agenda. *Perspectives on Politics, 2*(4), 725–740.

Isaksen, A., Jakobsen, S. E., Njøs, R., & Normann, R. (2019). Regional industrial restructuring resulting from individual and system agency. *Innovation: The European journal of social science research, 32*(1), 48–65.

Isenberg, D. J. (2010). How to start an entrepreneurial revolution. *Harvard Business Review*, *88*(6), 40–50.

Klincewicz, K., Marczewska, M., & Tucci, C. L. (2021). Regional smart specializations in Central and Eastern Europe: Between political decisions and revealed technological potential. In *Partnerships for regional innovation and development* (pp. 21–48). London: Routledge.

Kroehn, M., Maude, A., & Beer, A. (2013). Leadership of place in the rural periphery: Lessons from Australia's agricultural margins. In *Leadership and Place* (pp. 141–154). London: Routledge.

Langley, A., Smallman, C., Tsoukas, H., & Van de Ven, A. H. (2013). Process studies of change in organization and management: Unveiling temporality, activity, and flow. *Academy of Management Journal*, *56*(1), 1–13.

Locke, K., Feldman, M., & Golden-Biddle, K. (2022). Coding practices and iterativity: Beyond templates for analyzing qualitative data. *Organizational Research Methods*, *25*(2), 262–284.

Loewen, B., & Schulz, S. (2019). Questioning the convergence of cohesion and innovation policies in Central and Eastern Europe. In *Regional and local development in times of polarisation* (pp. 121–148). Singapore: Palgrave Macmillan.

Lowe, N. J., & Feldman, M. P. (2017). Institutional life within an entrepreneurial region. *Geography Compass*, *11*(3), e12306.

Ma, M., & Hassink, R. (2014). Path dependence and tourism area development: The case of Guilin, China. *Tourism Geographies*, *16*(4), 580–597.

Mason, C., & Brown, R. (2014). Entrepreneurial ecosystems and growth oriented entrepreneurship. *Final Report to OECD, Paris*, *30*(1), 77–102.

MC (Muszyna Commune). (2012). *Strategia rozwoju Miasta i Gminy Uzdrowiskowej Muszyna na lata 2013–2020* (Development strategy for Muszyna Health Resort 2013–2020) https://bip.malopolska.pl/umigmuszyna,a,633216,uchwala-nr-xxx4152013-rady-miasta-i-gminy-uzdrowiskowej-muszyna-z-dnia-28-lutego-2013-r-w-sprawie-pr.html

MC (Muszyna Commune). (2020). *Strategia rozwoju Miasta i Gminy Uzdrowiskowej Muszyna na lata 2021–2027. (Development strategy for Muszyna Health Resort 2021–2027)* https://bip.malopolska.pl/umigmuszyna,m,123479,strategia.html

MC (Muszyna Commune). (2021). *Newsletter.* http://muszyna.pl/mfiles/1939/28/0/z/Biueltyn-Informacyjny-63-grudzien-2021.pdf.pdf

MC (Muszyna Commune). (2022a). *Newsletter.* http://muszyna.pl/pl/965/6182/biuletyn-informacyjny-65-sierpien-222.html

MC (Muszyna Commune). (2022b). *Non-governmental organizations.* http://muszyna.pl/pl/1301/0/organizacje-pozarzadowe.html

MC (Muszyna Commune). (2022c). *Consultations with residents.* http://muszyna.pl/pl/1857/0/miasto-i-gmina.html

Ministry of Finance. (2014). Regulation on the classification of incomes, spending, revenues, and expenditures, as well as international financing sources (Dz. U. z 2014 r. poz. 1053, poz. 1382).

MRDO/Małopolska Regional Development Observatory. (2015). *Specjalizacja lokalna w gminach i powiatach województwa małopolskiego* (Local specialization in the communes and counties of Małopolska). Kraków: MRGO.

MRGO/Małopolska Regional Government Office. (2005). *Program strategiczny „Regionalna Strategia Innowacji Wojewodztwa Malopolskiego 2005–2013* (Regional Innovation Strategy of the Małopolska Region 2005–2013). Kraków: MRGO.

MRGO/Małopolska Regional Government Office. (2007). *Małopolski Regionalny Program Operacyjny na lata 2007–2013* (Regional Operational Program for Malopolska 2007–2013), CCI:2007PL161PO010, Kraków: MRGO, update approved by MRGO in 2016.

MRGO/Małopolska Regional Government Office. (2014). *Regionalny Program Operacyjny Województwa Małopolskiego na lata 2014–2020* (Regional Operational Program for Malopolska 2014–2020, CCI:2014PL16M2OP006). Kraków: MRGO, update approved by MRGO in 2019.

MRGO/Małopolska Regional Government Office. (2015). *Inteligentne specjalizacje województwa małopolskiego. Uszczegółowienie obszarów wskazanych w Regionalnej Strategii Innowacji województwa małopolskiego 2014–2020* (Smart specializations of the Małopolska region. Details of the areas indicated in the Regional Innovation Strategy of the Małopolska Region 2014–2020). Kraków: MRGO.

Murmann, J. P. (2013). The coevolution of industries and important features of their environments. *Organization Science, 24*(1), 58–78.

OECD. (2019). *Local entrepreneurship ecosystems and emerging industries: Case study of Malopolskie, Poland.* OECD Local Economic and Employment Development (LEED) Working Papers, No. 2019/03, Paris: OECD Publishing.

O'Shea, G., Farny, S., & Hakala, H. (2021). The buzz before business: A design science study of a sustainable entrepreneurial ecosystem. *Small Business Economics, 56*(3), 1097–1120.

Ostrom, E. (1986). An agenda for the study of institutions. *Public Choice, 48*(1), 3–25.

Ostrom, E. (2010). Beyond markets and states: Polycentric governance of complex economic systems. *American Economic Review, 100*(3), 641–672.

Piekkari, R., & Welch, C. (2018). The case study in management research: Beyond the positivist legacy of Eisenhardt and Yin. *The SAGE Handbook of Qualitative Business and Management Research Methods,* 345–358.

Polish Journal of Laws. (1990). *The law of March 8, 1990 on the commune government (Dz.U.2021.1372).* https://isap.sejm.gov.pl/isap.nsf/DocDetails.xsp?id=WDU19900160095 Access: 05.07.2021

Polish Journal of Laws. (2003). *The law of April 24, 2003 on public benefits and volunteering (Dz.U.2020.1057).* https://isap.sejm.gov.pl/isap.nsf/DocDetails.xsp?id=WDU20030960873 Access: 05.07.2021

Pushkarskaya, H., Fortunato, M. W. P., Breazeale, N., & Just, D. R. (2021). Enhancing measures of ESE to incorporate aspects of place: Personal reputation and place-based social legitimacy. *Journal of Business Venturing, 36*(3), 106004.

Putnam, R. D. (1992). *Making democracy work: Civic traditions in modern Italy.* Princeton: Princeton University Press.

Reichel, M., Danielska, M., Serafin, P., & Witowska, J. (2021). *Ocena aktywności gmin Subregionu Sądeckiego za 2020 rok.* Nowy Sącz: Instytut Ekonomiczny Państwowej Wyższej Szkoły Zawodowej w Nowym Sączu, Fundacja Sądecka.

Reichel, M., Peter-Bombik, K. et al. (2016). *Ocena aktywności gmin Subregionu Sądeckiego w 2015 r.* Nowy Sącz: Instytut Ekonomiczny Państwowej Wyższej Szkoły Zawodowej w Nowym Sączu, Fundacja Sądecka.

Rogerson, C. M. (1995). Forgotten places, abandoned places. *The Migration Experience in Africa, 109.*

Shatkin, G. (2004). Planning to forget: Informal settlements as' forgotten places' in globalising Metro Manila. *Urban Studies, 41*(12), 2469–2484.

Silverman, D. (2015). *Interpreting qualitative data.* London: Sage.

Spigel, B. (2017). The relational organization of entrepreneurial ecosystems. *Entrepreneurship Theory and Practice, 41*(1), 49–72.

Spigel, B. (2022). Examining the cohesiveness and nestedness entrepreneurial ecosystems: Evidence from British FinTechs. *Small Business Economics,* 1–19.

Spigel, B., & Harrison, R. (2018). Toward a process theory of entrepreneurial ecosystems. *Strategic Entrepreneurship Journal, 12*(1), 151–168.

Stam, E. (2015). Entrepreneurial ecosystems and regional policy: A sympathetic critique. *European Planning Studies*, *23*(9), 1759–1769.

Stam, F. C., & Spigel, B. (2016). Entrepreneurial ecosystems. *USE Discussion Paper Series*, *16*(13). file:///C:/Users/MG/Downloads/16_13.pdf Access: 05.07.2021

Stam, E., & Van de Ven, A. (2021). Entrepreneurial ecosystem elements. *Small Business Economics*, *56*(2), 809–832.

Statistics Poland, Regional Statistics. (2021). https://stat.gov.pl/en/regional-statistics/publications-and-studies/aggregated-studies/. (Access: 14.11.2021).

Statistics Poland, Local Data Bank. (2022). https://bdl.stat.gov.pl/bdl/start

Ter Wal, A. L., & Boschma, R. (2011). Co-evolution of firms, industries and networks in space. *Regional Studies*, *45*(7), 919–933.

Thompson, J., Alvy, G., & Lees, A. (2000). Social entrepreneurship – A new look at the people and the potential. *Management Decision*, *38*(5), 328–338.

Thompson, T. A., Purdy, J. M., & Ventresca, M. J. (2018). How entrepreneurial ecosystems take form: Evidence from social impact initiatives in Seattle. *Strategic Entrepreneurship Journal*, *12*(1), 96–116.

Tiwari, P., Bhat, A. K., & Tikoria, J. (2022). Mediating role of prosocial motivation in predicting social entrepreneurial intentions. *Journal of Social Entrepreneurship*, *13*(1), 118–141.

Van de Ven, H. (1993). The development of an infrastructure for entrepreneurship. *Journal of Business Venturing*, *8*(3), 211–230.

Villegas-Mateos, A., & Vázquez-Maguirre, M. (2020). Social entrepreneurial ecosystems: A regional perspective of Mexico. *International Journal of Entrepreneurship*, *24*(1).

Williamson, O. E. (2000). The new institutional economics: Taking stock, looking ahead. *Journal of Economic Literature*, *38*(3), 595–613.

Wojnicka-Sycz, E. (2020). *Paradygmat systemowy w innowacyjności: Geneza, ewolucja i ocena*. Gdańsk: Wydawnictwo Uniwersytetu Gdańskiego.

Wright, A. L., Middleton, S., Hibbert, P., & Brazil, V. (2020). Getting on with field research using participant deconstruction. *Organizational Research Methods*, *23*(2), 275–295.

Wurth, B., Stam, E., & Spigel, B. (2021). Toward an entrepreneurial ecosystem research program. *Entrepreneurship Theory and Practice*, 1042258721998948.

Yeung, H. W. (2019). Rethinking mechanism and process in the geographical analysis of uneven development. *Dialogues in Human Geography*, *9*(3), 226–255.

Yin, R. K. (2018). *Case study research and applications*. London: Sage.

Zukauskaite, E., Trippl, M., & Plechero, M. (2017). Institutional thickness revisited. *Economic Geography*, *93*(4), 325–345.

7 The specificity determinants of monetary and fiscal policy in the V4 countries

Comparative economics perspective[1]

Joanna Stawska[2]

Introduction

The aim of the chapter is the comparison of monetary and fiscal policy in the countries of Visegrad Group (V4) in the context of economic shocks in 2000–2020. The four countries that were selected for the analysis are part of the so-called Visegrad Group, which was founded in 1991. The V4 is an association of four countries: Poland, the Czech Republic, Slovakia, and Hungary, and its aim is, among others, to deepen economic cooperation and European integration. All of these countries have belonged to the structures of the European Union since 2004, and Slovakia has been a member of the euro area since 2009. The agreement within the V4 group has been going on for over 30 years and it should be emphasized that during this period there were moments characterized by a greater or lesser degree of cooperation. However, it is worth paying attention to the dynamics of development of these countries and their economic policies, especially in the context of economic shocks, such as the global financial and economic crisis of 2008–2009, or the COVID-19 crisis.

The study focuses on basic economic indicators that will allow for the interpretation of how the economies of selected countries function in the face of contemporary economic threats in the context of decisions made by monetary and fiscal authorities. The greatest attention was paid to the following economic variables: the gross domestic product (GDP) dynamics, GDP per capita, General Government (GG) debt, GG deficit, unemployment rate, government spending, private consumption expenditure, short-term and long-term interest rates, inflation, investments, exports and imports, and foreign direct investment (FDI) inflow to these countries. Solutions for the conduct of monetary and fiscal policy in selected countries will be presented in the context of the cooperation of economic authorities in these countries and their impact on the economy. The considerations focus on the policies pursued by individual governments and central banks of selected V4 countries, because of threats to their economies caused, inter alia, by external factors, such as the global financial crisis (which began in Europe in 2008) and the so-called the coronavirus crisis or the COVID-19 crisis that appeared in the world with the coronavirus pandemic at the end of 2019. Based on the analysis, relevant conclusions will be made taking into account the context of the strategies of economic entities, which aim at overcoming economic crises and shocks.

DOI: 10.4324/9781003256281-10

This chapter also analyzes the impact of monetary and fiscal policy variables on the economy. Therefore, it is worth emphasizing in this context that the goal of the central bank's monetary policy is the inflation target, which is to maintain a stable level of prices, while the goal of the government's fiscal policy is to strive for the highest possible economic growth and low unemployment. Taking this into account, it seems that the goals of the economic authorities can counter each other. In the event that the central bank tries to reduce inflation, it can often also contribute to an increase in unemployment, which the government tries to fight. Then, higher government spending may generate an increase in the budget deficit, often causing an increase in global demand, which is an inflationary phenomenon. As a result of, for example, the global financial crisis or other external shocks (such as the COVID-19 crisis), it seemed that the fiscal and monetary authorities were cooperating to revive economic activity. The policy mix is a combination of monetary and fiscal policies which, according to many authors, has a significant impact on the economy (Buti & Sapir, 1998; Clarida et al., 2000; Bennett & Loayza, 2001; Jacquet & Pisani-Ferry, 2001; Hughes et al., 2001; Beetsma & Debrun, 2004; Onorante, 2006; Buti & Franco, 2005; Krus & Woroniecka-Leciejewicz, 2017; Stawska, 2019; Stawska & Mourao, 2021). In pursuing its goal, the central bank uses an appropriate monetary policy strategy with a varying degree of expansiveness/restrictiveness, measured with the interest rate. On the other hand, the government, while implementing its goal, uses strategies with a varying degree of expansiveness or restrictiveness, measured by the level of the budget deficit in relation to GDP. At this point, it should also be emphasized that the decisions of the central bank and the government regarding the restrictiveness or expansiveness of monetary and fiscal policy are influenced by numerous heterogeneous factors, including financial and economic crises or other external shocks.

Blinder (1983) as well as Bennett and Loayza (2001) considered the strategies of the central bank and the government in the context of the monetary and fiscal game consequently leading to the coordination of these policies. On the other hand, Libich et al. (2014) compares selected countries in the context of monetary and fiscal leadership. For example, Keynes (1936) preferred expansive fiscal policy, which involved a departure from the classical theory of public finance – identified with the classic principle of a sustainable budget. Keynesians assumed that an expansionary fiscal policy and the budget deficit often resulting from such a policy made it possible to counteract short-term declines in economic activity. Subsequently, these additional budgetary expenses, through multiplier effects, will contribute to employment and product growth (Keynes, 1936; Hicks, 1937). In summary, Nordhaus (1994) Corsetti et al. (2016), Hein & Truger (2014), and others were of the opinion that in situations of recessionary shocks it is the common monetary and fiscal policy that are necessary to stabilize the economy. Moreover, they believed that monetary policy could not achieve the goals of stabilization without the support of fiscal policy.

The structure of the chapter is as follows: fist section is "Introduction". "Background" presents the background of the establishment and operation of the V4 Group, its place in the region, its goals, tasks, and results. In "Dynamics of economic development and economic policy in Visegrad Group countries in the years 2000–2020", the development dynamics of the economies of the V4 countries over 21 years (2000–2020) is presented, with a special discussion of the most important economic variables during the period of economic shocks. This section focuses mainly on variables in the area of fiscal and monetary policy. "Decisions of monetary and fiscal authorities in the Visegrad countries in the context of economic shocks" presents decisions of monetary and fiscal authorities in the V4 countries in the context of economic shocks. "Comparative economics perspective" summarizes the activities of the V4 countries. The last section presents the conclusions.

Background

The V4 Group is often called the Central European Quartet. If the V4 Group were treated as one nation-state, it would be the 6th largest economy in Europe and the 12th largest economy in the world. The total population of the Czech Republic, Poland, Slovakia, and Hungary is 64 million, making it the 22nd in the world and the 3rd among the EU-27 countries. These former Eastern bloc countries joined the North Atlantic Treaty Organization (NATO) in 1999 (Slovakia in 2004), and then joined the EU structures in 2004. The purpose of establishing the V4 Group was regional cooperation, integration with Euro-Atlantic structures and the European Union, which was to be facilitated by similar historical experiences, geographical proximity, and the convergence of goals in foreign policy. The V4 Group is involved in cross-border cooperation projects. In 2000, the International Visegrad Fund was launched to support projects in the field of education, culture, and science. During the 30 years of the V4 Group's existence, its GDP increased by over 150%, and its share in the global economy grew to 1.4%. Over the past 30 years, the V4 countries have been able to narrow the income gap separating them from the countries of the old EU, even though they were still developing. In 2000, the GDP per capita (in current prices) of the V4 countries according to PPP (purchasing power parity) accounted for 45% of the average level for the EU-15 countries. In turn, in 2019, GDP per capita in the V4 countries was nearly 72% of the EU-15 level. The V4 Group has become Germany's most important trade partner in terms of exports and imports, accounting for 1.5 times the amount of trade between Germany and China. In the years between 1991 and 2019, the value of imports in the V4 countries increased by over 16 times and the value of exports by 19 times. In the years 1995–2019, investments in fixed assets in the V4 countries increased more than three times faster than in the EU-15 countries. The inflow of FDI was of significant importance in the process of economic transformation of the V4 countries. The accumulated value of FDI inflows in 1991–2019 increased 118 times from USD 4.8 billion to USD 564.8 billion, which proves the region's attractiveness for investments. The economies of the V4 Group are characterized by a relatively high share of industry in gross value added, exceeding the EU-27 average. About 4.1 million nonfinancial enterprises operate in the V4 countries, of which 95.3% are microenterprises (Ambroziak et al., 2020).

What remains related to the labor market are social inequalities, often measured by the Gini index. While analyzing the inequality index in the income of a given society in the V4 countries, it should be noted that Slovakia was the leader in the region, where the Gini index was 25.9% in 2010, and it was 20% in 2020. Also in the Czech Republic, the Gini index remained at a relatively low level, falling from 24.9% in 2010 to 24.2% in 2020. Compared to the EU average of 30%, the situation in Poland improved, as from 31% in 2010, the social inequality index fell to 27% in 2020. The situation in Hungary, on the other hand, deteriorated as the Gini index was 24% in 2010 and increased to 28% in 2020 (Eurostat, 2022). Another significant challenge for the V4 economies is technological development, which is associated with expenditure on research and development (R&D). The V4 countries, in terms of R&D spending, along with the economic transformation, made up for a significant distance from the EU average at the beginning of the 1990s. None of the V4 countries, despite significant progress, achieved the ratio of R&D expenditure to GDP in 2019 at the level of the EU average (2.2% of the GDP). The Czech Republic is the region's leader in terms of R&D spending because it reduced this gap from 0.7 percentage points (in 2000) to 0.26 percentage points in 2019.

The region of the V4 countries is perceived as attractive in terms of development opportunities, which is a motive for foreign investors to enter these markets. What is also important for investors is the financial stability of the economy as reflected in the credit ratings awarded by international rating agencies. Each country strives to achieve the highest possible rating, which indicates an almost zero risk of default on its public debt and thus also shows a low risk of investment in that country. A high rating is achieved due to healthy economies, stable financial systems, and a safe political climate (Lesław & Paga Foundation, 2016). When analyzing the current ratings of the largest rating agencies, the Czech Republic is the best with the following ratings: S&P (AA−); Moody's (Aa3); and Fitch (AA−). Then, the next is Slovakia with ratings: S&P (A +); Moody's (A2); and Fitch (A). Third place in the V4 Group goes to Poland with the following ratings: S&P (A−); Moody's (A2); and Fitch (A−). On the other hand, Hungary ranks worst in the V4 Group with ratings: S&P (BBB); Moody's (Baa2); and Fitch (BBB) (Countryeconomy.com, 2022).

Slovakia is the only country from the V4 Group in the euro area, which may result in lower profitability of government bonds, compared to the other three V4 countries that have their own currency. Theoretically, joining the euro area in accordance with the theory of the optimal currency area (Mundell, 1961) should, thanks to the elimination of transaction costs, exchange rate risk and better behavior of money in exchange, lead to a reduction in macroeconomic risk, deeper integration, expansion of foreign trade, and thus investment growth, factor productivity, and GDP growth. It should be noted, however, that the free exchange rate, and hence the depreciation of the local currency, was an important factor supporting the economies of the Czech Republic, Poland, and Hungary during the global crisis of 2008–2009. It is also emphasized that the argument in favor of membership in the euro area is the growing investment rate (mainly due to low interest rates in the Euroland), but it is worth noting that this lower interest rate has led, for example, countries such as Greece, Spain, Ireland, and Portugal to overinvestment causing an unstable economic boom.

The main driving force of the V4 Group was the dynamics of economic trans-formation and convergence with the West. This economic convergence of Central Europe is supported by EU funds, mainly under the cohesion policy. In total, in the years 2000–2019, the V4 countries received EUR 239 billion net from EU funds (including pre-accession funds). The economic development of the V4 countries turned out to be largely resistant to the financial crisis of 2008–2009 as well as to the conditions related to the current COVID-19 crisis. Significant strengths of the V4 Group are also social changes, mainly in the labor market, which has become friendly to employees who enter this market. However, the worrying demographic trends are a challenge for this market. For the V4 countries, changes in the area of politics and security as well as energy security are of crucial importance. The essence of the operation of the V4 Group is also the coordination of EU policy between the countries of the region (Ambroziak et al., 2020). Despite many political and sometimes economic differences, cooperation within the V4 Group is necessary and valuable in many areas, for example: environmental protection, transport, infrastruc-ture, energy and tourism. The V4 countries are expected to promote the Central European region as an area with a clear and distinct identity.

Dynamics of economic development and economic policy in Visegrad Group countries in the years 2000–2020

When looking at the economies of the V4 Group countries in 2000–2020, it is worth analyzing the evolution of the variables important for their development, such as: GDP growth, GDP per capita, GG deficit/surplus, GG debt, unemploy-ment rate, export and import, short-term interest rates, long-term interest rates, in-flation (HICP – Harmonised Index of Consumer Prices), Direct Foreign Investment (FDI), Investment (as gross fixed capital formation), GG expenditure, and final con-sumption expenditure of households. Selected economic variables have a significant impact on the economy of each country and enable to notice certain trends in their development, especially in the context of the impact on the economy of variables in the field of monetary and fiscal policy.

The dynamics of GDP in the V4 countries in 2000–2020 (Figure 7.1) followed a similar course.

Before the 2008–2009 financial crisis, GDP increases can be observed in each of the economies discussed. The highest growth before the global financial crisis was recorded in Slovakia (10.8% in 2007) and the lowest in Hungary (0.3% in 2007). It was mainly the increase in labor productivity that contributed to the significantly highest economic growth in Slovakia in the V4 group. In addition to labor produc-tivity, the significant increase in the employment rate and the decline in unemploy-ment in Slovakia should also be mentioned. The changes in the age structure of the population were also significant for higher economic growth in Slovakia, which results from the increase in the share of working age population (15–64 years) from 69% (in 2000) to 72% (in 2008) (Bîea, 2015). During the crisis, in 2009, the larg-est declines in GDP were recorded in Hungary (−6.6%), Slovakia (−5.5%) and the Czech Republic (−4.7%). Poland is the only country in the V4 and one of the few

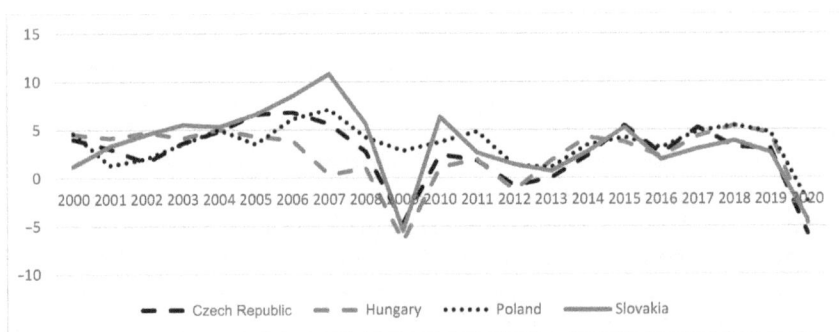

Figure 7.1 Gross domestic product (GDP) at market prices – percentage change on previous period in V4 Group in years 2000–2020

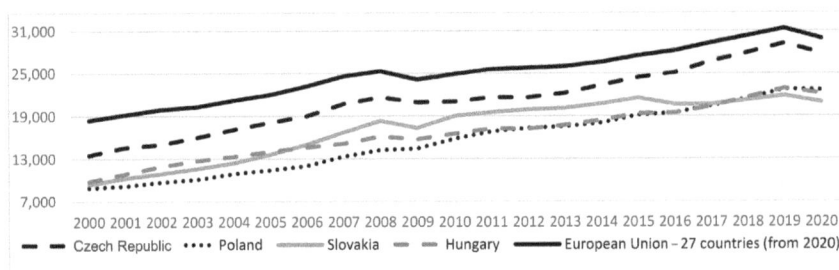

Figure 7.2 Purchasing power adjusted GDP per capita (in PPS EU27_2020) in V4 Group and average in EU in years 2000–2020

in Europe that recorded even a slight increase (2.8%). According to Drozdowicz-Bieć (2011), there were several factors that saved Poland from negative economic growth during the 2008–2009 financial crisis. These include, for example, a dynamic increase in the competitiveness of the Polish economy and increasing labor productivity, the inflow of EU funds, FDI as well as the flexible exchange rate of the Polish currency. Increased competitiveness and, most importantly, labor productivity contributed to the increase in wages, which in the era of rising raw material prices allowed stabilizing consumption during the economic slowdown. Further drops in GDP occurred in 2012 in Hungary (−1.3%) and the Czech Republic (−0.8%). It may seem that since 2014, the V4 economies have returned to the path of moderate GDP growth, but the situation changed in 2020 when, in the face of the COVID-19 pandemic, all V4 countries recorded declines, with the Czech Republic the highest (−5.8%) and Hungary (−4.7%).

In the case of GDP per capita in the V4 countries, in the years 2000–2020 (Figure 7.2) the situation is slightly different compared to the GDP dynamics in the analyzed countries. This variable was also presented in relation to the average GDP per capita in the EU.

First of all, it should be noted that in the V4 countries, GDP per capita grew according to the PPP, but was below the EU average. The Czech Republic was the closest to this average in the analyzed period, in 2020, it was almost 93%, while the indicator for Poland was 75.6%, for Hungary it was 74%, and the lowest value was in Slovakia, it was almost 70% of the EU average. It should be emphasized that 2020 is the time of the COVID-19 pandemic, and GDP per capita, compared to 2019, fell in all V4 countries (with a simultaneous decrease in the EU average). It is worth noting that at the beginning of the analyzed period, that is, in 2000, the highest GDP per capita in the V4 countries was unchanged in the Czech Republic (73.4% of the EU average), and the lowest in Poland (only 48.4% of the EU average). Some researchers indicate that those V4 countries that focused their policies on increasing innovation and competitiveness of their economies, using appropriately financial resources, including EU subsidies, are able to improve their market position and achieve better economic results (Kowalska et al., 2018).

Another important variable is GG deficit/surplus as percentage of GDP, which largely depends on the decisions of the fiscal authorities in a given country.

At the beginning of the analyzed period, in 2000, the highest deficit was recorded in Slovakia (−12.6% of the GDP) and the lowest in Hungary (−3.0% of the GDP), with the EU average (−1.2% of the GDP). Several factors contributed to such a high GG deficit in Slovakia. The main reasons include significant reductions in personal and corporate income tax rates, costs of bank restructuring, and honoring loan guarantees. Moreover, the phasing-out of the import subsidy was not matched by a comparable decrease in public expenditure (OECD Economic Survey, 2002). During the economic slowdown in 2001–2002, these deficits in all V4 countries remained high (above the Maastricht limit, i.e. 3% of the GDP). In the period of economic recovery, the lowest deficits in the V4 were recorded in the Czech Republic in 2004–2008 below 3% of the GDP, and in Slovakia in 2004–2005 and 2007–2008 (also below 3% of the GDP). As a result of the global financial crisis, budget deficits increased significantly above 3% of the GDP and the EU average in 2009–2010 amounted to 6% of the GDP, which was the result of the launch of fiscal packages saving European economies from the effects of the financial crisis. Starting from 2015, deficits in all V4 economies did not exceed the Maastricht criterion, and even in the years 2016–2019, a budget surplus was recorded in the Czech Republic. The situation changed in 2020, when the V4 countries re-triggered significant fiscal packages to mitigate the effects of the COVID-19 pandemic. In 2020, Hungary recorded a deficit of 8% of the GDP, Poland 7.1%, and the Czech Republic and Slovakia 5.6% and 5.5%, respectively (Figure 7.3).

The average GG debt in the EU countries in 2000 amounted to 66.3% of the GDP and in 2020 as much as 90.1% of the GDP (Figure 7.4).

This debt in the EU countries has significantly increased as a result of anti-crisis measures taken by the governments of European countries to mitigate the effects of the global financial crisis of 2008–2009. Then, during the debt crisis, GG debt remained elevated, but increased again during the COVID-19 pandemic. In the V4 Group countries, over the 21 years under study, the Czech Republic reported the lowest GG debt. Despite the implementation of additional fiscal packages as part of

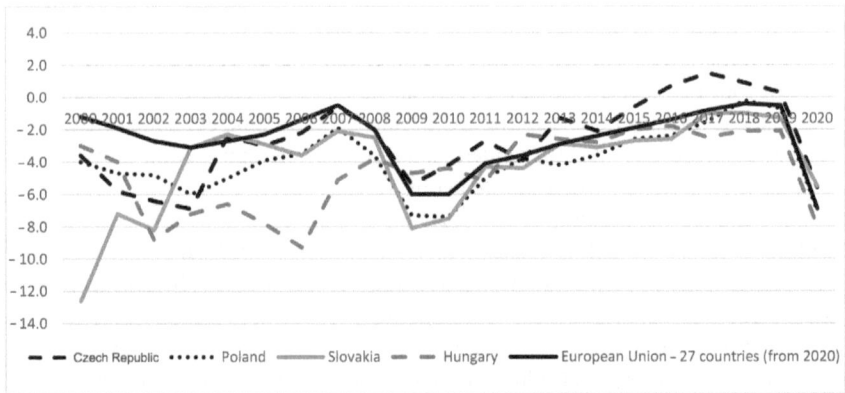

Figure 7.3 Government deficit/surplus – General Government deficit/surplus as % of GDP in V4 Group and average in EU in years 2000–2020

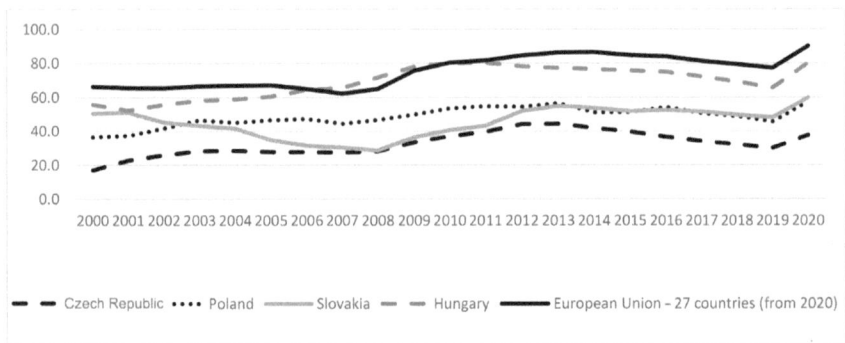

Figure 7.4 Government consolidated gross debt – General Government debt as % of GDP in V4 Group and average in EU in years 2000–2020

anti-crisis measures, both during the financial crisis and the COVID-19 pandemic, public debt in the Czech Republic remained the lowest in the V4 Group. In turn, the highest GG public debt was recorded in Hungary, and since 2005, it has exceeded the Maastricht public debt limit, which is 60%, every year. In 2010–2011 and in 2020, GG debt in Hungary amounted to over 80% of the GDP. In the analyzed period of 2000–2020, public debt in Poland and Slovakia did not exceed 60% of the GDP (Figure 7.5).

Public expenditure is an instrument of the state's fiscal influence on the expenditure side. Among budgetary expenses, there are expenses for education, health care, army, uniformed services, financing of pensions and disability pensions, social programs, costs of servicing public debt, and investments in infrastructure and public buildings. It is worth looking at the share of general government expenditure in the GDP of the V4 countries compared to the EU average.

Figure 7.5 General government expenditure – total general government expenditure - % of GDP in V4 Group and average in EU in years 2000–2019

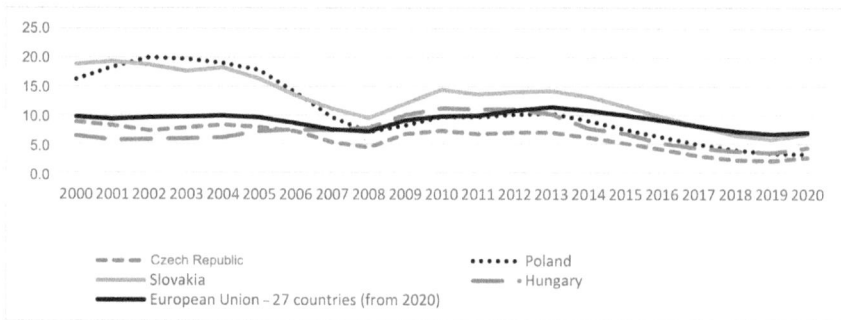

Figure 7.6 Unemployment as percentage of population in the labor force (from 15 to 74 years) in V4 Group and average in EU in years 2000–2020

In 2000, Slovakia recorded general government expenditure at the level of 52.8% of the GDP. It was the highest result in the V4 Group and definitely outnumbered the EU average. Since 2001, GG expenditure in Slovakia has decreased and in the years 2003–2013, it was the lowest in the region. In turn, Hungary recorded the highest share of GG expenditure in the V4 countries in 2001–2019. Public expenditure in Hungary in 2000–2009 and 2013–2015 even exceeded the EU average (Figure 7.6).

The pillar of economic development of each country is certainly a high level of employment or the lowest level of unemployment. The average unemployment in the EU countries in 2000 was 9.7%. In the years 2012–2015, it oscillated in the range of 10.0%–11.4%, dropping to 6.7% in 2019.

In the V4 countries, the relatively lowest unemployment in 2000–2020 was in the Czech Republic. Unemployment in the Czech Republic in the analyzed period never exceeded the average unemployment in the EU. In Hungary, the situation on the labor market deteriorated significantly in 2009–2013 as a result of the financial crisis and the debt crisis. In Poland, in the years 2002–2004, unemployment oscillated between 19% and 20%, then began to gradually decrease, reaching 3.2% in 2020. In the period 2000–2020, the highest unemployment was most often recorded in Slovakia, of which the highest unemployment (19.3%) was in 2001 (Figure 7.6). The highest unemployment level in Slovakia in the V4 group and the lowest unemployment level in the Czech Republic during the discussed period were due to several factors. They include the following: in Slovakia, compared to the Czech Republic, there was a greater share of the agricultural sector in the economy, the presence of a larger population in less integrated social groups and high regional economic concentration which fosters job segmentation and, moreover, facilitates job creation in the Czech Republic through government incentives (Havlat et al., 2018).

During the transformation, the economies of the V4 Group were increasingly opening up to the world economies. Analyzing the data on exports of goods and services expressed as a percentage of GDP, Slovakia and Hungary were by far the leaders among the V4 countries in the years 2000–2020.

In fact, since 2012, exports of the Slovak economy have exceeded 90% of the GDP, falling only to 85.4% of the GDP in 2020, which was the result of the COVID-19 crisis. Despite the fact that Slovakia joined the euro area in 2009 exactly during the financial crisis and this may have contributed to a certain weakening of exports, the share of exports in the Slovak economy grew significantly in the following years. The Slovak economy is on the way of changes in the sectoral structure, that is, the transition from an agrarian-predominant society to an export-oriented economy, as well as the shift of export orientation from the markets of the former Soviet bloc to developed Western economies. The most important export category in Slovakia are cars, car parts and video displays (Fidrmuc et al., 2019). It should also be emphasized that exports in Hungary and the Czech Republic over the 21 analyzed years significantly exceeded the average share of exports, expressed as percentage of GDP in the EU countries. In Poland, in the years 2000–2012, exports of goods and services expressed as percentage of GDP were below the average exports in the EU countries, and only from 2013, the Polish economy entered a trend exceeding the average EU share of exports in GDP. Comparing the results of the V4 countries, Poland records the lowest share of exports in GDP (Figure 7.7).

Figure 7.8 presents the import of goods and services as percentage of GDP in the Visegrad countries compared to the average import in the EU countries in the years 2000–2020.

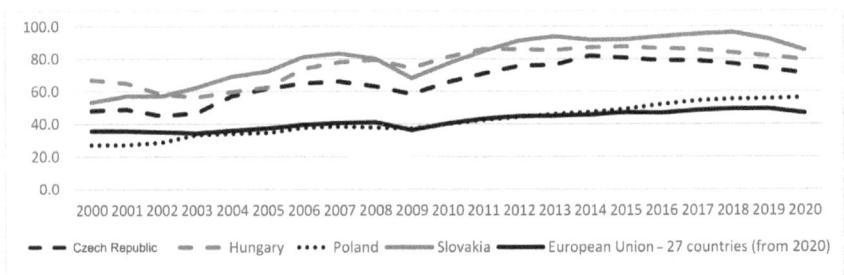

Figure 7.7 Exports of goods and services as % of GDP in V4 Group and average in EU in years 2000–2020

Figure 7.8 Imports of goods and services as % of GDP in V4 Group and average in EU in years 2000–2020

It is worth noting that during the discussed period, imports in all V4 countries exceeded the average EU import as a percentage of GDP. Slovakia is definitely the best in this area (imports over 90% of the GDP in 2016–2019) and Hungary (around 80% of the GDP in 2011–2019). High level of import, in Slovakia results from the import intensity of exports. Import grows, for example, along with the expected increase in car production (NBS, 2016). The share of imports in the Czech economy (in 2012–2018, imports above 70% of the GDP) was lower than in Slovakia and Hungary, but higher than in Poland (in 2016–2020, imports were around 50% of the GDP). Imports in Poland are slightly higher than the EU average of imports as a percentage of GDP in the EU countries. Slight drops in imports are noticeable in all countries of the V4 Group and the EU during the global financial crisis and in the first year of the COVID-19 pandemic. It is worth adding that the V4 countries are dependent on the import of energy resources.

Short-term interest rates in the interbank market depend on the basic interest rates of central banks. The three-month interest rates are most often the basis for the interest rate on bank loans and fluctuate close to the basic interest rate of the central bank. In the years 2000–2020, the level of short-term interest rates showed a downward trend in the V4 countries.

In the years 2000–2001, the highest short-term interest rates were recorded in Poland, 18.9% and 15.7%, respectively. At the beginning of the period under review, the National Bank of Poland decided to implement a restrictive monetary policy in connection with the persistent risk of depreciation of the zloty and the danger of an increase in inflation (NBP, 2002). In the period 2002–2013, the highest short-term interest rates were in Hungary. When the V4 countries joined the EU, the short-term interest rate in Hungary was 11.53%, while in the Czech Republic it was 2.4%. In 2009, Hungary also recorded the highest short-term interbank rate (9.14%), which only reached the lowest level in 2018 (0.12%). Thus, despite the relatively low GDP growth in Hungary and rising unemployment, the National Bank of Hungary did not use the interest rate tool intensively to improve the economic situation, as the nominal interest rates in 2002–2013 were relatively high compared to the analyzed countries

(Grabia, 2015) which was influenced, inter alia, by higher inflation relative to the V4 economies (in most of the analyzed period). The Czech Republic and Slovakia were actually characterized by the lowest short-term interest rates throughout the entire analyzed period. After Slovakia joined the euro area in 2009, short-term interest rates on the Slovak interbank market remained the lowest in the region. For comparison, in Slovakia, from 2016, the three-month short-term interest rate was below zero (Figure 7.9).

Figure 7.10 presents long-term interest rates as government bonds maturing in ten years, in the V4 countries and in the euro area in 2000–2020.

At the beginning of the analyzed period, the highest long-term interest rates in the V4 Group were in Poland, then from 2003 to 2016, Hungary showed the highest levels of these rates. Then, in 2017–2018, Poland took the lead in the V4 Group in terms of long-term interest rates. On average, the highest long-term interest rates during the period under review were recorded in Hungary and the lowest in the Czech Republic. During the 21 years under study, the level of long-term interest rates showed a downward trend. It is worth noting, however, that during the

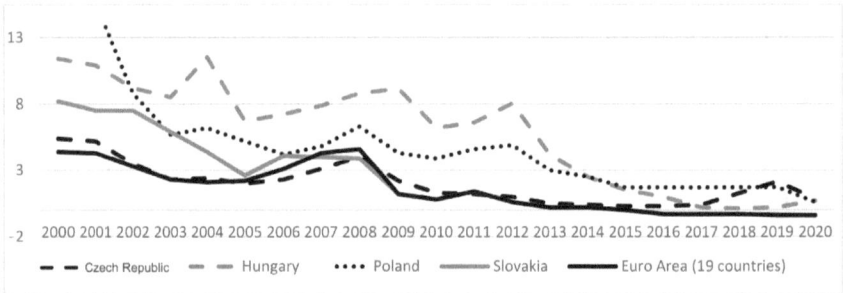

Figure 7.9 Short term interest rates - three-month interbank interest rates in V4 Group and average in Euro Area in years 2000–2020

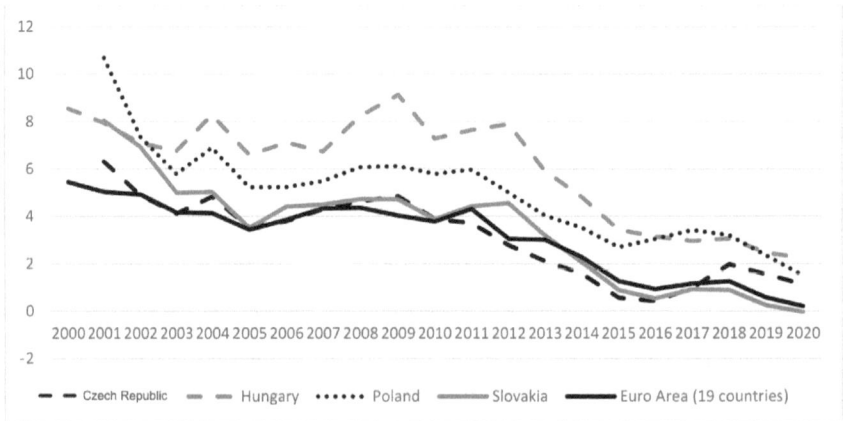

Figure 7.10 Long - term interest rates (government bonds maturing in ten years) in V4 Group and average in Euro Area in years 2000–2020

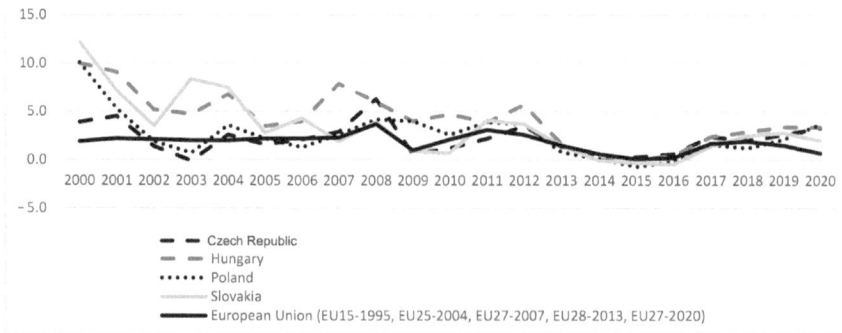

Figure 7.11 HICP - (annual average rate of change) in V4 Group and average in EU in years 2000–2020

2008–2009 financial crisis, the profitability of ten-year government bonds increased in all countries of the V4 Group.

When analyzing the level of inflation in the V4 countries and the average inflation in the EU countries during 2000–2020, it should be noted that in 2000, high inflation rate of 12.2% was recorded in Slovakia and 10% in Poland and Hungary.

On the other hand, in the Czech Republic, inflation in 2000 was 3.9%, and it was the lowest result in the V4 Group, while the average inflation in the EU was 1.9% at that time. Relatively in the discussed period, the highest inflation was recorded in Hungary. In the analyzed period, inflation in the Czech Republic was closest to the average inflation in the EU (except for 2008, when inflation in the Czech Republic increased to 6.3% and the EU average was 3.7% then). Slovakia in 2014–2016 was affected by deflation, as was Poland in 2015–2016 (Figure 7.11).

Hungary, where the FDI inflow in 2000–2006 does not differ much from the data from other members of the V4 Group, draws particular attention. It is already in the years 2007–2008 that a significant increase in FDI in Hungary can be noticed, that is, 49.5% and 47.6% of the GDP, respectively, which is an impressive result compared to the other V4 countries. In 2009–2010, a significant decline in FDI was recorded, which still took place in 2013, 2015 and 2018. In 2016 and 2019–2020, Hungary again stood out from the V4 Group with an impressive inflow of FDI. Hungary has largely attracted greenfield investments, which has contributed to the modernization of the economy by channeling new technologies and capital toward the Hungarian economy. It also had a positive effect on job creation. Hungary also shifted FDI from low-value textile and food processing sectors to wholesale, retail and vehicle repair (Xin, 2019).

Investments are essential to any economy as they fuel economic development. Investments contribute to production growth, increasing the competitiveness of the economy and exports, and the creation of new jobs. In the countries of the V4 Group in 2000–2020, the Czech Republic was definitely the leader in terms of the investment rate.

The ratio of gross fixed capital formation to GDP in the Czech Republic from 2000 (31.19% of the GDP) to 2020 (26.25%) was the highest not only in the region but also exceeded the average investment in the EU countries in each of the analyzed years. Similarly, the investment rate in Slovakia was often above the EU average during the period considered. In the Czech Republic and Slovakia, fixed investment was the second most important driver of economic growth behind TFP (Total-Factor Productivity – measured as the ratio of aggregate production to aggregate inputs). Additionally, the inflow of FDI required high investment productivity, which enabled the rapid transfer of technology and skills in the manufacturing sector. Moreover, the EU structural funds contributed to an increase in the level of investment, including, to a large extent, investment in infrastructure (Havlat et al., 2018). In Poland, the investment rate in 2000–2020 was the lowest among the V4 countries and was lower than the average investment rate in the EU countries (Figure 7.13).

Consumption is an indicator of the level, quality and lifestyle of a society. The level and dynamics of consumption are influenced by many factors that depend on

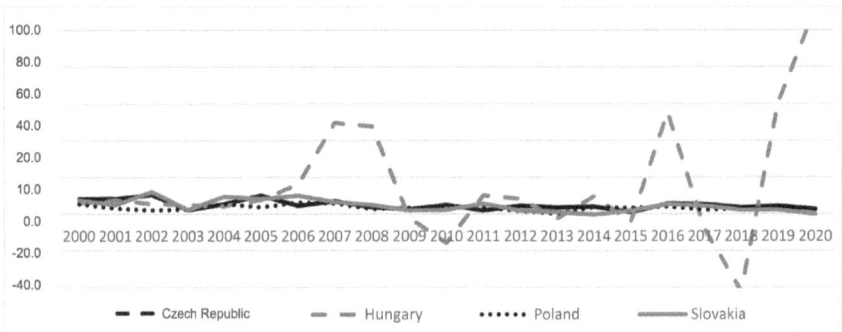

Figure 7.12 FDI – Foreign direct investment in the reporting economy (flows) - annual data, % of GDP in V4 Group in years 2000–2020

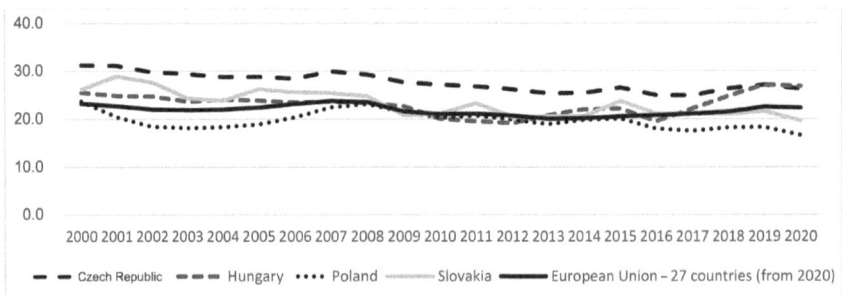

Figure 7.13 Investment share of GDP by institutional sectors (gross fixed capital formation) as % of GDP in V4 Group and average in EU in years 2000–2020

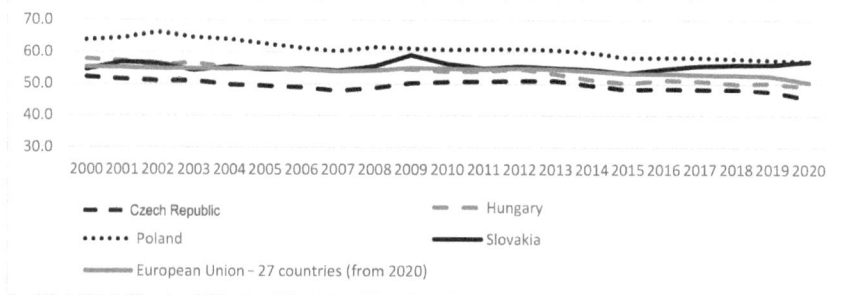

Figure 7.14 Final consumption expenditure of households as % of GDP in V4 Group and average in EU in years 2000–2020

the consumer and on the variables that make up the economic situation. It is also worth mentioning that the level, structure and dynamics of household consumption are largely influenced by macro- and microeconomic conditions, as well as the delayed impact of socioeconomic conditions from previous years (e.g., with economic crises).

In the years 2000–2020 (Figure 7.14), in the countries of the V4 Group, the Czech Republic had the lowest consumption expenditure of households, and Poland had the highest expenditure (definitely above the EU average).

Decisions of monetary and fiscal authorities in the Visegrad countries in the context of economic shocks

It is worth analyzing the anti-crisis measures taken by the economic authorities, mainly as part of fiscal and monetary policy, in response to emerging economic shocks. This is important in the context of observing how the authorities responsible for economic policy are able to counteract the effects of financial and economic crises. This will make it possible to see how the authorities in the V4 countries responded to emergency situations, which instruments were used and what decisions were made. These crises highlight the need for a better understanding of the interactions of fiscal and monetary policy. In response to the global financial crisis, the sovereign debt crisis and the COVID-19 crisis, policymakers have reacted decisively by using monetary and fiscal measures to counter the macroeconomic effects of the economic and financial crisis. Central banks lowered interest rates and, in many cases, applied unconventional monetary policies, as governments chose to run high budget deficits with falling incomes and higher spending to save the financial sector and stimulate demand in the economy.

Policy mix in Visegrad countries during the global financial crisis

Czech Republic

The Czech Republic is a country in Central Europe with 10.6 million citizens. The Czech Republic is a country that underwent an economic transformation from a

socialist economy to a market economy, which started after the collapse of the communist system in Central Europe. According to the World Bank ranking, the Czech
Republic was in the 36th position of countries in the world in terms of per capita
income in 2020 (theglobaleconomy.com, 2022).

The global financial crisis that started in Europe in 2008, and the sovereign debt
crisis in 2011–2013, followed by the COVID-19 crisis that started in 2020, have all
been an economic shock to most of the world's economies. In 2008, when the first
symptoms of the financial crisis appeared in Europe, the Czech economy also felt
the effects of these market turbulences. Initial concerns were directed to the possible
threat to Western European parent companies from banks in the Czech Republic
and other Central and Eastern European countries during the financial crisis. In the
case of the Czech Republic, however, these concerns were not fully justified because
banks in the Czech Republic are mostly subsidiaries of foreign parent companies
and their possible problems would not have such consequences for the parent companies. In the Czech economy, unlike, for example, the Hungarian economy, there
was no significant deterioration in the financial situation of bank debtors who took
out foreign currency loans. This was due to the limitation of such loans in the Czech
Republic, and therefore, changes in exchange rates did not affect foreign currency
loans in the Czech economy to such an extent. The effects of the global financial
crisis, that is, the crisis-induced recession, turned out to be more severe. The insol-
vency of companies and households increased, and thus the amount of unpaid loans
in total loans was estimated at 3.3% in 2008 (an increase by 0.6 percentage point
compared to 2007) (Hampl, 2009). The economic recession in 2008–2010 affected
the Czech economy mainly by lower industrial and construction production, limited investment in fixed assets and reduced exports and imports. At that time, the
budget deficit increased, the unemployment rate increased, the level of economic
activity decreased and the public debt increased significantly above the long-term
level of approximately 30%, which was recorded in 2003–2008 (Hronova & Hindls,
2012), i.e. starting from 2009, public debt gradually exceeded the level of approximately 30% of GDP.

In summer 2008, the Czech National Bank (CNB) decided to lower interest
rates. The two-week repo rate was lowered to a record low of 0.75% in May 2010.
Unlike many central banks that chose to use unconventional monetary policy tools,
the CNB was able to rely heavily on standard monetary policy instruments. It should
be added that the floating exchange rate regime proved to be an effective adjust-
ment mechanism, which manifested itself through the significant depreciation of the
Koruna exchange rate at the end of 2008 and helped the CNB in terms of quantitative easing. In the area of fiscal policy, in 2009 the Czech government approved an
anti-crisis package of fiscal measures intended to mitigate the impact of the crisis on
households and businesses. Prior to the global financial crisis, structural deficits in
the Czech Republic were relatively high as a result of the expansionary fiscal policy
pursued during the boom period between 2003 and 2007 (Tomšík, 2012). Explaining, a structural, cyclically adjusted balance (CAB) is defined as the excess of public
spending over revenues or vice versa that would persist if the economy were near its
potential. According to the recommendation of the Council under Article 104(7)

the medium-term objective for the budgetary position, was defined as a structural deficit of 1% of the GDP for the Czech Republic (*Recommendation for a Council Recommendation to the Czech Republic*, 2007). For example, in the Czech Republic, the CAB was −3.2% of the GDP in 2006, then it was −1.7% in 2007 and −2.8% in 2008. The structural balance in 2006 was −3% of the GDP, in 2007 it was −1.3% of the GDP and in 2008 it was −2.7% of the GDP (Ministry of Finance of the Czech Republic, 2007, 2008, 2010). Tomšík (2012) notes that before the global financial crisis, the Czech fiscal policy tended to be pro-cyclical, especially in the years of the economic boom – when additional revenues were spent. Two stimulus packages were adopted in the Czech Republic in response to the financial crisis. The first package in 2009 focused mainly on reducing employee social security contributions and additional expenditure on infrastructure investments. The second package adopted in February 2009 included income and expenditure measures aimed at supporting small- and medium-sized enterprises (SMEs), including tax reductions, grants, subsidies and others [Public Finances in EMU, 2009]. After the financial crisis, automatic stabilizers were activated in the Czech economy and the cyclical position of the Czech economy deteriorated significantly. After the introduction of the fiscal packages, the public deficit even deepened. However, it should be added that the financial and economic crisis hit the Czech economy mainly through the foreign demand channel, worsening export statistics and the results of the manufacturing sector. Nevertheless, the impact of the financial crisis was not as severe due to the resilience of the Czech banking sector to toxic foreign assets (Tomšík, 2012). In 2009, as a result of an increase in the GG deficit and exceeding the Maastricht deficit limit, the excessive deficit procedure was imposed on the Czech Republic and lifted in 2014. In 2011–2013, the Czech government decided to pursue a rather restrictive fiscal policy (Stawska, 2018).

It is also worth referring to the relationship between fiscal policy and monetary policy, which is manifested, for example, by the influence of fiscal policy on long-term interest rates. Dumičič and Ridzak (2011) noted that in the eight analyzed Central and Eastern European countries (including the Czech economy), if the ratio of GG debt to GDP increased by five percentage points, spreads would increase by 19 basis points. Wider spreads mean higher yields on government bonds and commercial interest rates. It was noted that during the financial crisis the relationship between the interest rate on mortgage loans and the yield on government bonds strengthened (Dumičič & Ridzak, 2011).

Hungary

Hungary is a country in Central Europe with a population of 9.7 million. Hungary is an emerging market with a free market economy that transformed from a centrally planned to a free market economy in the 1990s. According to the World Bank ranking in 2020, Hungary was the 44th in the world in terms of GDP per capita, purchasing power parity (Theglobaleconomy.Com, 2022).

The global financial crisis led to the first financial turmoil in Hungary as early as in autumn 2008. Support turned out to be necessary in the form of rescue packages from the International Monetary Fund (IMF) and the EU. The growing financial difficulties in the global markets resulted in a decrease in liquidity and an increase in risk aversion, which certainly influenced the valuation of Hungarian assets as very risky. The growing risk in the euro area has also increased the risk in Hungary due to Hungary's high external debt, high current account deficit and high demand for external financing. In addition, it should be emphasized that while Hungarian banks were not directly exposed to the subprime crisis, Hungary was sensitive to changes in the international capital markets because a significant part of financing depends on flows to Hungarian daughter banks from Western European parent banks. Another source of risk was the credit standing of the household and corporate sector, which took out a significant part of loans denominated in foreign currencies, which, in the event of turmoil in financial markets, led to an increase in net foreign currency liabilities in the Hungarian banking system. Even before the crisis, and more precisely in 2007, Hungary's performance in all basic macroeconomic statistics was weaker (the economic growth was lower and inflation and the current account were worse) than in other countries from the V4 Group (Horvath, 2009). In Hungary, it was decided in 2010 that Private Pension Act LXXXII of 1997 on Private Pensions and Private Pension Funds Funded was mandatory until November 3, 2010. This meant the nationalization of private pensions fund, which could, inter alia, improve some economic indicators (Maśniak & Lados, 2014).

On October 10, 2008, the National Bank of Hungary (MNB) and the European Central Bank (ECB) jointly announced an agreement to support MNB's euro liquidity instruments and new open market operations to support liquidity in the domestic FX swap market. A repurchase agreement was signed between the MNB and the ECB for EUR 5 billion. However, on October 20, 2008, it was announced that the EUR 5 billion bailout would not be launched immediately as the banking sector was not on the verge of bankruptcy. However, it was decided to help people who borrowed in foreign currency. In addition, MNB and major dealers of government securities committed to constantly fix the buying and selling prices, which was to reduce the volatility of profitability and to improve market transparency. In October 2008, the central bank raised its key interest rate by 300 basis points to 11.5% to support the forint, which fell significantly against the euro. A significant problem of the Hungarian economy was the fact that the public debt was largely owned by foreign investors. As the crisis unfolded, there was no demand for Hungarian government bonds. Despite the efforts of the MNB to promote currency liquidity and the government bond market, the organized new auctions were unsuccessful. As part of a rescue program, the IMF approved a loan of USD 15.7 billion to the Hungarian economy to ease tensions in the financial markets. The EU added USD 8.4 billion and the World Bank added USD 1.3 billion. The government undertook anti-crisis measures as part of the stabilization program, trying to carry out fiscal consolidation through cuts in the wage and pensions fund (Dapontas, 2011). It is worth noting that in 2004 the excessive deficit procedure was imposed on Hungary and, actually from 2005 to at least 2013, when the excessive deficit procedure was lifted, the Hungarian government pursued a rather restrictive fiscal policy (Stawska, 2018). In the banking sector, on the other hand, assistance comprised the recapitalization of eligible banks and the strengthening of supervisory and crisis management capacities. Research by Dapotas suggests that the Hungarian currency crisis had more to do with the structural inefficiency of the domestic economy following the shift from centrally planned to emerging market economy (Dapontas, 2011).

Poland

Poland is a country in Central Europe, inhabited by over 38 million people. In the 1990s, also in Poland, there was a transformation from a centrally directed economy to a market economy. According to the World Bank ranking in 2020, in terms of GDP per capita (purchasing power parity), Poland was ranked the 42nd in the world (Theglobaleconomy.Com, 2022).

The global financial crisis in Europe is considered to have started in September 2008 with the announcement of the collapse of the Lehman Brothers American bank (which had existed for over 150 years). The effects of the financial crisis also affected the Polish economy. In order to minimize the effects of the global financial crisis on the Polish economy, two comprehensive packages of measures were announced in October 2008 to restore confidence and proper functioning of the financial market. These packages were developed by the Ministry of Finance and the National Bank of Poland (NBP). The first regulatory package announced by the government concerned the Act on the Financial Stability Committee and consisted in strengthening cooperation among safety net institutions in Poland. In addition, it was decided to increase the level of deposit protection from EUR 22,500 to EUR 50,000 as part of the Bank Guarantee Fund operation and a full deposit guarantee was provided (previously only deposits up to EUR 1,000 were subject to 100% coverage). The NBP developed the second package, the so-called Confidence Package, which was based mainly on enabling banks to obtain funds in PLN for periods longer than one day, obtain funds in foreign currencies and obtain liquidity in PLN by banks as a result of extending the security of operations with the central bank. Moreover, the activities of the NBP included measures such as early redemption of NBP bonds (PLN 8.2 billion) in January 2009; reduction of the required reserve rate from 3.5% to 3%; introduction of the Package for the Development of Credit Action and the introduction of a bill of exchange loan. This package is a continuation of the "Confidence Package", which was aimed at supporting liquidity in the Polish banking system and thus counteracting the tendency of banks to reduce lending activity (Polański, 2017). During the global recession in 2007–2009, the Polish banking sector was in good shape. Banks' profits in 2008 were among the best in the last 20 years, and in 2009 they decreased by only 30% compared to the previous year. The Polish banking sector has not suffered from poor liquidity. Banks' own assets grew steadily and were invested in financial instruments other than loans, mainly in government securities. It is worth adding that the Polish banking sector was not involved in risky subprime securities (Maria Drozdowicz-Bieć, 2011). It should be noted that in 2009, in Poland, as a result of the amendment to the act on personal income tax made by the act of November 16, 2006, amending the act on personal income tax and some other acts [Act of November 16, 2006] in 2009, advance payments for income tax, including employment contracts will be charged at different rates than in 2008. Instead of the rates of 19%, 30% and 40%, two rates will apply, that is, 18% and 32%. The changes therefore consist essentially in lowering the lowest rate and liquidating the highest rate, which could have contributed to an increase in consumption and thus to support the GDP growth.

Due to the fact that the deficit limit according to the Maastricht criterion was exceeded, the excessive deficit procedure was imposed on Poland in 2009. Therefore, fiscal authorities in Poland decided to pursue a rather restrictive fiscal policy in 2011–2016. The excessive deficit procedure was abolished in 2015 (Ministry of Finance of Poland, 2016). As a result of the growing deficit and public debt, one of the government's decisions was to increase all value-added tax (VAT) rates by one percentage point, starting from January 2011. Taking into account the share of household expenditure on individual food groups, it was expected that the reduction in food prices subject to the change in the VAT rate from 7% to 5% will compensate for the price increases in the group subject to the VAT rate increase from 3% to 5% and from 22% to 23% (Polish Investment & Trade Agency, PFR Group, 2011).

Slovakia

Slovakia is a country located in Central Europe with a population of nearly 5.5 million. It is also a country that underwent an economic transformation in the 1990s. According to the World Bank ranking in 2020, Slovakia was ranked the 46th in the world in terms of GDP per capita, purchasing power parity (theglobaleconomy. com, 2022).

The small, open and export-oriented Slovak economy influenced by foreign markets has been hit by the 2008–2009 global financial crises. Slovakia's largest trading partners remained in deep recession as a result of the crisis, which also caused the Slovak economy to slow down. The financial problems of many European banks and the growing distrust in the markets resulted in a decline in demand and consumption in Slovakia as well. It is worth adding, however, that banks in Slovakia were not affected by the mortgage crisis and the government did not have to intervene to calm the situation and increase confidence in banks. The effects of the global economic depression spread to the real economy of Slovakia through the credit crisis, and in this respect, the government decided to introduce three anti-crisis packages. The total costs of these anti-crisis measures in 2009 amounted to EUR 1.46 billion (2.3% of the GDP). The government has been engaged in supporting public-private partnership projects to stimulate employment and production in the construction industry, which has picked up significant losses during the crisis. The government also decided to support SMEs through two state-owned banks, for example, in the form of financing export loans in the SME segment. As part of the anti-crisis packages, the government also focused on the labor market by helping employers save jobs and create the new ones (Ručinská et al., 2009).

Certainly, the increased budget deficit, especially in 2009, reflects the shortfall in revenues related to worse economic development during the financial crisis. The fiscal authorities hoped that the fiscal impulse in the form of the anti-crisis package would have an expansive impact on the economy. The fiscal impulse was also significantly influenced by the increase in the use of EU funds and the launch of projects for the construction of motorways. Fiscal and structural policies aimed at making the labor market more flexible, as well as the goods and services market, are also helpful in maintaining price stability, which is a key goal of the central bank. In connection with Slovakia's entry to the euro area, the Slovak government adopted a package of anti-inflation measures to curb speculative price increases (*Stability Programme . . .*, 2009).

It seems that if it were not for the strategic plan to join the euro area, Slovakia would not be able to maintain a balanced budget policy. On the other hand, the condition of joining the euro area regarding the requirement to meet the Maastricht convergence criteria prevented the Slovak government from increasing social spending and thus increasing the budget deficit. In addition, Slovakia's accession to the euro area helped mitigate the negative effects of the crisis. This was reflected in a more credible perception of Slovak markets by investors and creditors. Moreover, cuts in foreign investment could be smaller than in other countries of the region and Slovakia could obtain credit financing at lower costs in the global financial markets. The only threat to the competitiveness of the Slovak economy could be the high exchange rate of the koruna to the euro, but the benefits of joining the euro area outweighed the losses (Dąbrowski, 2009; Hanus & Vacha, 2015; Havlat et al., 2018).

Policy mix in Visegrad countries in COVID-19 crisis

Czech Republic

From the beginning of March 2020, the fight against the COVID-19 pandemic began in the Czech Republic. Many measures have been implemented to support the population, jobs and enterprises (Czech Republic: Staff Concluding Statement of the 2021 *Article IV Mission*, IMF, 2021). However, in 2020, GDP fell by 5.6%. The government implemented a fiscal package worth EUR 8.6 billion (CZK 228.6 billion) in 2020, representing 4% of the GDP, and another fiscal package of CZK 332.1 billion (approximately EUR 12.5 billion) in 2021. In 2020, the Czech government decided to abolish social security contributions paid by employers (24.8%) who employ a maximum number of 50 employees. The state paid 50% of rents of all companies after ordering a 30% reduction and 20% coverage by tenants in the period between April and June 2020. They also introduced a lump sum of CZK 500 per day from March 12 to June 8 for self-employed persons and small businesses. The government paid one-off benefits to pensioners (CZK 15 billion in total) and bonuses for health workers and social services (CZK 15.1 billion in total) and subsidies for tourism (CZK 8.4 billion) (European Commission, 2020; *Policy Responses to COVID-19*, IMF). During the second wave of coronavirus, the government once again supported self-employed and small businesses that could apply for a lump sum from October 5, 2020, to February 15, 2021. Tourism, sport, restaurants, culture, transport and businesses that were closed due to the COVID-19 crisis were again supported (CZK 20.4 billion was spent in total). The government approved a six-month moratorium on bank loans (*Policy Responses to COVID-19*, IMF).

The Czech government decided to protect jobs, among other things, until the end of October 2021, it paid 80% of wages to employees sent to quarantine, and until the end of May 2021, it paid 100% of wages to employees if the company was closed as a result of crisis management. A tax package was launched, introducing an extraordinarily accelerated depreciation of assets acquired in 2020 and 2021, and personal income tax rates lowered from 2021. The government, trying to help enterprises, launched two support programs (the "COVID 2021" program and the "COVID-uncovered costs" program – (The Council on Czech Competitiveness, 2022)) based on the criterion of a 50% decrease in the company's turnover. In addition to the Antivirus Program and compensation bonuses (for small businesses and self-employed persons earning 1,000 CZK per day from the end of February to the end of May 2021), these programs provided a significant support to businesses and self-employed persons. The government undertook to provide state guarantees in the amount of CZK 500 billion (EUR 19 billion or 8.9% of the GDP), additionally, the VAT rate was reduced from 15% to 10% for selected services, and the road tax was reduced by 25% for vehicles over 3.5 tons (*Policy Responses to COVID-19*, IMF).

The CNB, in response to the first symptoms of the COVID-19 pandemic, decided to lower interest rates on March 16, 2020 by 50 basis points, then on March 26 by 75 basis points and also in May by 75 basis points. In May 2020, the basic interest rate (2W repo rate) in the Czech Republic was 0.25%. The frequency of repo operations has been increased from one to three times a week. In 2020, the countercyclical buffer rate was lowered. The CNB eased its credit ratios for new mortgage loans, increasing the recommended LTV ratio from 80% to 90%, and expanded the list of types of securities (through an amendment to the CNB Act) that CNB can engage in on secondary markets. The amendment to the CNB Act allowed for a wider range of monetary policy instruments as well as the scope of entities with which CNB may conclude open market transactions, which in turn allowed the CNB to purchase government bonds, corporate bonds and other high-risk debt (European Commission, 2020). In June 2021, it raised the interest rate by 0.25 basis points to 0.50%. Following further interest rate increases by the CNB between August and December 2021, the interest rate was 3.75%. In February 2022, the CNB raised its reference rate to 4.5%. It is worth emphasizing here that the inflation target in the Czech Republic is 2%, year-on-year growth in the consumer price index (*Bank Board decisions*, CNB).

The Czech Republic used a wide range of fiscal, monetary and macroprudential policy instruments to mitigate the effects of the shock caused by the global financial crisis and later by the COVID-19 pandemic in the economy. The labor market relatively well endured the effects of a pandemic (compared to the effect of global financial crisis). However, at the end of 2021, inflation increased significantly, which, combined with the increase in real estate prices caused by risk-taking by households, may pose an uneasy challenge for monetary and fiscal policymakers (Czech Republic: Staff Concluding Statement of the 2021 *Article IV Mission*, IMF, 2021).

Hungary

Another crisis that severely affected the Hungarian economy was the COVID-19 pandemic, the first symptoms of which appeared in March 2020. The Hungarian economy is closely linked globally through supply chains and tourism, which certainly, as a result of the pandemic, adversely affected Hungarian economic indicators. In response to the COVID-19 crisis, the Hungarian government introduced the first part of the anti-crisis package to ease the fiscal burden. Employers' social contributions in the sectors most affected by the pandemic have been abolished. In addition, health-care contributions have been reduced until June 30, 2020, and around 80,000 SME companies have been exempt from the small business tax (European Commission, 2020). Contributions to the development of tourism have also been temporarily canceled. The government has decided to spend HUF 245 billion (0.6% of the GDP) on the health-care sector. In addition, a package of tax reliefs for families and companies was introduced, as well as state support through salaries, subsidies and exemptions from taxes on salaries, was given to the tourism, arts, entertainment and leisure sectors. In April 2020, a new package of measures was announced, which was supported by the creation of two funds: the Anti-epidemic Protection Fund and the Economy Protection Fund (National Reform Programme of Hungary, 2021). As part of the new package, it was decided, inter alia, to support and protect jobs, in particular by subsidizing wages for employees with shortened working hours and creating jobs by supporting investments worth a total of HUF 450 billion (OECD Policy Responses to Coronavirus (COVID-19), 2020). It was also decided to provide companies with loans with interest rate subsidies and guaranteed loans, and to pay out additional pensions each February in the years 2021–2024. The government decided to support exports through Exim Bank, which will provide subsidies (EUR 800,000) for investments by export companies, preferential working capital loans and a new guarantee and insurance system. The State Development Bank has launched a package that includes financial support for companies worth HUF 1,490 billion. The government declared that it would buy up to HUF 150 billion (0.3% of the GDP) of bonds issued by banks, thus supporting lending. Interest-free loans for SMEs have also been introduced (*Policy Responses to COVID-19*, IMF).

As part of the monetary policy, among the anti-crisis measures in response to the COVID-19 pandemic, several steps were taken, such as increasing liquidity by increasing the regular forint-liquidity swap stock at regular auctions, extending eligible collateral or introducing long-term unlimited secured credit. In April 2020, a loan program was announced to support the SME sector, inter alia, through interest rate subsidies. In May, a quantitative easing program was launched consisting of purchasing government securities on the secondary market, and the covered bond purchase program was resumed. The central bank in Hungary in June and July 2020 cut interest rates twice, leaving the central bank basic rate at 0.6% (lowering it from 0.9% by 30 basis points). The overnight collateralized loan interest rate was 1.85% (up from April 8, 2020, up 95 bps) and the overnight central bank deposit rate remained at −0.05%. In September 2020, the MNB introduced a liquidity exchange facility to improve the effectiveness of the monetary policy transmission mechanism and to reduce the volatility of the forex swap yield (MNB press releases, 2020). Only in June 2021, in the face of rising inflation, it was decided to increase the central bank's basic rate from 0.60% to 0.90%, and the remaining rates were left unchanged. On the other hand, in July 2021, monthly increases in all key interest rates began, leaving the basic rate of the central bank at 2.4% at the end of 2021; overnight central bank deposit at 2.40% and overnight collateralized loan at 4.4%. There were moratoria on the repayment of all existing corporate and retail loans. Under the macroprudential policy, the Foreign Exchange Coverage Ratio was reduced from 15% to 10%, and from July 1, 2020, the requirement for an additional capital buffer for systemically important banks was temporarily abolished. In January 2022, the basic rate of the central bank was increased to 2.9% (overnight central bank deposit up to 2.90% and overnight collateralized loan up to 4.9%) (MNB press releases, 2021).

Poland

In response to the COVID-19 crisis, which also affected Poland, the economic authorities took the necessary anti-crisis measures. An important pillar of the Polish economy is the banking sector, which has built a strong capital base, thanks to which banks are immune to potential risks and maintain their credibility on the financial markets. One of the activities of the safety net institutions in Poland at the beginning of the pandemic in 2020 was, inter alia, the announcement by the Polish Financial Supervision Authority that banks and insurance companies may retain all the earned profits from previous years. Additionally, the so-called The Package of Supervisory Impulses for Safety and Development (PIN), was launched and its aim was to strengthen the resilience of the banking sector and to improve financing of the economy in response to the COVID-19 pandemic (Report, DLA Piper, March, 2020).

In March 2020, the Polish government decided to introduce the first edition of the action package entitled the "Anti-Crisis Shield" (worth of PLN 43–50 billion, approximately 2% of the GDP), aimed at supporting economic entities, households, the health-care sector and the financial system. Moreover, a program of financial support for enterprises was launched, worth of PLN 100 billion (approximately 4% of the GDP), implemented by the Polish Development Fund (European Commission, 2020). In April 2020, another part was introduced – the so-called Anti-crisis Shield 2.0, then in May 2020, the so-called Anti-crisis Shield 3.0 and in June 2020, Anti-crisis Shield 4.0. As part of these Shields, financial rules were relaxed, which meant that local governments could take on more debt; credit holidays (credit moratoria) have been announced; loans, sureties and guarantees for investment and operational purposes were offered; packages were introduced to prevent job losses, bankruptcies, closure of workplaces and a reduction in turnover and revenues of enterprises (Report, DLA Piper, July, 2020; Government of Poland, 2020).

Sobanski (2021) analyzed the economic policy tools used in the first phase of the COVID-19 crisis and noted that the scope of economic policy adjustments can be considered relatively wide in Poland. The monetary policy instruments used and the fiscal packages introduced had profound consequences for the Polish economy. At the same time, he pointed to some related risks, such as the fact that the funds used in anti-crisis measures caused an increase in the budget deficit and public debt. Additionally, he warned against an increase in the price level of Poland over a longer period of time perspective because of the weakening Polish zloty and the unprecedented increase in the balance sheet of the NBP.

The government announced that the total value of the Anti-Crisis Shield package was estimated at PLN 212 billion, or approximately 10% of the GDP. The next edition of the Anti-Crisis Shield 5.0, the so-called The Industry Shield was introduced in October 2020, under which the support was offered to the operations of enterprises that were significantly affected by the COVID-19 pandemic, that is, companies from the tourism and hotel sectors, as well as the organization and service of fairs, conferences and exhibitions. Enterprises operating in the tourism and exhibition industries that meet certain conditions could apply for exemption from Social Insurance Institution (ZUS) contributions or for downtime benefits. The next edition of the act is the so-called The Anti-Crisis Shield 6.0, covering aid for selected industries affected by the second wave of the COVID-19 pandemic, including further exemptions from ZUS contributions; additional cash benefits resulting from downtime; the so-called small subsidy in the amount of PLN 5,000; subsidizing jobs; compensation for municipalities in connection with lost revenues from the market fee. In December 2020, the so-called Anti-Crisis Shield 6.0 covered entrepreneurs from around 40 industries, such as trade, tourism, transport, as well as the educational, cultural and entertainment industries. The next Anti-Crisis Shields appeared in 2021. In February, Shield 7.0 was introduced, covering downtime benefits, wage subsidies, subsidies to cover current operating costs and further exemptions from paying ZUS contributions. In turn, Shield 8.0 included downtime benefits from ZUS, exemptions from ZUS contributions, subsidies to cover the running costs of business operation or benefits for the protection of jobs. As part of Shield 9.0, the list of industries that may benefit from the exemption from ZUS has been expanded (OECD Policy Responses to Coronavirus (COVID-19), 2020; Official Polish government website, 2022).

In turn, as part of the anti-crisis measures of the National Bank of Poland (NBP), the following decisions were made: NBP lowered interest rates to 0.1% (reference rate); the required reserve rate was reduced from 3.5% to 0.5%, then the interest rate on funds kept in the form of a required reserve – established at the level of the NBP reference rate; repo operations providing liquidity to the banking sector were used; the purchase of Treasury bonds and debt securities guaranteed by the State Treasury on the secondary market under structural open market operations commenced; the list of collaterals accepted in operations providing liquidity to the central bank was extended to include bonds guaranteed by the State Treasury and the offer included a bill of exchange loan for the refinancing of loans granted by banks to enterprises. In 2021, due to the increase in inflation in Poland and exceeding the inflation target, the NBP decided to increase the interest rates three times, including the reference rate to 1.75%. In turn, in early 2022, the reference rate was increased to 2.75% (NBP, MPC decisions).

Slovakia

The main anti-crisis measures of the government in response to the COVID-19 pandemic in Slovakia include: wage compensation for enterprises and the self-employed and subsidies for people with no income; postponement and exemption of payment of social security contributions by employers and self-employed persons; the possibility of deferring the payment of salaries and corporate tax for companies whose revenues fell by 40%; the ability to carry losses from 2014 by companies; rental surcharges; and higher health-care spending [European Commission, 2020]. In 2020, a total of EUR 1.9 billion (2.1% of the GDP) was disbursed in anti-crisis measures, which contributed to an increase in the deficit to 6.1% of the GDP in 2020. In addition, it was decided to launch state guarantee schemes, up to a total amount of EUR 4 billion (4.4% of the GDP) for SMEs and large companies (although the inflow of guarantees in 2020 amounted to EUR 1.04 billion). It was allowed to defer the repayment of loans to consumers, the self-employed and SMEs. There is also a moratorium on rent payments and temporary protection of the state against creditors for aggrieved companies. The Stability Program included a revised budget for 2021, which encompassed 4.2% of the GDP for the fight against the COVID-19 pandemic. The budget deficit was assumed in 2021 at 9.9% of the GDP (*Policy Responses to COVID-19*, IMF).

Monetary policy in Slovakia is conducted by the European Central Bank (ECB) at the level of the monetary union. The National Bank of Slovakia (NBS), as part of a coordinated approach with the ECB and the Banking Supervision Authority (EBA), implemented several of the following solutions in response to the COVID-19 crisis: banks were allowed to partially meet the Pillar 2 requirement (P2R); used capital instruments that did not qualify as Common Equity Tier 1 (CET1) capital; in addition, it was found that banks may, in some cases, operate below the capital level set by the conservation buffer; in justified cases, banks were temporarily released from full compliance with the LCR (Liquidity Coverage Ratio). The NBS also decided to lower the CCyB (Countercyclical capital buffer) rate from 1.5% to 1.0% from August 1, 2020. The capital buffer for one of the systemically important banks, Postova Banka, in Slovakia, was also reduced from 1% to 0.25% (NBS, press releases, 2021).

When it comes to monetary policy, it should be remembered that on January 1, 2009, Slovakia joined the euro area. The ECB's monetary transmission mechanism through the interest channel had a positive impact on the Slovak credit market from the first year of membership. Even before Slovakia joined the euro area, the level of basic interest rates was successively adjusted to the ECB interest rates. Thus, at the end of 2008, the basic interest rate of the NBS was equal to the basic interest rate of the ECB and was 2.5%. In 2009, the ECB applied four interest rate cuts, leaving the basic rate temporarily at 1% [Nagy, 2016]. Ultimately, after a few minor changes, the main refinancing operations rate as the key interest rate in the euro area has been 0% from March 2016 to July 2022. There were two increases in the main refinancing operations rate in the euro area between July and September 2022. In July, the key interest rate in the eurozone increased from 0.00% to 0.50%, and in September it increased to 1.25% [ECB, 2022].

Comparative economics perspective

In the period of economic shocks, government interventions are expected, but in relatively calm times, these direct interventions have both supporters and opponents. Government interventions or regulatory actions vary from levying taxes to creating entities to deploy public money. Block and Keller (2011) discovered, based on their data, that 88% of key US innovations in 1971–2006 were funded at least in part by government subsidies. Krugman concluded that it was only through intervention and encouragement from governments that the world avoided another Great Depression, and these economic depressions are a kind of punishment for globalization (The Associated Press, 2009).

Generally, recessions reduce the state budget revenues along with measures stimulating the economy and increase the public finance deficit. Reinhart and Rogoff (2009)[3] found that recessions are always accompanied by significant increases in public debt. The financial crisis and its consequences, for example, influenced the increase in unemployment in the V4 countries. There has been an increase in unemployment among young workers. Along with the increase in unemployment, the expenditures on general labor market policy as well as on passive labor market policy and its service increased (Zieliński, 2015).

In the context of the analysis of the global financial crisis of 2008–2009, which appeared in the V4 countries as well, it is worth emphasizing the observations of Harvey (2011), who noted that in the long run the state cannot compensate for the problems generated by capital because the efficient functioning of the state depends on the capital itself and the capital never solves its own crisis. Then, Solow (2000) believes that the capitalist system can deal with smaller problems and copes with crisis issues but cannot solve global crises. Stawska and Mourao (2021), on the basis of the research conducted on the restrictiveness and expansiveness of monetary, fiscal and economic policies in the economies of the euro area in 1999–2018, noted that in the discussed period, the economic authorities tried to coordinate monetary and fiscal policies in order to stabilize the economy.

Cotella (2006) rightly notices that as a consequence of the global financial crisis, the countries of Central and Eastern Europe decided to follow various paths of economic, political and social changes. The diversity of these Central European countries was further exacerbated by the financial crisis. An apt example is Hungary, which until recently during the transformation period had a leading role in the region. As Egedy (2012) quotes, Hungary is characterized by double marginalization, that is, first, the country's position has weakened not only in the EU but also in Central and Eastern Europe, and second, the role of Budapest in the region has weakened. Many experts even believe that it was as a result of many irresponsible political decisions that the global financial crisis led to the weakening of the state and that Hungary was one of the biggest losers of the crisis in the region. The crisis had a negative impact on export-oriented sectors, the size of the industry and the financial sector (mainly due to the credit crisis) and thus a social crisis appeared. To a large extent, the situation in Hungary can be attributed to the nonexistent, effective state (political) regulations of the credit market, or to credit institutions that applied interest rate indicators that were not adjusted to the economy. However, Stawska et al. (2021) note that in the years 2004–2019 in Hungary there was a relatively strong reaction of the central bank to changes in the budget deficit, which indicates that the Hungarian central bank is making a significant correction of interest rates as a result of changes in the budget deficit.

By making a certain synthetic comparison of selected economic variables in the V4 countries only in 2020, that is, in the initial waves of the COVID-19 pandemic, it can be seen that on the one hand, the Czech Republic recorded the largest decline in GDP (−5.8%), and on the other hand, in the V4 Group this country saw the highest GDP per capita. In the Czech Republic, the lowest GG debt (37.7% of the GDP) and the highest short-term interest rates (0.86%) were also noted in 2020. The Czech Republic recorded the lowest GG expenditure (41.3% of the GDP) in 2019 and the lowest consumption expenditure of households (45.3% of the GDP) in 2020. In turn, Hungary had the highest GG deficit in 2020 (8.0% of the GDP) and the largest GG debt (80.1% of the GDP). Hungary had the highest long-term interest rates in 2020 (2.23%). In 2020, Hungary showed the highest inflow of FDI (111.5% of the GDP) and also the highest investment rate (26.79%). In 2019, the highest level of GG expenditure was recorded in Hungary (45.6% of the GDP). As for Poland, in 2020 the country recorded the lowest GDP decrease (−2.5%) among the countries of the V4 Group, but it recorded the lowest GDP per capita. In 2020, Poland had the lowest unemployment rate (3.2%), but the lowest value of exports (56.2% of the GDP) and imports (49.4%). In 2020, Poland had the highest HICP inflation (3.7%) and the lowest investment rate (16.6% of the GDP). The highest consumption expenditure of households was in Poland and Slovakia (57.1% of the GDP each). Slovakia in 2020 recorded the lowest GG deficit (5.5% of the GDP) among the V4 countries, while it had the highest unemployment rate (6.7%). Slovakia had the highest volume of exports (85.4% of the GDP) and imports (84.5% of the GDP) as well as the lowest short-term and long-term interest rates, −0.43% and −0.04%, respectively. In 2020, Slovakia saw the lowest HICP inflation (2%), but also the lowest inflow of FDI to the country (−0.2% of the GDP).

It can be generally observed that in the analyzed V4 countries the expansionary monetary policy was used mainly during crises. Hungary proves to be an exception here, as despite the tendency to ease monetary policy, it did not significantly lower interest rates during the 2008–2009 financial crises. However, since 2014, short-term interest rates have also been significantly reduced. Similarly, in the case of fiscal policy, governments have decided to increase fiscal expansion when faced with crises. As a result of the 2007–2009 crisis, a public finance crisis occurred in many countries, which led to a change in the direction of fiscal policy from expansionary to restrictive. In turn, in the time of the COVID-19 pandemic, the fiscal authorities also decided to pursue an expansionary fiscal policy, opting for excessively high budget deficits and public debts.

Certainly, both during the 2008–2009 financial crises and during the COVID-19 crisis, as well as after these external shocks, the economies of the V4 countries were and still are supported by EU funds. The European Economic Recovery Plan was a proposal for an anti-cyclical macroeconomic response to the crisis, introduced to support the real economy. This plan is anchored in Stability and Growth Pact and the Lisbon Strategy for Growth and Jobs [Commission of the European Communities, 2008]. V4 economies should benefit from the Next Generation EU (NGEU) recovery fund, which is the fiscal policy response to the COVID-19 crisis. The purpose of this fund is to support economic recovery in the EU countries and structural reforms in the Member States (Astrov et al., 2022).

Conclusion

Summing up, it is worthwhile taking a look at some successes, failures, as well as threats and challenges faced by the countries of the V4 Group after 30 years of operation. The analysis of the last 21 years of the V4 Group's existence showed how these countries were facing economic shocks, mainly the global financial crisis, then the debt crisis and the COVID-19 pandemic.

Despite significant progress in terms of GDP per capita in the V4 countries, this indicator still remains below the EU average, which is certainly a challenge for these four countries. The labor market in the V4 countries has become more resistant to the effects of crises than in the so-called old EU. Despite various problems on the labor market, the countries of the V4 Group in 2017–2020 record unemployment below the EU average. The V4 Group achieves quite good results in terms of imports and exports. Virtually, all V4 countries import and export is above the EU average. Investments are an important economic variable for any economy. Poland has the most to catch up in this matter, as the investment rate has been below the EU average for many years. The Czechs are doing the best when it comes to investments, as their investment rate is far above the EU average. Interest rates are related to investments, which in the Czech Republic, Poland and Hungary are not far more but still higher than in Slovakia (belonging to the euro area). As a result of the pandemic, interest rates not only in the V4 countries fell significantly, which, despite many positive effects, has also a considerable impact on rising inflation levels. Inflation rose above the EU average in all V4 countries. Therefore, the central banks of Hungary, the Czech Republic and Poland have decided to raise interest rates since mid-2021 (the ECB only started raising interest rates in July 2022, and thus in Slovakia interest rates are the lowest in the region). A considerable challenge for the economies of the V4 Group will be related to the fiscal policy of the governments, with much higher public spending in response to the COVID-19 pandemic, and thus increasing public debts.

Notes

1 The chapter is a part of the research project financed by the National Science Centre, Poland; grant number: UMO-2017/26/D/HS4/0095
2 Ph.D., Assistant Professor at University of Lodz, Faculty of Economics and Sociology, Poland email: joanna.stawska@uni.lodz.pl (ORCID: 0000–0001–6863–1210).
3 It is also worth referring to other studies by Reinhart and Rogoff (2010) who found that the relationship between public debt and permanent growth is weak in those countries where the debt-to-GDP ratio is above 90%. On the other hand, in the case of countries where public debt to GDP exceeds 90%, the median growth rate drops by 1 percentage point. In this context, Checherita and Rother (2010) argue that in 12 euro area countries the relationship between public debt and economic growth is concave (with the turning point of public debt at around 90%–100% of the GDP). If the debt-to-GDP ratio is above the threshold, public debt reduces long-term economic growth.

References

Act of November 16, 2006 amending the act on personal income tax and some other acts – Journal of Laws no., item 1588, as amended.
Ambroziak, Ł., Chojna, J., Gniadek, J., Juszczak, A., Miniszewski, M., Strzelecki, J., Szpor, A., Śliwowski, P., Święcicki, I., & Wąsiński, M. (2020). *Grupa Wyszehradzka – 30 lat transformacji, integracji i rozwoju [Visegrad Group – 30 years of transformation, integration and development]*. Warsaw: Polish Economic Institute.
Astrov, V., Stehrer R., & Zavarská, Z. (2022). Recovery and resilience facility funding in the visegrad countries and its impact on Austria. *Policy Notes and Reports, 56.* https://wiiw.ac.at/recovery-and-resilience-facility-funding-in-the-visegrad-countries-and-its-impact-on-austria-dlp-6122.pdf (Access: 18.01.2022).
Bank Board decisions. *CNB.* www.cnb.cz/en/monetary-policy/bank-board-decisions/ (Access: 22.01.2022).
Bennett H., & Loayza N. (2001). Policy biases when the monetary and fiscal authorities have different objectives. *Central Bank of Chile Working Papers*, no. 66.
Bîea, N. (2015). Economic growth in Slovakia: Past successes and future challenges. *European Economy Economic Briefs, 008*, 3–4.
Beetsma, R., & Debrun, X. (2004). The interaction between monetary and fiscal policies in monetary union: a review of recent literature. In R. Beetsma et. al. (Ed.), *Monetary policies and labour markets: Key aspects of European macroeconomic policies after monetary unification.* Cambridge: Cambridge University Press.
Blinder, A. S. (1983). Issues in the coordination of monetary and fiscal policy. In *Monetary policy in the 1980s*. Missouri: Federal Reserve Bank of Kansas City.
Block, F., & Keller, M. R. (2011). *State of innovation: The U.S. government's role in technology development.* Boulder: Paradigm Publishers.
Buti, M., & Franco, D. (2005). *Fiscal policy in EMU.* Cheltenham: Edward Elgar Publishing Limited.
Buti, M., & Sapir, A. (1998). *Economic policy in EMU: A study by the European commission services.* Oxford: Clarendon Press.
Checherita, C., & Rother, P. (2010). The impact of high and growing government debt on economic growth: an empirical investigation for the Euro Area. *ECB Working Paper, Series No. 1237,* August 2010. European Central Bank.
Clarida, R., Galí, J., & Gertler, M. (2000). Monetary policy rules and macroeconomic stability: Evidence and some theory. *Quarterly Journal of Economics, 115*(1), 147–180.

Commission of the European Communities. (2008). Communication from the Commission to the European council. *A European Economic Recovery Plan* (COM (2008) 800 final). Brussels: Commission of the European Communities.

Corsetti, G., Dedola, L., Jarociński, M., Maćkowiak, B., & Schmidt, S. (2016). Macroeconomic stabilization, monetary-fiscal interactions, and Europe's monetary union. *ECB Working Paper, 1988*.

Cotella, G. (2006). Economic growth and territorial cohesion in CEECs: What chances for local development. *Geografický Časopis, 58*(4), 259–277.

Countryeconomy.com. (2022). https://countryeconomy.com/ratings (Access: 05.02.2022).

Czech Republic: Staff Concluding Statement of the 2021 Article IV Mission. *IMF 2021.* www.imf.org/en/News/Articles/2021/11/22/mcs-czech-republic-staff-concluding-statement-of-the-2021-article-iv-mission (Access: 22.01.2022).

Dąbrowski, T. (2009). Slovakia's economic success and the global crisis. *CESCommentary, 19*.

Dapontas, D. (2011). Currency crisis: The case of Hungary (2008–2009) using two stage least squares. *Special Conference Paper.* Bank of Greece, 5–21, https://www.bankofgreece.gr/Publications/SCP201113.pdf (Access: 23.01.2022).

Drozdowicz-Bieć, M. (2011). Reasons why Poland avoided the 2007–2009 recession. *Prace i Materiały* (Instytut Rozwoju Gospodarczego (SGH)), *86*(2), 39–66.

Dumičič, M., & Ridzak T. (2011). Determinants of sovereign risk premia for European emerging markets. *Financial Theory and Practice, 35*(3), 277–299.

ECB. (2022). *Key ECB interest rates.* www.ecb.europa.eu/stats/policy_and_exchange_rates/key_ecb_interest_rates/html/index.en.html (Access: 12.09.2022)

Egedy, T. (2012). The effects of global economic crisis in Hungary. *Hungarian Geographical Bulletin, 61*(2), 155–173.

European Commission. (2020). *Policy measures taken against the spread and impact of the coronavirus – 30 April 2020.* https://pracodawcyrp.pl/upload/files/2020/05/coronovirus-policy-measures30-april-ue-krajami.pdf (Access: 21.02.2022).

Eurostat. (2022). https://ec.europa.eu/eurostat/databrowser/view/tessi190/default/table?lang=en (Access: 04.02.2022)

Fidrmuc, J., Gardoňová, K., Hulényi, M., & Zavarská, Z. (2019). *Report on productivity and competitiveness of the Slovak Republic.* National Productivity Board of the Slovak Republic. https://economy-finance.ec.europa.eu/system/files/2020-06/7814_report-on-productivity-and-competitiveness-of-the-slovak-republic-npb-isa-final2.pdf (Access: 03.09.2022).

Government of Poland. (2020). *Anti-crisis shield 4.0 budgetary support to local government.* www.gov.pl/web/development-labour-technology/shield-40-signed-by-the-polish-president

Grabia, T. (2015). Interest rate policy of selected central banks in Central and Eastern Europe. *Comparative Economic Research, 18*(1).

Hampl, M. (2009). The Czech financial sector successfully copes with crisis thus far. *Ekonom,* May 21 (Czech National Bank). www.cnb.cz/en/public/media-service/interviews-articles/The-Czech-financial-sector-successfully-copes-with-crisis-thus-far# (Access: 20.01.2022).

Hanus, L., & Vacha, L. (2015). Business cycle synchronization of the Visegrad Four and the European Union (No. 19/2015). *IES Working Paper,* Prague. https://www.econstor.eu/bitstream/10419/120435/1/833040154.pdf (Access: 02.09.2022).

Harvey, D. (2011). Roepke lecture in economic geography – Crises, geographic disruptions and the uneven development of political responses. *Economic Geography, 87*(1), 1–22.

Havlat, M., Havrlant, D., Kuenzel, R., & Monks, A. (2018). Economic Convergence in Czech Republic and Slovakia, European Economy. *Economic Brief, 034*, 2–3.

Hein, E., & Truger, A. (2014). Fiscal policy and rebalancing in the euro area: A critique of the German debt brake from a Post-Keynesian perspective. *Panoeconomicus, 61*(1), 21–38.

Hicks, John, R. (1937). Mr Keynes and the classics: A suggested interpretation. *Econometrica*, *5*, 147–159.

Hughes, H., Mooslechner, P., & Schuerz, M. (2001). *Challenges of economic policy coordination within European Monetary Union*. Dordrecht: Kluwer Academic Publishers.

Horvath, J. (2009). 2008 Hungarian financial crisis. *CASE Network E-briefs*. https://case-research.eu/files/?id_plik=3789 (Access: 24.01.2022).

Hronova, S., & Hindls, R. (2012). Economic crisis in the results of the non-financial corporations sector in the Czech Republic. *Statistika*, *49*(3), 4.

Jacquet, P., & Pisani-Ferry, J. (2001). *Economic policy co-ordination in the Eurozone: What has been achieved? What should be done?* London: Centre for European Reform.

Keynes, J.M. (1936). *The general theory of employment, interest and money*. London: Macmillan.

Kowalska, A., Kovarnik, J., Hamplova, E., & Prazak, P. (2018). The selected topics for comparison in visegrad four countries. *Economies*, *6*(3), 50. https://doi.org/10.3390/economies6030050

Krus, L., & Woroniecka – Leciejewicz, I. (2017). Monetary-fiscal game analyzed using a macroeconomic model for Poland. *Przegląd Statystyczny*, *3*.

Lesław, A. (2016). Paga foundation. *Future of the Visegrad Group*. https://paga.org.pl/wp-content/uploads/2021/05/v4_future_of_the_visegrad_group.pdf (Access: 02.02.2022).

Libich, J., Nguyen, D., & Stehlik, P. (2014). *Monetary exit and fiscal spillovers*. Munich: MPRA.

Maśniak, D., & Lados D. J. (2014). Pension reforms in Poland and Hungary from the legal perspective – Similarities and differences. *Insurance Review*, *4*(2014), 123–142.

Ministry of Finance of the Czech Republic. (2007). *Convergence programme Czech Republic, March 2007*. https://www.mfcr.cz/assets/en/media/Convergence-Programme-of-the-Czech-Republic-March-2007.pdf (Access: 03.09.2022).

Ministry of Finance of the Czech Republic. (2008). *Convergence programme Czech Republic, November 2008*. https://ec.europa.eu/economy_finance/economic_governance/sgp/pdf/20_scps/2008-09/01_programme/cz_2008-11-20_cp_en.pdf

Ministry of Finance of the Czech Republic. (2010). *Convergence programme Czech Republic, January 2010*. https://www.mfcr.cz/assets/en/media/Convergence-Programme-of-the-Czech-Republic-January-2010.pdf (Access: 03.09.2022).

Ministry of Finance of Poland. (2016). *Convergence Programme Poland*, April 2016. https://mf-arch2.mf.gov.pl/en/c/document_library/get_file?uuid=46d0767b-26d4-4f0d-bb1a-cd82d6d92f3f&groupId=764034 (Access: 02.09.2022).

MNB Press Releases. (2020). www.mnb.hu/en/pressroom/press-releases/press-releases-2020 (Access: 24.01.2022).

MNB Press Releases. (2021). www.mnb.hu/en/pressroom/press-releases/press-releases-2021 (Access: 24.01.2022).

Mundell, R. A. (1961). A theory of optimal currency area. *The American Economic Review*, *51*(4).

Nagy, L. (2016). From independent Slovakian central bank policy to the monetary policy of the Euro area. *Public Finance Quarterly*, *1*, 49–64.

National Reform Programme of Hungary. (2021). *Government of Hungary*, April. https://commission.europa.eu/system/files/2021-11/nrp_2021_hungary_en.pdf (Access: 22.01.2022).

NBP. (2002). *Inflation report 2001*. Warsaw: Monetary Policy Council, National Bank of Poland.

NBP, MPC Decisions. www.nbp.pl/homen.aspx?f=/en/dzienne/stopy.htm (Access: 02.01.2022).

NBS. (2016). *Annual report 2015*. https://nbs.sk/_img/documents/_publikacie/annual-report/arnbs15.pdf (Access: 24.01.2022).

NBS, Press Releases. (2021). www.nbs.sk/en/press/all-press-releases/press-releases-archive (Access: 28.01.2022).

Nordhaus, W. D. (1994). Policy games: coordination and independence in monetary and fiscal policies. *Brookings Papers on Economic Activity*, *2*, 139–216.

OECD Economic Surveys: Slovak Republic. (2002). Vol. 2002/11 – June https://books. google.pl/books?id=skiM_pHnIvgC&printsec=frontcover&hl=pl&source=gbs_ge_summ ary_r&cad=0#v=onepage&q&f=false (Access: 18.01.2022).

OECD Policy Responses to Coronavirus (COVID-19). (2020). *Coronavirus (COVID-19): SME policy responses*, July. https://www.oecd.org/coronavirus/policy-responses/coronavi rus-covid-19-sme-policy-responses-04440101/ (Access: 11.01.2022).

Official Polish government website. (2022). www.gov.pl/web/tarczaantykryzysowa (Access: 27.01.2022).

Onorante, L. (2006). Interaction of fiscal policies in the Euro area: How much pressure on the EBC? *Economics Working Papers from European University Institute, ECO2006/9*.

Polański, Z. (2017). Stabilization policies and structural developments: Poland and the crises of 1929 and 2008, *CASE Working Papers*, *9*(133), 86.

Policy Responses to COVID-19. *IMF*. www.imf.org/en/Topics/imf-and-covid19/Policy-Responses-to-COVID-19 (Access: 11.01.2022).

Polish Investment & Trade Agency, PFR Group (2011). *Tax on Goods and Services (VAT) '11*. www.paih.gov.pl/polish_law/taxation/vat_2011, (Access: 03.09.2022).

Public finances in EMU 2009. (2009). *European Economy 5*. https://ec.europa.eu/economy_ finance/publications/pages/publication15390_en.pdf (Access: 12.01.2022).

Recommendation for a Council Recommendation to the Czech Republic with a view to bringing an end to the situation of an excessive government deficit Application of Article 104(7) of the Treaty/* SEC/2007/1154 final */

Reinhart, C. M., & Rogoff, K. S. (2009). The aftermath of financial crises. *American Economic Review*, *99*(2), 466–472. http://dx.doi.org/10.1257/aer.99.2.466

Reinhart, C. M., & Rogoff, K. S. (2010). Growth in a time of debt. *NBER Working Paper* No. *15639*. Cambridge: National Bureau of Economic Research, Inc.

Report, DLA Piper, July. (2020). *Report: Aid measures encompassed by the Anti-Crisis Shield acts introduced by the Polish government*. file:///C:/Users/user/Downloads/Report%20with%20 aid%20measures%20July%202020.pdf (27.01.2022)

Report, DLA Piper, March. (2020). *Report: Aid measures encompassed by the anti-crisis shield acts introduced by the Polish government*. https://psik.org.pl/images/publikacje-i-raporty – pub likacje/covid-19/DLA-Piper_Aid-measures-encompassed-by-the-anti-crisis-shield-act-introduced-by-the-Polish-government.pdf (Access: 26.01.2022).

Ručinská, S., Urge, D., & Ručinský, R. (2009). Competitiveness of Slovakia and the economic crisis. *Central European Journal of Public Policy*, *3*,(2), 50–78.

Sobanski, K. (2021). Economic policy response to the COVID-19 Crisis: The case of Poland. *Eurasian Business and Economics Perspectives, EBES*, *18*, 107–118.

Solow, R. M. (2000). *Growth theory: An exposition*, P. 304. Oxford: Oxford University Press.

Stability Programme of the Slovak Republic for 2008–2012. (2009). *Ministry of finance of the Slovak Republic*, April. https://ec.europa.eu/economy_finance/economic_governance/sgp/ pdf/20_scps/2008-09/01_programme/sk_2009-04-30_sp_en.pdf (Access: 03.09.2022).

Stawska, J. (2018). Expansiveness/Restrictiveness of monetary and fiscal policy in the Czech Republic and Hungary – Comparative analysis. *Ad Alta- Journal of Interdisciplinary Research*, *8*(2).

Stawska, J. (2019). Do monetary and fiscal policy variables matter for the economy in Poland? *Ad Alta: Journal of Interdisciplinary Research*, *9*(2).

Stawska, J., Malaczewski, M., Malaczewska, P., & Stawasz- Grabowska, E. (2021). The Nash equilibrium in the policy mix model for Czechia, Hungary, and Romania. *Cogent Econom ics & Finance*, *9*(1), 1869380. https://doi.org/10.1080/23322039.2020.1869380

Stawska, J., & Mourao Reis, P. J. (2021). Expansionary or restrictive policies in the Eurozone? Dominating trends in the first two decades. *Acta Oeconomica, 71*(3), 405–430. https://doi.org/10.1556/032.2021.00020

The Associated Press. (2009). *Krugman says world avoided second Great Depression.* https://usato-day30.usatoday.com/money/world/2009-08-10-krugman_N.htm (05.02.2022).

The Council on Czech Competitiveness. (2022). *Government measures supporting business,* February 22. http://www.czechcompete.cz/economic-policy/business-and-industry/government-measures-supporting-business (Access: 02.09.2022).

Theglobaleconomy.com. www.theglobaleconomy.com/rankings/gdp_per_capita_ppp/ (Access: 05.09.2022).

Tomšík, V. (2012). Some insights into monetary and fiscal policy interactions in the Czech Republic. *BIS Papers No 67,* 161–171.

Xin, Ch. (2019). *Foreign direct investment in Central and Eastern European Countries.* Budapest: China-CEE Institute Nonprofit.

Zieliński, M. (2015). Unemployment and labor market policy in visegrad group countries. Equilibrium. *Quarterly Journal of Economics and Economic Policy, 10*(3), 185–201. http://dx.doi.org/10.12775/EQUIL.2015.032

8 Public procurement as a transformative innovation policy instrument

Urban rehabilitation in Malmö

Stephanie Francis Grimbert[1] *and Jon Mikel Zabala-Iturriagagoitia*[2]

Introduction

The implementation of the 2030 Agenda for Sustainable Development defined by the United Nations requires forging a new framework of urban development, in the light of vertiginous urbanization pace projected for the coming decades. At present, around 56% of the population in the world live in cities, and it is expected that this value may increase up to 70% by 2050 (World Bank, 2020). This calls for the need to turn cities into more sustainable living environments. Urbanization generates economic development and well-being, but also brings problems with water and sewage, traffic, poor energy systems and over consumption of resources associated to it, to mention a few. Solving cities' environmental problems is therefore the key to a sustainable future (European Union, 2011). Concomitantly, just as industrialization led to urbanization, so too has deindustrialization led to suburbanization, hence littering cities with the vestiges of long-gone economic activities. Reconciling the revitalization of empty urban spaces with sustainability agendas requires ambitious and innovative urban planning. In the words of Rodríguez Pose (2018, p. 189) "place-sensitive development policies need . . . to focus on tapping into untapped potential and on providing opportunities to those people living in the places that 'don't matter'".

In urban sustainability, best practices can be understood as "a discursive process [in which] not only is new knowledge created about a policy problem, but [also in which] the nature and interpretation of the policy problem itself are challenged and reframed" Bulkeley (2006, p. 1029). The purpose of this chapter is to illustrate the lessons that can be learned from the local investment program for ecological development developed in the city of Malmö (Sweden), which aimed at accelerating the environmental sustainability of the city. This program included a series of projects (see Figure 8.1)[3] to build 'ecological' districts that would function as inspiration on how to reach the goal of sustainability. In particular, the chapter will focus on the ecological city district in the Western Harbor. The chapter focuses on a particular case study, but similar projects have been developed in many other cities all around the globe supported by the Inter-American Development Bank, as part of its emerging and sustainable cities program.[4]

The Western Harbor (Västra Hamnen in Swedish) was reclaimed from the seabed in the 18th century to accommodate the strong Swedish shipbuilding industry.

DOI: 10.4324/9781003256281-11

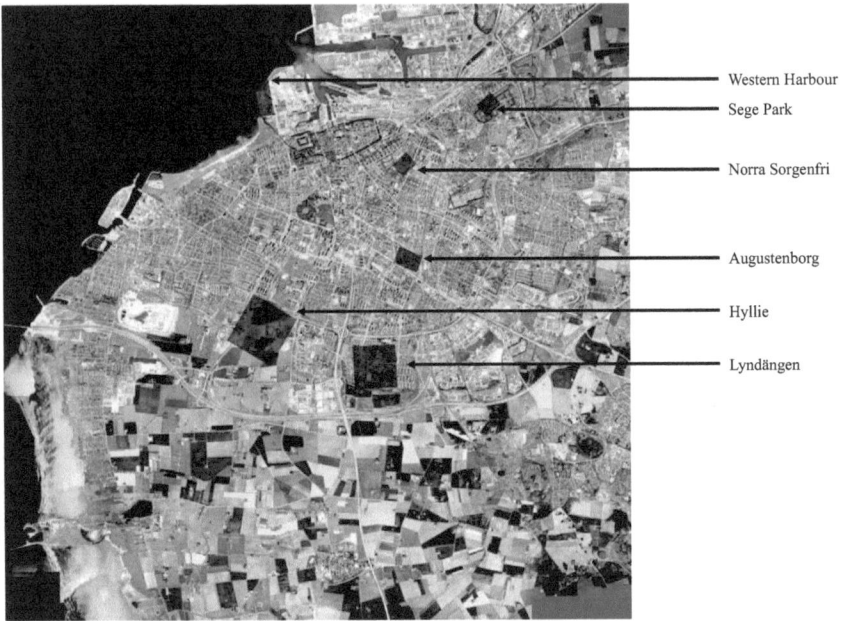

Figure 8.1 Sustainable projects in the city of Malmö
Source: Fossum (2008)

Kockums Industries was founded in the area back in the 1870s (Figure 8.2). At its peak, 6,000 people worked among docks, cranes, and big industrial buildings. The decision to close the business was made in 1986 (City of Malmö, 2009a, p. 4). Saab-Scania was then established in Malmö and one of Europe's most modern car manufacturers operated out of Kockums Hall. But the plant was closed in 1996 due to a decline in profit and restructured when Saab-Scania merged with General Motors. The area became an old industrial land with environmental contamination issues, but also with problems of crime, addiction, violence and poverty (Andrén, 2010).

Today, Västra Hamnen has become the flagship of Malmö's sustainable urban development. In a couple of decades, it has transformed from being an old industrial district into becoming an area for knowledge and sustainable living (Moodysson et al., 2017). The Kockums machine halls and cranes have given way for parks, schools, renewed industrial activities related to the environment and living accommodations (City of Malmö, 2009a).

The following environmental issues were judged as problematic in Malmö (Andrén, 2010, p. 54): urban air quality, traffic situation, contaminated soil and ground water and the use of chemicals, eutrophication, and linear flows of phosphorous and landscape threats from urban activities. Some of the goals aimed at with this initiative included:

• meet 100% of the energy needs from renewable energy sources by 2020, by providing innovative energy generation plant and distribution systems;

Figure 8.2 The Kockums cranes in the old Västra Hamnen
Source: Fossum (2008)

- energy consumption reductions of at least 40% per capita by 2030 (based on consumption levels from 2001 to 2005) and a 40% decrease in greenhouse gas emissions by 2020 (calculated from 1990);
- the emissions of carbon dioxide shall be reduced by 25% by 2005 and by 60%–75 % by 2050;
- the emissions of nitrogen to the Öresund sea via waterways in the municipality shall be reduced by at least 30% by 2005; and
- combine appropriate technologies (e.g. solar and wind production units, together with a heat pump and an aquifer storage system) to produce clean heat and electricity cost-effectively.

The execution of Malmö's local investment program for ecological development was targeted by public procurement (Erdmenger, 2003; Simcoe & Toffel, 2012).[5] One of the reasons why public procurement was chosen as one of the main instruments is related to the long history Sweden has counted on the use of this policy instrument (Natuvårdsverket, 2009) and the previous successes achieved in many of these experiences where it was implemented (Edquist et al., 2000).

Accordingly, the chapter provides evidence on how Public Procurement for Innovation (PPI), besides its direct purchase power and capacity to meet given objectives (i.e. first-degree effects), can also be used as a tool to achieve additional policy objectives, such as environmental, economic and social goals (i.e. second-degree effects) (McCrudden, 2004; Edquist & Zabala-Iturriagagoitia, 2012; OECD, 2017). Following previous studies (e.g. Uyarra et al., 2020; Zabala-Iturriagagoitia, 2022) we adopt a single case study approach (Eisenhardt, 1989), as it is regarded as an appropriate methodological choice when the target of the research is to respond to questions such as 'when', 'how' or 'why', as it is the case of this chapter. Adopting the case study method is also aligned with the overall ambitions of the book, as it aims to disentangle the experiences observed in Forgotten Spaces and their global policy implications. The analysis of atypical cases such as the ones included in this chapter, and overall, in the book, reveals the underlying mechanisms behind the dynamics observed in certain realities, but which often remain indiscernible (Flyvbjerg, 2006), and hence, the identification of these intangible (policy) dimensions allow their subsequent transfer to other contexts.

The research process started from desk study research, collecting secondary data, checking existing literature, policy documents (e.g. tender calls, laws, plans, white papers, evaluations), and other written materials and reports (i.e. articles in newspapers, websites of the City of Malmö), in which we particularly looked for evidence on the way PPI processes were being articulated. Further data was collected through semi-structured interviews and focus groups with a range of actors from the city of Malmö. In particular we focused on meeting policymakers and technicians who had either been involved in the definition, implementation or monitoring of either the regional innovation strategy in Skåne or the procurement initiative in the city of Malmö. These interviews were also complemented with the direct observation of the transformative effects of the city by the authors during the period 2009–2015.

So far, policy and scholarly interest on PPI have to a great extent been limited to the national level, paying little attention to the rationales for, and implementation of, procurement policies and practices at the subnational level (Uyarra et al., 2020). However, cities can be spaces for experimentation and development of niche innovations (Hodson & Marvin, 2010; Lember et al., 2011), and therefore their relevance should not be underestimated nor underexplored. As the case will illustrate, PPI was instrumental for meeting sustainability goals through the realization of energy efficiency objectives. With the example of this urban success story, we delve into the practice of 'Transformative PPI', identifying the key conditions that made the procurement process work, so as to make it transferable to other forgotten places that also aim to counter affect environmentally related grand challenges at subnational levels. Extrapolating from the Malmö case, we characterize *transformative* PPI as both an *ambitious* PPI in its specifications and an *inclusive* PPI in its process.

The transformative potential of PPI

One of the main purposes of demand side interventions, such as public procurement, is to increase the demand for innovations, to improve the conditions for the uptake of innovations and to improve the articulation of demand (Edler & Georghiou, 2007, p. 952). The aim of public procurement is to meet an identified need by achieving the best possible performance in terms of cost and service or expected functionalities (Saussier & Tirole, 2015, p. 7).

The focus of PPI is to support and stimulate the demand for and the adoption and diffusion of innovations, to generate economic benefits for suppliers and supply chains, on top of the social benefit generated by the public sector (Edler & Yeow, 2016, p. 415). The potential of PPI for prioritization is higher than other traditional R&D and innovation instruments, as it necessarily implies a proactive process of prioritization linked to thematic areas (i.e. societal needs), something less directly achievable with the implementation of supply-oriented measures. Despite the new policy rhetoric that has emerged, particularly in Europe, in relation to PPI, it is mostly conceptualized in terms of short-term efficiency gains. As discussed by Lember et al. (2015, p. 404), governments mostly attempt to make the process of public procurement more innovation-friendly but do not acknowledge the wider role public procurement can play in long-term structural change.

PPI can become a transformative instrument (i.e. a game changer) because it helps create the conditions for creativity, and ultimately for the development, diffusion and uptake of innovations. PPI puts governments as 'lead customers' for innovative products and/or services (Beise & Cleff, 2004; European Commission, 2007). This leads to several benefits, such as the possibility of producing economies of scale due to substantial early purchases, reduction of costs in products and improvements in quality due to production-related learning effects, as well as learning effects related to reduction in production costs, and improvements in product quality and performance. PPI can also encourage innovation by articulating the demand, signaling to innovation producers the existence of unmet needs and by facilitating interaction between users and producers (Bleda & Chicot, 2019). Finally public procurement can have a 'transformational role' (Neij, 2001), and influence the evolution of an existing market, by changing its structure.

PPI can be characterized not only as a process but also as an interactive learning space. Interaction between procurers and suppliers is required to mitigate the potential drawbacks of information asymmetries, and to create the conditions for the subsequent development of innovations (Roberts & Siemiatycki, 2015). Both users and producers need some degree of interaction to face the several challenges and risks associated to the uncertainties underlying innovation processes. On the one hand, users' uncertainties are related to the technological characteristics of the products or systems to be procured, their performance, their potential impact, the risk aversion in the definition and the later granting of contracts, financial risks and the organizational and societal risks associated to the procuring organization (Edler et al., 2015, Chapter 4, p. 92). On the other hand, producers' challenges are mostly associated to the capabilities required to meet the demands and needs signaled by contracting authorities, and the technological challenges related to the performance requirements defined by these (Mazzucato, 2018). The communication of these potential needs also constitutes another central feature of the PPI, as it signals both the state and the level of sophistication of the demand. In this sense, engaging suppliers at an early stage in procurement processes is argued to reduce procurement risks (Zsidisin & Smith, 2005). Early supplier involvement in PPI processes is seen as generating improvements in suppliers' solutions, not only influencing the efficiency and effectiveness of their solutions but also having benefits for the territory in which these products will be further exploited and used. Given the central role that the interaction between suppliers and contracting authorities play in the effectiveness of PPI, the European directives of public procurement have included multiple procedures which aim to facilitate the dialogue and exchange between the two parties during the whole procurement process (i.e. Directive 2014/24/EU of 26 February 2014 on public procurement and Directive 2014/25/EU of 26 February 2014 on procurement by entities operating in the water, energy, transport and postal services sectors). These procedures include: open procedures (Article 27), restricted procedures (Article 28), competitive procedure with negotiation (Article 29), competitive dialogue (Article 30), innovation partnership (Article 31) and design contest (Article 78).

First- and second-degree effects of PPI in Malmö

This section is structured into three parts. The first subsection (3.1) provides the general policy context in which the Malmö's local investment program for ecological development emerged. The second one (3.2) illustrates the main direct outputs (i.e. first-degree effects) achieved through the use of PPI. Finally, the third one (3.3) highlights its environmental, economic and social outcomes (i.e. second-degree effects). The figure below (Figure 8.3) provides a comprehensive view of those processual effects of PPI applied to Malmö's sustainable urban development.

Policy context

The departing point for this urban transformation goes back to 1996, when the Swedish government started funding Local Investment Programs to promote the

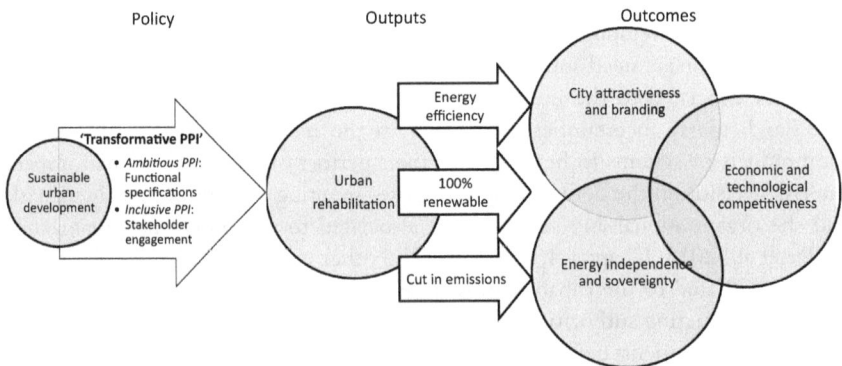

Figure 8.3 Outputs and outcomes of 'Transformative PPI'

Source: Own elaboration

transition to an ecologically sustainable society in Swedish municipalities.[6] The Swedish government allocated SEK 7.2 billion (approx. $0.9 billion) for the period 1998–2003 for grants supporting the Local Investment Programs. In 1998, the City of Malmö allocated SEK 147 million (approx. $18.3 million) in grants for sustainability projects. Only in year 2000, Malmö's Local Agenda 21 efforts amounted to SEK 4 million (approx. $0.47 million). Other sources of funding also came from the European Commission, €1.9 million through the SURE/RESECO-project in the 5th Framework Program, and the cofunding provided by Sydkraft AB (approx. €10 million). In 2000, the city of Malmö received funding for the transformation of Malmö into ecological sustainability, according to strategies in the 'Local Agenda 21', which specified the long-term sustainable development objectives of the city. One of the mechanisms used by the city of Malmö to implement this Local Agenda 21 was the 1998–2002 Environmental Plan, which later turned into the Environmental Program 2003–2008.

The European Housing Exhibition (Bo01-City of Tomorrow) held in Malmö in 2001 was a key determinant in triggering a move toward sustainability in the city. The theme of the housing exhibition and the city district was "The City of Tomorrow in the ecologically sustainable information and welfare society". The objective of the exhibition was to define a city of the future in a sustainable society, and Västra Hamnen was chosen as the area to host the exhibition. As mentioned above, Västra Hamnen constituted a totally abandoned old industrial area in Malmö, with environmental problems of contamination due to the already extinct shipbuilding industry that had operated for more than 130 years. Hence, the location of this housing exhibition represented a strategic choice to drive the city toward a sustainable path.

Malmö decided to direct its efforts toward achieving socially responsible public procurement due to the political commitment of one of the city Majors. In 1995, the association of local authorities in the Skåne region (where the city of Malmö is located) decided that all public purchasing should be environmentally adapted, and recommended a common policy for the municipalities in the region. As a result, the city of Malmö established a procurement framework under which a centralized procurement department (Serviceförvaltningen) had authority to integrate, manage and negotiate purchase agreements with suppliers according to the eco-standards established by the city council (Christensson et al., 2002). In 1997, the city of Malmö set up its own environmental policy. This policy stated that the procurement done by the city of Malmö should be used as an enforcing power in the work toward ecological sustainability. One of the main tools used in the implementation of this policy was a binder with quality criteria, including environmental criteria, for a large series of products. The systematic application of multi-criteria methods made the evaluation process transparent to bidders, avoiding corruption and favoritism toward large companies. Hence, the city had several political guidelines that identified how procurement should be undertaken and that, for example, low environmental impact and socially responsible products should be the first choice (Santos et al., 2012, p. 4).

As it can be observed, the city adopted a very active role at the initial stages of the Local Agenda 21 program, particularly concerning the requirements to be met by the potential supplying companies. In order to identify and define the needs to be addressed in the procurement process, the city of Malmö worked with experts from municipal departments, local urban district committees, and established dialogues with citizen groups, college and university, public agencies, NGOs and other European cities (Environment Department, 2009). Remarkably, local energy utility providers and private construction companies were also involved in the early stages (ICLEI, 2012). Together with local developers, architects and citizens Malmö launched a new communication process known as 'The Creative Dialogue'(City of Malmö, 2009b). This dialogue was one way to implement public-private partnerships within PPI (Stilgoe, 2012), as it provided a platform bringing together various stakeholder groups to discuss common themes related to the environment (Roberts & Siemiatycki, 2015). The intention of these dialogues was to pull different stakeholders together so that both public and private actors would benefit from sharing knowledge before the call was launched, building upon their collective expertise.

Officials in the city of Malmö met the previous social actors every two weeks over a period of two years, building a relationship based on reciprocity, interdependence and complementary strategic interests (ibid: 790). Including the capabilities of these stakeholders in these early-stage dialogues (i.e. equivalent to market consultations) helped to create a common understanding of the program's ambitious goals and defining the (mainly functional) requirements that should be addressed by the suppliers.[7] These dialogues are a reflection of the traditional Swedish culture of seeking consensus (Billing, 2000), and are not intrinsic to PPI processes.

Besides acting as a catalyst during the initial stages of the project, the city of Malmö also played a strong role as a regulator. It decided to specify more demanding environmental requirements than those established by the Swedish Environmental Protection Agency for new construction areas (Naturvårdsverket, 2009). These strong demands created synergies that led the companies involved in the construction work to develop innovations that were beyond what they may have generated in the absence of such demands. The goals set by Malmö to be climate neutral by 2020 and with all municipal operations being run on 100% renewable energy by 2030 were significantly more ambitious than those set by the European Union for Sweden (49% by 2020) and the national plan (50% by 2020) (ICLEI, 2012). Since the program counted with a strong political support and leadership that developed the city's vision and guided the revitalization process, sustainable development was integrated into every department's policy decision-making within the city of Malmö.

An important characteristic of the PPI initiatives undertaken in Västra Hamnen is that the city of Malmö embraced public-private partnerships as a supporting factor for their development, due to the strong cooperation that was established between the multiple parties (Roberts & Siemiatycki, 2015). Several initiatives were established, seeking to foster dialogues with citizens and public bodies (Björgvinsson et al., 2012). These participatory mechanisms were used for example in the city budget formulation, the organization of the districts, the central political organization or the participation in the quality of education of primary schools. The mechanisms were variable, from pure customer surveys to projects in which citizens' influence was of crucial importance to the content and design of the operation (City of Malmö, 2009a). The city now uses a variety of methods to educate and inform both citizens and visitors and to improve their understanding and commitment to sustainable development such as educational materials in the local schools, a newsletter on greening issues or exhibits in the Malmö Museum (Dale, 2011). A special form of consultation/dialogue was also developed during the construction of this city district, what came to be known as the "Hej city district projects". The Hej city district projects were implemented in open meetings, focus groups and dialogue meetings with various special interest groups. Each local initiative was followed up with an action plan that was sent to the administration. Until 2010, 5,800 proposals had been submitted concerning changes within the city district area (City of Malmö, 2009a).

An example of these consultation/dialogue building initiatives can be found at the Flagghusen residential area (also known as Bo02), which consists of 16 buildings and more than 600 apartments, both rental and cooperative apartments. Before this area was built within Västra Hamnen, a so called Good dialogue was initiated, in which both citizens and the winning bidder were invited to participate in the planning of the area from the start. In this dialogue, the plan, the architecture, safety and security, costs of living, maintenance costs, parking, energy efficiency, use of nontoxic substances, local surface, water handling and the environmental adaptation were discussed to come up with the best solutions (City of Malmö, 2009b, p. 7). Through dialogue with residents and people working in the city district, contracting authorities gathered insights on how to improve its organization, for it to live up to the needs and aspirations of the local ecosystem.

The Malmö Panel and the Malmö Initiative are other two examples of how the residents of the city participate and influence the content of the municipal decision-making. The Malmö Panel, established in 2008, is a forum of 1,600 Malmö residents that, twice each year, have a say on issues brought up by Malmö's councils. Matching the establishment of the Malmö Panel, the City of Malmö created a special site on the Internet in which citizens, organizations and parties were able to share their views on the city's development etc. Via the 'Malmö Initiative', citizens can also make suggestions and comments pertaining to various areas related to the city or their own districts (City of Malmö, 2009b, p. 9).

The environmental outputs: urban rehabilitation

Västra Hamnen turned into Sweden's first urban area with a climate-neutral energy system, using entirely locally produced energy from renewable sources such as solar, wind and waterpower (Delegation for sustainable cities, 2012, p. 10). The buildings in the district were designed to minimize energy demands for heating, while the installed electrical equipment was highly energy efficient.[8] A large proportion of the heating needs are extracted from seawater and groundwater and complimented with solar collectors. Electricity is generated by wind power and solar panels connected to

Figure 8.4 Solar collectors in the buildings in Västra Hamnen

Source: Fossum (2008)

the district heating grid (see Figure 8.4).[9] The solar cells placed on semitransparent glass roofs allow the light through to the balconies below (City of Malmö, 2009b, p. 22), and recyclable and organic materials are sorted and contribute to energy production by the city's biogas plant. Office properties met the 'Green Building Standard', which implies that they are 25% more energy efficient than the national mandatory requirements. In addition, healthy materials in the dwellings and surroundings are given high priority.

In every household, residuals are separated into food waste, residual waste and wastewater via waste grinders and separate pipe networks. The household waste that is not separated for recycling goes into vacuum waste chutes where the waste is separated into organic waste and other waste. First, wastewater is treated in a treatment plant before it is circulated back to the Öresund sea. Then, food waste is collected and brought into digesters. These digesters produce (i) biogas, which is used to heat homes and as fuel for vehicles,[10] (ii) sludge, from this mud it is possible to extract nutrients and heavy metals so that nutrients such as phosphorus can be returned to agriculture and those metals used in the treatment process can be reused, and (iii) residual waste, which is collected and brought into an incineration facility where it is transformed into clean air, sludge, ash and heat.

The household waste that is not separated for recycling goes into the vacuum waste chutes where the waste is separated into organic waste and other waste. The organic waste is taken to the biogas plant for digestion into biogas, which is then returned to the housing area through the existing natural gas network or used for car fuel. The remaining waste is driven in lorries to Malmö's waste incineration plant, where heat is extracted in the incineration process.

As a result, Västra Hamnen has managed to meet the target of 100% of the energy needs coming from renewable energy sources. For a comparison, the share of renewable energy in the gross final energy consumption in Sweden in 2017 was 53.758%, while in the EU-28 it amounted to 17.021% (Eurostat, 2022). The leading countries in this respect would be Iceland (72.658%) and Norway (69.822%).

The outcomes

The previously stated formal regulations were also complemented with other informal mechanisms such as the promotion of a culture of entrepreneurship, which is one of the key determinants of the urban transformation that Malmö has experienced since the launch of its local investment program for ecological development. The city of Malmö developed this program as a possible way to achieve urban rehabilitation goals, rather than focusing on employment creation and economic growth, city attractiveness or energy independence and sovereignty, although these outcomes have also been achieved.

Västra Hamnen has managed to undergo a transition from hosting old (and polluting) shipyards to becoming the location for the headquarters of some of the high-tech companies that have developed in Malmö in recent years in sectors such as clean-tech, packaging, information and communications technology, life sciences, media, computer games, education, energy and design, creating new employment opportunities in the area (Moodysson & Zukauskaite, 2014; Moodysson et al., 2017). For example, Västra Hamnen has witnessed the establishment of the Media Evolution City (Ruoppila et al., 2007). The Media Evolution City aims to create an innovation setting for everything in and surrounding the film, TV and computer games industries in new media. It also accommodates Malmö University and two business incubators – MINC (Malmö Incubator) and MEDEON (i.e. a Science park that supports knowledge-intensive companies in the life science field).

This knowledge environment attracts established companies as well as start-ups. In particular, the life science sector, which includes pharmaceuticals, medical devices, biotechnology and health care, has expanded rapidly. Together with the Copenhagen region, the Skåne region constitutes the largest center for pharmaceuticals and biotechnology in Scandinavia (i.e. Medicon Valley). The city of Malmö has initiated the marketing organization 'Medical Malmö', which links trade and industry with medical research, and which takes place through partnerships with Malmö University and Lund University (Malmö Stad, 2010).

One of the lessons that can be learned from this case is that the economic impact of PPI cannot only be assessed according to the benefits gained by the companies that have been granted procurement contracts. Instead, economic outcomes should consider the related spillover effects (positive or negative) that may take place once the initiative is concluded. Attributing the creation of an innovation-friendly entrepreneurial ecosystem to the public intervention in Västra Hamnen is not a straightforward issue.

Moreover, and acknowledging its unintended character, it also seems sensible to think that the new economic activities generated in it are to a great extent influenced by the branding, recognition and reputation the city has built around this program. Malmö has developed a strong trademark as a sustainable city, attracting visitors, residents and industry (Environment Department, 2009; Anderson, 2014; Grimbert et al., 2023). This program, by requesting efforts from many stakeholders for the development of the city, has also captured a lot of media attention, and has raised awareness as to the potential of environmentally sustainable policies.

Finally, the case of Västra Hamnen evidences that (i) *ambitious* PPI (in its specifications, for achieving energy independence) and (ii) *inclusive* PPI (in its process, for achieving energy sovereignty), by leading to 100% renewable and increased energy efficiency, has broader effects on the energy policy of the area. This has important implications in the context of an amplified use by local authorities of stricter environmental specifications in public procurement (Aldenius et al., 2021), and their exploration of energy savings and carbon reduction opportunities as part of the sustainable and smart city agenda (Preston et al., 2020).

The strong consultation building initiatives for residential areas, such as in the Flagghusen neighborhood of Västra Hamnen, provides interesting perspectives. The 600 rental and cooperative apartment area was constructed following a dialogue between the winning developer and citizens around urban planning. Hence, the plan, the architecture, safety and security, costs of living, maintenance costs, parking, energy efficiency, use of nontoxic substances, local surface, water handling and the environmental adaptation were discussed in order to come up with the best solutions (City of Malmö, 2009a, p. 7). This sheds light on the potential of citizen engagement "to support local authorities to increase their ambitions and vision for meeting the needs of their constituents and escape the path dependency and bounded rationality that appears to deflate ambitions for innovation" (Dale-Clough, 2015, p. 239).

Energy independence can be considered here as a natural outcome for PPI, following the urban rehabilitation which it contributed to foster. However, it is worth noting that the participatory dynamics at the core of the PPI process also contribute to energy sovereignty. Policies to enhance energy sovereignty promote the use of renewable energies for accelerating electricity decarbonization, "while also empowering community scale decision making and offering communities control to reduce the myriad externalities associated with the fossil fuel energy system" (Schelly et al., 2020, p. 109). Local authorities, as epitomized here in the case of a subnational PPI initiative, make full use of their proximity to citizens to cocreate the city of the future, by encouraging long-term and meaningful relationships between service providers and service users.

Conclusion

The case presented in this chapter is interesting for multiple reasons. First, Malmö counts with a long trajectory in preserving the environment. This trajectory is explained by the industrial structure that dominated the city of Malmö in the previous century, which had strong environmental impacts (e.g. Kockums shipyards). Second, despite public procurement has been (and still is) prone to corruption, the involvement of multiple stakeholders, before, during and after the implementation of the initiative led to the definition of demanding requirements, which requested innovative efforts on the supply side. This dialogue between public and private spheres limits path dependence resulting from the domination of incumbent suppliers and promotes disruptive innovation. Finally, the urban planning project in Västra Hamnen also generated positive externalities, mainly through the intense support to entrepreneurial projects, in the regenerated neighborhoods. As a result, the city has turned into a reference not only in the achievement of sustainable goals but also in the promotion of a fertile business environment and of its energy independence and sovereignty, contributing to Malmö's attractiveness.

The Västra Hamnen trajectory illustrates the potential of PPI policies at the urban level leading to first- and second-degree effects. The case shows the clear additionality of PPI as a policy instrument when it is used as part of a wider, intended and holistic strategic innovation policy (Borrás & Edquist, 2019). The priorities of the city of Malmö respond to grand challenges that are relevant to the region, aiming to generate and exploit radical innovations, while (unintendedly) creating new industries. The case study provides evidence for the transformative effects of policy interventions that go beyond their original intended outputs and prove how these can also have deep societal and economic implications (Nijaki & Worrel, 2012). However, reaping the full effects of PPI requires designing procurement calls differently, in other words (i) not demanding products, but rather demanding needs (i.e. *functional specifications*), and (ii) promoting constant *stakeholder engagement* for the cocreation of superior solutions. This shift in policymaking mirrors the evolution from a world of certainty to a world of uncertainty and sets the ground not only for the emergence of innovations but also for the generation of positive spillovers that transcend the policy goals aimed at with the intervention. Scholarly contributions (e.g. Barbieri et al., 2016) acknowledge that environmental regulation and standards provide valuable incentives for the uptake and diffusion of environmental innovations. We would like to add that this case study illustrates how moving beyond existing standards (i.e. ambitious PPI) may lead to energy independence, while creative dialogue processes (i.e. inclusive PPI) pave the way for energy sovereignty.

Finally, we acknowledge that there is not a one-size-fits-all policy to address grand societal challenges, or in this case to roll out PPI as a transformative policy instrument. Implementation stages should take into account the specificities of the innovation system, its legacies, policy traditions, organizational structures, paths and inertias, institutional settings and the capabilities in place (Roberts & Siemiatycki, 2015). However, there is a set of key conditions that explain the effective implementation of PPI as a transformative policy instrument in the Malmö case, and which could be institutionalized (see Table 8.1).

Exploring the strategies to successfully implement PPI at the local level is inherently associated to some challenges that need to be further explored (ICLEI, 2016). First, political competences and financial resources are not always found within cities and/or regions, which requires the implementation of multilevel co-funding

Table 8.1 Recommendations for an effective roll out of PPI as a transformative policy instrument

Recommendations	Conditions for effective implementation
Request explicit political ownership, and support of operational levels	Develop the entrepreneurial mindset of public service leaders. This requires strong political ownership, backing top management and providing support to procurers and technicians.
Identify needs and use functional procurement	Start with the problem, not the solution, and open up for variety, even considering unsolicited ideas. If possible, define the tender in functional terms, demanding requirements beyond the state of the art.
Integrate and balance goals with other political objectives	Use public demand to spur innovation, as a means to achieve wider societal goals: improving public services can also contribute to innovation dynamics in the economy.
Communicate ambition to the market	Signal the potential of the local demand for local firms (lead markets), but also create a platform for them to scale up and reach other potential markets with similar needs.
Engage the community through conversations	Collaborate (with everyone, public and private stakeholders), particularly at the early stages of the procurement process: this calls for the establishment of early market engagement dialogues, not only with potential providers but also with potential buyers, problem owners and end users.
Define public–private partnerships	Build innovation partnerships where co-creation, co-development and co-learning can take place.
Develop capabilities internally and/or externally	Being an 'intelligent customer' requires knowing your needs but also being aware of your limited capacities: if needed, bring in external expertise to increase the capabilities of the public sector.
Use co-funding schemes	Manage the available financing mechanisms effectively, searching for the complementarity among the funding schemes from different governmental levels (i.e. local, regional, national, transnational).
Use procurement-related instrument-mixes	Ensure the coherent application of procurement-related instruments in a comprehensive mix: public–private innovation partnerships, pre-commercial procurement, circular procurement, functional procurement, regular procurement.
Develop monitoring, evaluation and impact assessment	The execution of the contract requires continuous evaluation, not only ex post but also ex ante and during the procurement process. The evaluation should not only be limited to the direct outputs achieved but also include their impacts or potential spillovers.

Source: Own elaboration

schemes. Second, by moving in a subnational level, the potential benefits associated to the scale of operations can be rather limited. Lastly, PPI requires certain organizational routines and government (managerial) capabilities, since the products to be purchased are not yet developed, which differ to a great extent from those required in regular procurement practices (Kattel & Mazzucato, 2018). Examples of capabilities required for the implementation of policies aiming at societal transformations include capabilities related to experimentation, translation of functional requirements into technical specifications, coordination and engagement, evaluation and policy learning. Besides, public organizations also need to build organizational routines to identify opportunities for anticipating policy changes, setting organizational strategy, planning investments, quality improvement of service delivery and collaboration with suppliers and stakeholders. The evidence to date points to officials in charge of PPI normally lacking the capabilities required to implement PPI processes, so developing these capabilities becomes essential for the effective use of PPI (Edquist et al., 2018). This lack of capabilities can be even larger at the local and regional levels rather than at the national one, which poses clear and deep challenges for the implementation of PPI processes.

The Malmö case provides an example of the mobilization of local authorities through PPI providing directionality to innovation activities, and also defining a set of key strategic sectors. The Västra Hamnen experience shows that large infrastructure projects can have large positive externalities. Beyond the policy outputs constituted by improvements in living conditions and energy efficiency, the emergence of new industries and the support of entrepreneurship eventually provide an alignment of the technological configuration opted for at the city level with the principles of energy sovereignty (Schelly et al., 2020), as long as local authorities acknowledge the PPI process as a community-driven endeavor.

Acknowledgments

Stephanie Francis Grimbert acknowledges financial support from the University of Deusto Research Training Grant Programme.

Jon Mikel Zabala-Iturriagagoitia acknowledges financial support from the Basque Government Department of Education, Language Policy and Culture (IT 1429–22).

Notes

1 Stephanie Francis Grimbert, Ph.D. candidate, Deusto Business School, University of Deusto, Spain; CIRCLE, Lund University, Sweden, email: s.grimbert@deusto.es (ORCID: 0000–0001–9295–5813).
2 Jon Mikel Zabala-Iturriagagoitia, Associate Professor, Deusto Business School, University of Deusto, Spain; South Eastern University Norway, Norway; CIRCLE, Lund University, Lund, email: jmzabala@deusto.es (ORCID: 0000–0003–1975–2555).
3 Some of these projects included: Ekostaden Augustenborg, Malmö Cycle City, refitting and extension of Ängslättsschool, Photovoltaic System for Municipality-owned Premises, Malmö Traffic Environment Program, Environmental Building Program, the City Tunnel Project, Malmö in Green and Blue and ecological adaptation of Rosengård.

4 See: www.iadb.org/en/urban-development-and-housing/emerging-and-sustainable-cities-program.
5 Naturally, there are many other instruments which have also been used in this program (e.g. the environmental strategy for the city of Malmö 1998–2002, urban development plans, city district participatory structures, programs related to food, alcohol and smoking, city initiatives dealing with traffic, waste, water and open and green spaces). However, here we focus on the use of public procurement as a driver of sustainability, environmental protection and economic development (Lember et al., 2007; Claes et al., 2012).
6 The Local Investment Program was replaced in 2002 by the Climate Investment Program, which is more specifically intended to reduce emissions of greenhouse gases.
7 Several information campaigns, early dialogues and market consultations were arranged for these purposes. As a result, the city of Malmö, the construction companies involved, the society at large, and other relevant stakeholders (e.g. energy companies) worked together from the start of the project to produce a common knowledge base. Issues such as energy-efficiency, dampproof construction, ventilation, green urban areas, open storm water treatment, carpools and forms of tenure were at the center of these conversations (Delegation for sustainable cities, 2012, p. 11).
8 For example, substances listed in the Swedish Chemicals Inspectorate's list of hazardous materials cannot be used in the building process, and building materials should be reusable when the buildings are demolished. As stated, these environmental criteria were set by the city of Malmö and agreed upon by the stakeholders involved in the definition of the program.
9 The total sum of solar panels in Malmö is currently 2,350 m^2.
10 Organic waste is expected to lead to the production of about 270 MWh of biogas per year, the equivalent of 70,500 liters of petrol.

References

Aldenius, M., Tsaxiri, P., & Lidestam, H. (2021). The role of environmental requirements in Swedish public procurement of bus transports. *International Journal of Sustainable Transportation*, *16*(5), 391–405. http://dx.doi.org/10.1080/15568318.2021.1879975

Anderson, T. (2014). Malmo: A city in transition. *Cities*, *39*, 10–20. http://dx.doi.org/10.1016/j.cities.2014.01.005

Andrén, S. (2010). *Visions and realities. Tensions in the field of urban sustainable development with Malmö and energy as a case study* [Unpublished doctoral dissertation]. Human Ecology Division, Lund University.

Barbieri, N., Ghisetti, C., Gilli, M., Marin, G., & Nicolli, F. (2016). A survey of the literature on environmental innovation based on main path analysis. *Journal of Economic Surveys*, *30*(3), 596–623. http://dx.doi.org/10.1111/joes.12149

Beise, M., & Cleff, T. (2004). Assessing the lead market potential of countries for innovation projects. *Journal of International Management*, *10*(4), 453–477. http://dx.doi.org/10.1016/j.intman.2004.08.003

Billing, P. (2000). *Skilda världar?: Malmös 1990-tal i ett kort historiskt perspektiv*. In *Part of a project called 'Malmö 2000'*. City of Malmö. https://books.google.fr/books/about/Skilda_v%C3%A4rldar.html?id=bkejMQAACAAJ&redir_esc=y

Björgvinsson, E., Ehn, P., & Hillgren, P. A. (2012). Agonistic participatory design: Working with marginalised social movements. *CoDesign*, *8*(2–3), 127–144. http://dx.doi.org/10.1080/15710882.2012.672577

Bleda, M., & Chicot, J. (2019). The role of public procurement in the formation of markets for innovation. *Journal of Business Research*, *107*, 186–196. http://dx.doi.org/10.1016/j.jbusres.2018.11.032

Borrás, S., & Edquist, C. (2019). *Holistic innovation policy: Theoretical foundations, policy problems and instrument choices.* Oxford: Oxford University Press. http://dx.doi.org/10.1093/oso/9780198809807.001.0001

Bulkeley, H. (2006). Urban sustainability: Learning from best practice? *Environment and Planning A*, *38*(6), 1029–1044. http://dx.doi.org/10.1068/a37300

Christensson, K., Günther, E., Hell, S., Klauke, I., Olsthoorn, X., & Wollmann, R. (2002). *Malmö Green Purchasing Status Report* (IVM Report No. W-02/01). City of Malmö: Dept of Economics and Technology, Amsterdam. https://research.vu.nl/en/publications/malm%C3%B6-green-purchasing-status-report

City of Malmö. (2009a). *Guide western harbour.* City of Malmö: Environmental Department. https://malmo.se/Welcome-to-Malmo/Technical-visits/Theme-Sustainable-City/Sustainable-Urban-Development/Western-Harbour.html

City of Malmö. (2009b). *Flagghusen: The creative dialogue.* City of Malmö. https://climate-adapt.eea.europa.eu/en/metadata/case-studies/optimization-of-the-mix-of-private-and-public-funding-to-realise-climate-adaptation-measures-in-malmo/malmo_document1.pdf

Claes, K., Vandenbussche, L., Versele, A., Klein, R., & Verbist, B. (2012). Sustainable urban planning and construction in the South. In *KLIMOS Working Paper 7*. Leuven: KLIMOS. https://ees.kuleuven.be/eng/klimos/papers/wp7sustainableurbanplanningandconstructioninthesouth.pdf

Dale, A. (2011). *Malmö, Sweden: Integrating policy development for climate change and sustainable development.* Royal Roads University, School of Environment and Sustainability. www.crcresearch.org/book/export/html/3851

Dale-Clough, L. (2015). Public procurement of innovation and local authority procurement: Procurement modes and framework conditions in three European cities. *Innovation: The European Journal of Social Science Research*, *28*(3), 220–242. http://dx.doi.org/10.1080/13511610.2015.1012709

Delegation for Sustainable Cities. (2012). *Sustainable urban development projects: Projects that have received financial support from the delegation for sustainable cities.* Stockholm. https://symbiocity.org/wp-content/uploads/2020/01/SusCit-in-Sweden_REVhela-mail.pdf

Edler, J., & Georghiou, L. (2007). Public procurement and innovation – Resurrecting the demand side. *Research Policy*, *36*(7), 949–963. http://dx.doi.org/10.1016/j.respol.2007.03.003

Edler, J., Georghiou, L., Uyarra, E., & Yeow, J. (2015). The meaning and limitations of public procurement for innovation: A supplier's experience. In C. Edquist, N. S. Vonortas, J. M. Zabala-Iturriagagoitia, & J. Edler (Eds.), *Public procurement for innovation* (pp. 35–64). Cheltenham: Edward Elgar. http://dx.doi.org/10.4337/9781783471898.00008

Edler, J., & Yeow, J. (2016). Connecting demand and supply: The role of intermediation in public procurement of innovation. *Research Policy*, *45*(2), 414–426. http://dx.doi.org/10.1016/j.respol.2015.10.010

Edquist, C., Buchinger, E., Whyles, G., & Zabala-Iturriagagoitia, J. M. (2018). *Mutual learning exercise on innovation-related procurement – Final report.* Brussels: European Commission, Directorate-General for Research & Innovation, Directorate Policy Development and Co-ordination, Unit A. Brussels. https://ec.europa.eu/research-and-innovation/en/statistics/policy-support-facility/mle-innovation-related-public-procurement

Edquist, C., Hommen, L., & Tsipouri, L. (Eds.) (2000). *Public technology procurement and innovation.* Dordrecht: Kluwer Academic Publishers. https://link.springer.com/book/10.1007/978-1-4615-4611-5

Edquist, C., & Zabala-Iturriagagoitia, J. M. (2012). Public procurement for innovation as mission-oriented innovation policy. *Research Policy*, *41*(10), 1757–1769. http://dx.doi.org/10.1016/j.respol.2012.04.022

Eisenhardt, K. M. (1989). Building theories from case study research. *Academy of Management Review*, *14*(4), 532–550. https://doi.org/10.5465/amr.1989.4308385

Environment Department. (2009). *Environmental programme for the City of Malmö 2009–2020.* City of Malmö. https://docplayer.net/21328017-Environmental-programme-for-the-city-of-malmo-2009-2020.html

Erdmenger, C. (2003). *Buying into the environment: Experiences, opportunities, and potential for eco-procurement.* London: Routledge. https://dx.doi.org/10.4324/9781351281409

European Commission. (2007). *A lead market initiative for Europe. COM(2007) 860.* Brussels: Publications Office of the European Union. http://eur-lex.europa.eu/LexUriServ/Lex-UriServ.do?uri=COM:2007:0860:FIN:en:PDF

European Union. (2011). *Cities of tomorrow: Challenges, visions, ways forward.* Brussels: Publications Office of the European Union. https://ec.europa.eu/regional_policy/sources/doc-gener/studies/pdf/citiesoftomorrow/citiesoftomorrow_final.pdf

Eurostat. (2022). *Share of renewable energy in gross final energy consumption.* https://ec.europa.eu/eurostat/data/database?node_code=t2020_rd330

Flyvbjerg, B. (2006). Five misunderstandings about case-study research. *Qualitative Inquiry*, *12*(2), 219–245. https://doi.org/10.1177/1077800405284363

Fossum, T. (2008). *Sustainable urban development in Malmö, Augustenborg and Bo01/Western Harbour.* City of Malmö: Environment Department. www.fomento.gob.es/NR/rdonlyres/9D6A5DD0-D460-4728-9882-71E4E5EDD3EF/95899/5.pdf

Grimbert, S.F., Zabala-Iturriagagoitia, J.M., & Pesme, J.O. (2023) Deconstructing cluster identity: place branding and trademarking by cluster organizations. *Regional Studies.* in press. DOI: 10.1080/00343404.2023.2181951

Hodson, M., & Marvin, S. (2010). Can cities shape socio-technical transitions and how would we know if they were? *Research Policy*, *39*(4), 477–485. http://dx.doi.org/10.1016/j.respol.2010.01.020

ICLEI. (2012). *Integrating ambitious renewable energy targets in city planning.* Bonn: Local Governments for Sustainability. www.irena.org/-/media/Files/IRENA/Agency/Publication/2013/Jan/IRENA-cities-case-7-Malmo.pdf

ICLEI. (2016). *The Procura+ Manual. A guide to implementing sustainable procurement* (3rd ed.). Freiburg: Local Governments for Sustainability. https://procuraplus.org/fileadmin/user_upload/Manual/ManualProcura_online_version_new_logo.pdf

Kattel, R., & Mazzucato, M. (2018). Mission-oriented innovation policy and dynamic capabilities in the public sector. *Industrial and Corporate Change*, *27*(5), 787–801. http://dx.doi.org/10.1093/icc/dty032

Lember, V., Kalvet, T., & Kattel, R. (2011). Urban competitiveness and public procurement for innovation. *Urban Studies*, *48*(7), 1373–1395. https://doi.org/10.1177/0042098010374512

Lember, V., Kalvet, T., Kattel, R., Penna, C., & Suurna, M. (2007). Public procurement for innovation in Baltic Metropolises. In *Research report to baltmet inno organization.* Tallinn: Tallinn University of Technology. www.academia.edu/17497566/Public_procurement_for_innovation_in_Baltic_metropolises

Lember, V., Kattel, R., & Kalvet, T. (2015). Quo vadis public procurement of innovation? *Innovation: The European Journal of Social Science Research*, *28*(3), 403–421. http://dx.doi.org/10.1080/13511610.2015.1043245

Malmö Stad, 2010. *Malmö Snapshot. Facts and figures on trade and industry in Malmö. A summary from the Malmö City Office.* https://issuu.com/jesjon/docs/malmosnapshot2010

Mazzucato, M. (2018). Mission-oriented innovation policies: Challenges and opportunities. *Industrial and Corporate Change*, *27*(5), 803–815. http://dx.doi.org/10.1093/icc/dty034

McCrudden, C. (2004). Using public procurement to achieve social outcomes. *Natural Resources Forum, 28*(4), 257–267. http://dx.doi.org/10.1111/j.1477-8947.2004.00099.x

Moodysson, J., Trippl, M., & Zukauskaite, E. (2017). Policy learning and smart specialization: Balancing policy change and continuity for new regional industrial paths. *Science and Public Policy, 44*(3), 382–391. http://dx.doi.org/10.1093/scipol/scw071

Moodysson, J., & Zukauskaite, E. (2014). Institutional conditions and innovation systems: On the impact of regional policy on firms in different sectors. *Regional Studies, 48*(1), 127–138. http://dx.doi.org/10.1080/00343404.2011.649004

Naturvårdsverket. (2009). *Green public procurement in Sweden.* Stockholm: The Swedish Environmental Protection Agency. https://silo.tips/download/green-public-procurement-in-sweden

Neij, L. (2001). Methods of evaluating market transformation programmes: Experience in Sweden. *Energy Policy, 29*(1), 67–79. http://dx.doi.org/10.1016/S0301-4215(00)00100-2

Nijaki, L. K., & Worrel, G., (2012). Procurement for sustainable local economic development. *International Journal of Public Sector Management, 25*(2), 133–153. http://dx.doi.org/10.1108/09513551211223785

OECD. (2017). *Government at a Glance 2017.* Paris: OECD. https://doi.org/10.1787/gov_glance-2017-en

Preston, S., Mazhar, M. U., & Bull, R. (2020). Citizen engagement for co-creating low carbon smart cities: Practical lessons from Nottingham City Council in the UK. *Energies, 13*(24), 6615. http://dx.doi.org/10.3390/en13246615

Roberts, D. J., & Siemiatycki, M. (2015). Fostering meaningful partnerships in public – Private partnerships: Innovations in partnership design and process management to create value. *Environment and Planning C: Government and Policy, 33*(4), 780–793. http://dx.doi.org/10.1068/c12250

Rodríguez-Pose, A. (2018). The revenge of the places that don't matter (and what to do about it). *Cambridge Journal of Regions, Economy and Society, 11*(1), 189–209. http://dx.doi.org/10.1093/cjres/rsx024

Ruoppila, S., Lehtovuori, P., & von Hertzen, N. (2007). Infrastructures for innovation. Enhancing innovation activity through urban planning in Baltic metropolises. *BaltMet Inno Project.* www.academia.edu/64790571/Infrastructures_for_innovation_enhancing_innovation_activity_through_urban_planning_in_Baltic_metropolises

Santos, A. T., Hooper, M., Evans, N., & Dannenmaier, V. (2012). Good practice in socially responsible public procurement: Approaches to verification from across Europe. *The Landmark Consortium.* www.socioeco.org/bdf_fiche-document-4640_en.html

Saussier, S., & Tirole, J. (2015). Strengthening the efficiency of public procurement. *Notes du conseil d'analyse économique, 22*(3), 1–12. www.cae-eco.fr/en/Renforcer-l-efficacite-de-la-commande-publique

Schelly, C., Bessette, D., Brosemer, K., Gagnon, V., Arola, K. L., Fiss, A., & Halvorsen, K. E. (2020). Energy policy for energy sovereignty: Can policy tools enhance energy sovereignty? *Solar Energy, 205,* 109–112. http://dx.doi.org/10.1016/j.solener.2020.05.056

Simcoe, T., & Toffel, M. W. (2012). Public procurement and the private supply of green buildings. In *Working paper 13–030.* Boston: Harvard Business School. http://dx.doi.org/10.2139/ssrn.2142085

Stilgoe, J. (2012). Experiments in science policy: An autobiographical note. *Minerva, 50*(2), 197–204. http://dx.doi.org/10.1007/s11024-012-9199-1

Uyarra, E., Zabala-Iturriagagoitia, J. M., Flanagan, K., & Magro, E. (2020). Public procurement, innovation and industrial policy: Rationales, roles, capabilities and implementation. *Research Policy, 49*(1), 103844. http://dx.doi.org/10.1016/j.respol.2019.103844

World Bank. (2020). *Urban development.* www.worldbank.org/en/topic/urbandevelopment/overview

Zabala-Iturriagagoitia, J. M. (2022). Fostering regional innovation, entrepreneurship and growth through public procurement. *Small Business Economics*, *58*(2), 1205–1222. https://doi.org/10.1007/s11187-021-00466-9

Zsidisin, G. A., & Smith, M. E. (2005). Managing supply risk with early supplier involvement: A case study and research propositions. *Journal of Supply Chain Management*, *41*(4), 44–57. http://dx.doi.org/10.1111/j.1745-493X.2005.04104005.x

9 Conclusions

Regional policies, development, and Forgotten Spaces in Europe

María del Carmen Sánchez-Carreira,[1] *Paulo Jorge Reis Mourão,*[2] *and Bruno Blanco-Varela*[3]

This final chapter discusses the main findings of the book. It also approaches the main lessons and policy implications arising from the addressed experiences. The future paths in the topic are also tackled, as well as the transferability of these European cases to other regions worldwide.

Main conclusions: shedding light on the forgotten Europe

This book deals with the Forgotten Spaces of Europe. The region can be studied from a macro perspective, hence the term European region. In addition, it can be studied from a micro perspective: European regions as a subnational territory, which is more pertinent in the framework of this book. This last idea is more relevant if one considers how the local is inserted and related to the global. Although the world is deeply interconnected, most economic activity takes place at the local level. Another concurrent phenomenon to economic globalization is polarization. At the territorial level, there is a trend to concentrate. Thus, there are centers of high economic activity, dynamism, and innovation. They represent one side of the coin. The other side of the coin is constituted by territories with lower capabilities and potential for attracting human and financial resources, as well as greater difficulty in establishing a solid business structure. Thus, within a dichotomous Europe, the opportunities and possibilities for development of the weaker areas are presented.

This book contributes to the existing literature on European regional policies, focusing on Forgotten Spaces. It comprises a diverse analysis of different territories that are defined as "Forgotten Spaces" and how they have implemented their own initiatives and development models. Different situations have been addressed, such as the nature of the territory and the rural environment, while other urban territories have used tools for development, such as public procurement, promoting image, or local leadership. Other key aspects of the Forgotten Spaces have been tackled, such as the relevance of demographic trends and their interaction with economic phenomena. Territorial dynamics and political orientation influence migratory flows. The persistent trend toward rural abandonment implies fewer opportunities for the population living in rural environments and with a business structure that is low innovative, technological or knowledge intensive. This trend is also typical of territories with higher economic weakness and less dynamism in their productive base,

DOI: 10.4324/9781003256281-12

even urban or high areas, such as small or shrinking cities. To that extent, knowledge is crucial for the insertion of territories into the global economy, social, political, and economic challenges. Some of these problems are social cohesion, inequality, loss of competitiveness, and political fragmentation.

The variety of places analyzed shows different European experiences, such as the Portuguese and Spanish rural areas, Swedish, Danish, Estonian, German, Polish, or Italian cities, with different background situations and own development models. Among the different experiences, a set of similar features can be appreciated, but the need for knowledge of the specificities of each territory to promote the economic development of the area is also emphasized.

Forgotten Spaces show a close relationship with migratory movements. Endogenous development models are articulated as the key to maintaining the population and avoiding the desertification of those areas. In this sense, the links between the territory and the economy are crucial elements with an impact on demography. A higher territorial balance also has external effects. For example, the loss of rural or urban population in less dynamic territories is a factor in the danger of desertification in some areas and overcongestion in others, leading to increase environmental, economic, and social problems of the urban areas.

Common aspects have been found among the development models analyzed for forgotten areas. The main concern of the various actors in rural areas is to create a social and economic dynamic, that is, to promote employment and prevent their desertification. Agricultural and rural policies, as well as the diversification of activities and the multifunctionality of the agricultural sector, are crucial to increase the resilience of rural frameworks.

The role of resources is key to the success of development models, and, in turn, resources should be used to diversify the economy and create new activities. Resources are classified according to own and external resources. In terms of own resources, development processes depend on crucial elements, such as existing clusters, key sectors, educational and research institutions, and capabilities. External resources refer to financing and cofinancing policies that are not based on the contribution of the residents themselves. For example, the experiences analyzed in this book highlight the need to implement financing programs and policies that increasingly consider and address the specific needs and challenges of each territory. This highlights that territorial policies cannot be applied universally, since the defining circumstances and historical process are particularly relevant. As it is analyzed in this book, there are challenges that have been more invisible and with a deficit of structural attention, such as the case of small cities. Although resources are provided by agents and authorities outside the territorial reality, political deliberation and the allocation of resources are an element specific to the territory. Local and bottom-up processes based on a multifaceted understanding of the specific potentials of each place can help to slow down the accelerated decline in population and employment, as well as to reduce the perception that places are forgotten and increase the well-being of territories.

Other chapters focus on tools for development. These include smart specialization strategies and place reconceptualization. Tailored smart specialization strategies for distressed places address the challenges associated with a weak technology base in order to identify related diversification pathways. The technology or research and development-based innovation strategy expands by paying higher attention to the intangible qualities of places. For development strategies, intangible elements should be combined with a focus on how the physical environment of a place shapes and interacts with the social narratives and processes that exist and occur among stakeholders. Moreover, an appropriate implementation of the "smart" concept can open new perspectives for these contexts, as well as a higher involvement of population (all kinds of players, including civil society) in the design and implementation of the different strategies. The smart concept represents a turning point even in rural areas or territories with low knowledge-intensive economic specialization.

One of the key drivers to success and, therefore, crucial for getting good practices is to promote participation. The participation of stakeholders is really relevant in territorial development processes. The involvement of agents is analyzed from different perspectives. This implies higher participation of the business structure, civil society, nongovernmental organizations, and local entities. Multilevel co-decision makes it possible to identify effective place-based development strategies at the local level. This highlights the importance of actors and stakeholders in local development, as well as the leadership of the initiatives. A deep knowledge of the territory is a useful tool for designing strategies and proposing systemic measures. Strategies developed at the local level propose place-based solutions framed in a general orientation that could overcome the problems of lock-in policy design. However, it is also crucial to identify and engage key stakeholders to establish a systematic understanding of the areas with the highest potential for development.

In addition, participation is related to another key element, which is social support and perceptions of a place. These perceptions drive local development activities. Social ties can be considered as an additional element of intangible resources, which gather subjective meanings, conceptions, and emotional aspects. This allows settling down stakeholders to a specific place, mobilizing them and increasing their sense of belonging. A higher involvement can drive a more active contribution from stakeholders. Promoting ties to the communities can be done through different measures. Among them, the Muszyna experience can be highlighted, with key features in the local development process, such as the recovery of historical industrial and place identity through a series of renovations of the historic center and landmarks.

Other experiences also highlight external factors, such as the decentralization of regional development policies from the national level and the availability of structural funds for investments and infrastructure.

Regional disparities and remote areas play a relevant role in the relationships of local development actors. The relations of national and regional authorities with local development actors are relevant. A larger distancing of actors from these institutions may lead to greater disaffection or less involvement and cooperation of local development actors with these institutions. Furthermore, the cultural aspect of public-private or individual-state collaboration is a determinant of local development processes. Public-private collaboration is also relevant in public procurement. In some cases, such as the municipality of Poland, the neglect of the central government may be compensated by local leadership. Mayors were animators of local social capital for collective action, activating people and their capacity for self-organization.

Public procurement can also function as a driver of local development. With the participation of multiple stakeholders and the definition of demanding requirements, innovative efforts by the business base were promoted. Leveraging public procurement of innovation as a vehicle for development requires designing procurement calls specifically, that is, demanding needs and not products, and promoting the constant participation of stakeholders for the cocreation of solutions.

The environment has also been shown to be another fundamental element in development. Thus, the ecological transition can be a useful tool in both rural and urban areas. Some experiences, such as the Portuguese rural areas and the Swedish experience of Malmö, show how a greater diversification of the economy can be articulated focusing on environment.

However, many of the experiences analyzed focus on very local development processes. In this sense, very local development processes may lose regional potential. This implies that a cohesive political commitment at the regional level can ensure coherence between local sub-strategies and an overall regional strategy to support development at a broader geographic level.

Main challenges and policy recommendations

By way of summary, the main lessons learned from the experiences analyzed are highlighted below. The objective is to take these details into account as critical and key issues for the design of strategies for the development of spaces, specifically for Forgotten Spaces. It should be noted that a number of themes are mentioned, but that it is necessary to describe and analyze the singularities of the areas in which they could be applied.

- First, the systematic nature of the policies is highlighted. Decision-making is not an isolated issue. The socioeconomic configuration is interrelated and there may be external effects or modification of the incentive system of economic agents. Therefore, for the design and orientation of the different policies it is necessary to consider the structure and network of actors in the territories.
- Second, and related to the previous point, strategies must be designed and based on place. The historical and economic configuration of places is relevant. Their agents and productive structure have developed in a given environment, and the strategy can be adjusted to the global and knowledge economy without having repercussions on the dismantling or total substitution of the previous productive base. In this regard, path dependence is clear.
- Third, the nature of the agents and their level of commitment to the policies should be highlighted. Thus, the development requires a joint participation of public and private agents. Excluding or limiting the private character of development can lead strategies to failure. It facilitates commitment and accountability and helps to promote ownership.

- Fourth, the role of policies for overcoming the less development of certain areas should be emphasized. In this sense, it should be considered that all actors are relevant in development. Development is a process that should go through governance and accountability. Giving explanations and submitting the results to debate and dialogue enriches the process and makes it more holistic. Governance enables multi-stakeholder and multilevel cooperation, as well as fostering more democratic societies.
- Finally, it should be considered how policies are evaluated, in terms of both results and process. Results cannot be analyzed only in the short term, since certain development conditions materialize in the medium and long term. On other occasions, process analysis is useful because it provides resilience and flexibility to the implemented policies. Moreover, evaluation allows for learning both from the good and bad practices. Learning is not always taking the right path, but the opportunity to correct in the future, adjust, fine-tune, and ponder.

In addition to the lessons learned, there are also challenges to be faced. The strategic orientation of reducing disparities has consequences. The formulation of objectives may present contradictory or unexpected results. For example, the reduction of disparities between two different territories may lead to an increase in their internal differences and even between close areas. Moreover, the regional or cohesion policy of the European Union can conflict with other policies, such as innovation or industrial one. It should be considered that each policy has different territorial effects. Therefore, it is essential to coordinate and create synergies among European policies to avoid contradictions and increase the need for public funds to correct the imbalances generated.

Limitations and future lines of research

The main limitations of this book lie in its diversity. Although the experiences of different European countries, such as Portugal, Spain, Italy, Denmark, Sweden, Poland, Estonia, and Germany, have been studied, Europe as a whole is very rich in diversity, also from a territorial development perspective. Another important limitation derives from the availability of data. There are less available statistics for the local realities, which limits the capabilities of the study. In addition, comparison among different areas (rural, urban) is another limitation, because no two areas are the same, which makes comparison more complicated. For example, the Portuguese rural reality cannot be compared with a Polish city. Even though these territories have in common that they are not mainstream and that they are not economic and innovation centers, the differences among the territories are higher.

Some future lines of research that could have additional potential in this area are to address success stories on some of the topics studied, such as the rural area in the European context. The rural aspect could be an identifying feature of the territories and could generate learning lessons applicable in different contexts. Another possible extension is related to the strategic orientation of the Forgotten Spaces through policies of sustainability and development based on circular economy. It is also proposed to study the effects that COVID-19 has had on Forgotten Spaces, especially from the sanitary point of view. Another interesting issue refers to the opportunities that Forgotten Spaces can offer in this new context and how these areas can take advantage of these new circumstances to their revitalization. In this sense, the rural and smaller areas can provide good conditions for quality of life or even for teleworking. However, difficulties such as available services and, in particular, connectivity, emerge. Furthermore, it is interesting to ask how European funds can affect the development of Forgotten Spaces in the context of the new programming period 2021–2027, when funds for local areas increase. Finally, another line of extension proposed is to analyze the processes of gentrification in cities, especially in those that have received more population as a cause of the depopulation of less dynamic places. In this sense, the marginal and most vulnerable neighborhoods of the large European capitals could also be studied.

Notes

1   Associate Professor, Department of Applied Economics, ICEDE Research Group, Faculty of Economics, CRETUS, Universidade de Santiago de Compostela, Spain, email: carmela.sanchez@usc.es (ORCID: 0000–0001–9265–2521).
2   Associate Professor with habilitation, Department of Economics & NIPE, Economics & Management School, University of Minho, Portugal, email: paulom@eeg.uminho.pt (ORCID: 0000–0001–6046–645X).
3   Lecturer, Department of Applied Economics, Faculty of Economics and Business Administration, University of Santiago de Compostela, email: b.blanco.varela@usc.es (ORCID: 0000–0001–5319–6578).

Index

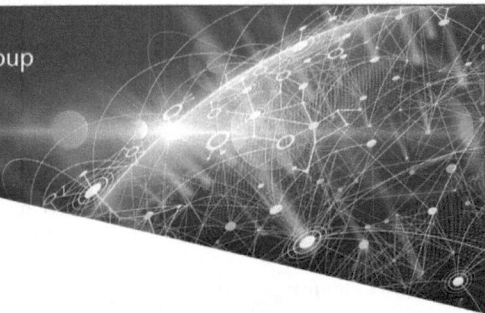